T0291913

OPENVX PROGRAMMING GUIDE

OPENVX PROGRAMMING GUIDE

FRANK BRILL

VICTOR ERUKHIMOV

RADHAKRISHNA GIDUTHURI

STEPHEN RAMM

ACADEMIC PRESS

An imprint of Elsevier

Academic Press is an imprint of Elsevier
125 London Wall, London EC2Y 5AS, United Kingdom
525 B Street, Suite 1650, San Diego, CA 92101, United States
50 Hampshire Street, 5th Floor, Cambridge, MA 02139, United States
The Boulevard, Langford Lane, Kidlington, Oxford OX5 1GB, United Kingdom

Copyright © 2020 Elsevier Inc. All rights reserved.

No part of this publication may be reproduced or transmitted in any form or by any means,
electronic or mechanical, including photocopying, recording, or any information storage and
retrieval system, without permission in writing from the publisher. Details on how to seek
permission, further information about the Publisher's permissions policies and our arrangements
with organizations such as the Copyright Clearance Center and the Copyright Licensing Agency,
can be found at our website: www.elsevier.com/permissions.

This book and the individual contributions contained in it are protected under copyright by the
Publisher (other than as may be noted herein).

Notices

Knowledge and best practice in this field are constantly changing. As new research and experience
broaden our understanding, changes in research methods, professional practices, or medical
treatment may become necessary.

Practitioners and researchers must always rely on their own experience and knowledge in
evaluating and using any information, methods, compounds, or experiments described herein. In
using such information or methods they should be mindful of their own safety and the safety of
others, including parties for whom they have a professional responsibility.

To the fullest extent of the law, neither the Publisher nor the authors, contributors, or editors,
assume any liability for any injury and/or damage to persons or property as a matter of products
liability, negligence or otherwise, or from any use or operation of any methods, products,
instructions, or ideas contained in the material herein.

Library of Congress Cataloging-in-Publication Data
A catalog record for this book is available from the Library of Congress

British Library Cataloguing-in-Publication Data
A catalogue record for this book is available from the British Library

ISBN: 978-0-12-816425-9

For information on all Academic Press publications
visit our website at https://www.elsevier.com/books-and-journals

Publisher: Mara Conner
Acquisitions Editor: Tim Pitts
Editorial Project Manager: Joshua Mearns
Production Project Manager: Kamesh Ramajogi
Designer: Miles Hitchen

Typeset by VTeX

Working together
to grow libraries in
developing countries

www.elsevier.com • www.bookaid.org

Contents

About the authors

Frank Brill manages Vision and AI software development for Cadence's Tensilica Imaging and Vision DSP organization. He began his professional career developing network management software at Bell Communications Research. He then returned to school to earn a Ph.D., which he took to Texas Instruments to do computer vision research and development for video surveillance applications. He then moved into silicon device program management, where he was responsible for several systems-on-chip for digital still cameras and other multimedia devices. Since then, Frank has managed computer vision R&D groups at TI, NVIDIA, Samsung, and now at Cadence, and has represented all four companies in the Khronos OpenVX working group. He joined Cadence in 2016 and served as the chairperson of the OpenVX working group from 2016 to 2019. Frank holds Bachelor's degrees in Mathematics and Computer Science from the University of Alaska, Fairbanks, and Master's and Ph.D degrees in Computer Science from the University of Virginia.

Victor Erukhimov is currently the CEO of Itseez3D, the company that democratizes 3D model creation. He also cofounded Itseez, Inc., which focused on developing computer vision solutions running on embedded platforms, specifically automotive safety systems. He successively held the positions of CTO, CEO, and President at Itseez when the company was acquired by Intel Corporation in 2016. Victor was the chair of the OpenVX working group in 2012–2016, helping to create the standard for cross-platform computer vision API. Before moving to the field of computer vision, he studied plasma physics at the Institute of Applied Physics, Russian Academy of Sciences, and tried to solve (without much success) the problem of electron cyclotron heating. Victor was a member of the OpenCV development team. He participates in the development and maintenance of the OpenCV library and serves as the director of the OpenCV Foundation board. He is the author of about 30 papers and several US and international patents.

Radhakrishna Giduthuri is currently a Principal Engineer at Intel, focusing on software architecture for Intel AI Accelerators. Prior to working at Intel, he built computer vision, deep learning, and video compression software acceleration libraries for AMD GPUs & CPUs. He has an extensive background with software architecture, development, and performance tuning for various computer architectures ranging from general purpose DSPs, customizable DSPs, media processors, heterogeneous processors, GPUs, and several CPUs. He is the current editor of the Khronos OpenVX working group and a member of Khronos NNEF (Neural Network Exchange Format) and OpenCL Safety-Critical working groups. For several years, he was a member of the SMPTE Video Compression Standardizing Committee. He was the Outstanding Leadership and Professional Services Award Recipient for the IEEE Central Area in 2016. Radhakrishna earned a Master's degree from IIT Kharagpur, India.

Stephen Ramm is currently a principal software engineer with ETAS, a subsidiary of Bosch, where he is working on reliable frameworks and development environments for advanced functionality in the automotive, rail and other safety-critical industries. Until late 2017, he was Director of AI and Vision software at Imagination Technologies, where one of his responsibilities was the team producing an implementation of OpenVX accelerated by proprietary GPU architecture. Prior to that, Stephen has held various positions in technical management, research, design, and applied mathematics with experience in fields as varied as optical design, nutritional analysis, advanced statistics and calibration techniques, RF electronics, NMR, seismic analysis and detonators, electronics at board and silicon level, and development tools for the games industry. Stephen was formerly an editor of the OpenVX specification, the former chair of the OpenVX Safety-critical subcommittee, and a former member of the OpenGL Safety Critical group and Safety Critical Advisory Panel within Khronos. He studied Physics and Computer Science at York University in the UK, and is a member of the Institute of Physics and a Chartered Physicist.

Foreword

While preparing to write this preface I was reminded that I have been involved in creating standards for image and vision processing for thirty years, and the work is not yet done. But now, finally, the Khronos Group's OpenVX API for vision and inferencing is established as the industry's leading open standard for effectively connecting vision developers to the power of acceleration silicon, enabling a new generation of applications that are visually aware.

Why did it take so long to architect an effective vision acceleration API? The earliest efforts took the most obvious approach, simply listing all the potentially useful image and vision operators and creating an API function call for each—done! But not so fast! In hindsight, that approach was too simplistic and suffered from two fatal issues. Firstly, the list of potential functions grew unsustainably large, exacerbated by the combinatorial explosion of different input and output parameter types. Those early specifications became lists of hundreds (and hundreds) of functions, an impossibly large and diffuse API surface area for silicon vendors to implement effectively. Secondly, sending each function to the hardware in isolation did not provide the silicon implementors enough context to undertake holistic optimizations. Each function call would have to read inputs and write results to default memory positions, with no way to know what operations had gone before and what was about to follow, leaving huge amounts of potential optimizations on the table.

OpenVX's key innovation is enabling application developers to holistically describe the complete flow of vision operators in their application as a graph connecting a network of nodes, each node defining a vision function from a carefully curated menu. Handing the complete graph to the silicon enables a groundbreaking level of optimization, for example, avoiding memory round trips or slicing and dicing images to fit in cache memory. Best of all, the graph description is high-level enough to be hardware agnostic, so each processor vendor can optimize the graph; however, they wish to execute optimally on their accelerator architecture, and they have all the information they need to do so.

But that is not all. An additional key ingredient in OpenVX's success derives from Khronos' long expertise in creating specifications that are carefully crafted, and conformance tested, to enable a vibrant ecosystem containing multiple OpenVX implementations, each optimized for a particular silicon processor while still providing application portability. This is directly analogous to GPU vendors shipping highly optimized 3D drivers for their silicon. It is in contrast to opensource projects where a single library implementation is ported across many platforms—and so may be less optimized than dedicated out-of-the-box vendor drivers.

It is a testament to the strength of OpenVX's underlying design that while early OpenVX implementations were gaining their first users, deep learning burst onto the scene, providing a new and powerful technique for solving complex pattern-matching and image recognition problems. OpenVX was able to leverage its extensible architecture to rapidly incorporate neural network inferencing into its graph description through a new tensor data type and associated operations. Today, OpenVX provides a uniquely powerful framework that can mix and combine both traditional image operators and hardware accelerated inferencing.

Now here we are in 2020, and we have the recently released OpenVX 1.3, which both consolidates proven extensions into the core specification and provides significant vertical market-targeted deployment flexibility through feature sets. OpenVX now even enables accelerated extensions to be integrated into an application's graph—an elegant solution to the "100s of functions" problem that plagued the early attempts at vision library standardization.

Optimized OpenVX implementations are shipping from multiple hardware vendors and routinely delivering superior performance to handcrafted vision processing code with far great portability and significantly reduced development costs.

Strong open standards such as OpenVX result from a wide need for a proven technology in the industry, and in the long view, an open standard that is not controlled by, or dependent on, any single company can often be the thread of continuity for industry forward progress as technologies, platforms, and market positions swirl and evolve. Open standards need the passion, patience, and participation of those that understand their value. OpenVX has been fortunate indeed in benefitting from the passion and patience of the authors of this book, that it has been my pleasure and honor to have worked with, as they have played a central role in creating the OpenVX ecosystem and continue to nurture and evolve this key vision acceleration standard into the future. The thirty-year journey continues.

Neil Trevett, President of the Khronos Group

Acknowledgments

We thank all of our current and former colleagues at the OpenVX committee for their hard and productive work on the standard. This standard would not be possible without Khronos President Neil Trevett, who guided and inspired us, and whose wonderful sense of humor saved us many times when the group was stuck trying to reach a consensus. The anonymous book reviewers provided useful comments on the book structure, and we want to thank Dmitry Matveev and Jesse Villarreal for the feedback on the contents. Our special thanks go to Susheel Gautam, who was the editor of the OpenVX 1.0 and 1.1 specifications, Erik Rainey, who was the editor of OpenVX 1.0 specification and the developer of the first version of the OpenVX sample implementation, and Kari Pulli, who helped to create the standard and was instrumental in promoting it. We are also very grateful to our families, who tolerated us spending long hours on weekends writing this book.

CHAPTER 1

Introduction

Contents

OpenVX[1] [1] is an Application Programming Interface (API) that was created to make computer vision programs run faster on mobile and embedded devices. It is different from other computer vision libraries, because from the very beginning it was designed as a Hardware Abstraction Layer (HAL) that helps software run efficiently on a wide range of hardware platforms. OpenVX is developed by the OpenVX committee, which is a part of the Khronos Group [2]. Khronos is an open and nonprofit consortium; any company or individual can become its member and participate in the development of OpenVX and other standards, including OpenGL, Vulkan, and WebGL. OpenVX is royalty free, but at the same time, it is developed by the industry: some of the world largest silicon vendors are members of the OpenVX committee.

If you are impatient to get started with OpenVX, you might want to skip to the next chapter. The introduction discusses the challenges of running computer vision algorithms in real-time that OpenVX attempts to solve. It will help you get familiar with the OpenVX high-level concepts, such as objects with opaque memory model and the OpenVX Graph.

---

[1] OpenVX is a Khronos Group trademark.

1.1 What is OpenVX and why do we need it?

Computer vision can be defined as extracting high-level information from images and video. Nowadays it is in the process of changing many industries, including automotive (Advanced Driver Assistance Systems, self-driving cars), agriculture and logistics (robotics), surveillance and banking (face recognition), and many more. A significant part of these scenarios require a computer vision algorithm to run in real time on a low-power embedded hardware. A pedestrian detection algorithm running in a car has to process each input frame; a delay makes a car less safe. For example, in a car moving at 65 miles per hour, each skipped frame adds about 3 feet to the braking distance. A robot that makes decisions slowly can become a bottleneck in the manufacturing process. AR and VR glasses that track their position slower than 30 frames per second cause motion sickness for many users.

Solving a practical computer vision problem in real time is usually a challenging task. The algorithms are much more complicated than running a single linear filter over an image, and image resolution is high enough to cause a bottleneck in a memory bus. In many cases, significant speedups can be reached by choosing the right algorithm. For example, the Viola–Jones face detector algorithm [3] enables detection of human faces in real time on relatively low-power hardware. The FAST [4] feature detector and BRIEF [5] and ORB [6] descriptors allow quick generation of features for tracking. However, in the most of cases, it is not possible to achieve the required performance by just algorithmic optimizations.

The concept of optimizing a computer vision pipeline for specific hardware is not new to the community, to say the least. One of the first major efforts in this direction was done by Intel, which released the first version of OpenCV library [7] in 2000 along with the optimized layer for Intel CPUs. Other hardware vendors provided their libraries too (see, e.g., [8–10]), and others followed with developing dedicated hardware for computer vision processing, such as the Mobileye solution for automotive [11]. NVIDIA GPUs with their high level of parallelism, and a wide bandwidth memory bus enabled processing of deep learning algorithms that, at the time of writing this book, are the best-known methods of solving a range of computer vision tasks, from segmentation to object recognition.

The computer vision applications on mobile/embedded platforms differ from server-based applications: real-time operation is critical. If a web image search algorithm keeps a user waiting, then it is still useful, and we can throw in more servers to make it faster. This is not possible for a car, where many computer vision tasks (pedestrian detection, forward car collision warning, lane departure warning, traffic sign recognition, driver monitoring) have to work in real time on a relatively low-power hardware. In this context, computer vision optimization for mobile/embedded applications is much more important than for server applications. This is why OpenVX is focused on mobile and embedded platforms, although it can be efficiently implemented for the cloud too.

Low-power mobile and embedded architectures typically are heterogeneous, consisting of a CPU and a set of *accelerators* dedicated to solving a specific compute intense problem, such as 3D graphics rendering, video coding, digital signal processing, and so on. There are multiple challenges for computer vision developers who want to run their algorithms on such a system. A CPU is too slow to run compute- and data-intense algorithms such as pedestrian detection in real time. One of the reasons is that a memory bus has a relatively low throughput, which limits multicore processing. Executing code on GPU and DSP can help, but writing code that will employ such processing units efficiently across multiple vendors is next to impossible. GPUs and DSPs have no standard memory model. Some of them share RAM with CPU, and some have their own memory with a substantial latency for data input/output. There are ways to write code that will execute on both CPU and GPU, such as [12]. However, developers want higher-level abstraction, which may be implemented over low-level API, such as OpenCL, or coded directly in the hardware. Chapter 13 discusses how OpenVX and OpenCL code can coexist and benefit from each other. Also, there are architectures that do not have full IEEE 754 floating point calculations support (required in the current version of OpenCL); they implement fixed-point arithmetic instead (where a real number is represented with a fixed amount of digits after the radix point). Finding a balance between precision and speed on such architectures is a serious challenge, and we have to tune an algorithm for such platforms. Computer vision is too important to allow such an overhead, and there has to be a way to write an algorithm that will run efficiently on a wide variety of accelerators, implemented and tuned for a specific mobile or embedded platform. This is the problem solved by OpenVX. The OpenVX library is usually developed, optimized, and shipped by silicon vendors, just like a 3D driver for a GPU. It has a graph API, which is convenient to use and efficient for executing on heterogeneous platforms. One of the most important requirements for this API is its portability across platforms.

1.2 Portability

OpenVX is the API that allows a computer vision developer to write a program once and have it efficiently executed on hardware, assuming that an efficient OpenVX implementation exists for that hardware. A reasonable expectation for this API is that it produces the same results across different platforms. But what does "same results" actually mean? How do we test if two implementations of the same function return the same results? There are several ways to answer this question:

- *Bit-exact tests*: the output of an implementation should not differ from the ground truth by a single bit. Such a test is useful to ensure that the results are going to be the same. However, there are many cases where bit-exact tests make no sense. For example, a simple function for correcting camera lens distortion [13] uses floating point calculations, and even if a method to compute an image transformation is well specified, a bit exact requirement may be too strong. For instance, a conformance to IEEE 754 floating point calculation standard may result in a very inefficient implementation on a fixed-point architecture. So, in many cases, it is beneficial to allow for a limited variety in the results.

- *Tolerance-based comparison*: for example, we can require that the output image is not different from the reference implementation output by more than ϵ in each pixel and each channel. There is no exact science in choosing the value of the threshold ϵ. The higher the threshold, the more space there is for optimizing functions for a specific platform, and the higher the variability of the results across different platforms. Computer vision means extracting high-level information from images, and if greater variability in this high-level information prevents solving the problem, then the thresholds are too high. For instance, an image arithmetic operation involved in an image stitching algorithm that results in a high-quality image on one platform and produces a visible stitch line on another should not pass a tolerance-based test.

- Algorithmic tests: a useful test to ensure a function returns correct results is to test some properties of this result. For instance, a face detector should return an image rectangle that contains a face. A text segmentation algorithm should return areas in an image that contain text. Although algorithmic tests are useful for any computer vision library, they usually are a poor choice for ensuring portability. Whereas a face detector returns a rectangle with a face, the algorithm processing this rectangle can work differently depending on the size and position of the rectangle. If the rectangle parameters vary across platforms, then the overall results may also depend on the platform.

As we can see, portability is a fine balance between precision and optimization. A set of tests that check for portability called *conformance tests* is an essential part of any cross-platform standard. Conformance tests are different from algorithmic tests: their objective is not only to check whether a function returns results according to the specification, but also to ensure the results to be consistent across different platforms. This is why conformance tests usually consist of bit-exact and tolerance-based tests, rarely using algorithmic tests.

OpenVX has its own set of conformance tests [14,15], designed by the OpenVX committee and available to all implementers of the standard. Passing conformance tests is an essential requirement for an implementation to be called "OpenVX."

1.3 OpenVX data objects

OpenVX defines several objects that are needed for common computer vision algorithms. This list includes images, pyramids, matrices, tensors, and several other constructs. All the data objects share some high-level design properties.

1.3.1 Opaque memory model

An efficient cross-platform computer vision API should be able to execute the same function on different accelerators. A function implementing a stereo matching algorithm should be computed on a GPU, provided that a GPU is present on the platform and is powerful enough to execute this function faster than a CPU. However, a GPU has its own memory, and executing stereo matching on a GPU will require moving image data to the GPU memory. Giving a user control over memory that stores image data requires exposing a memory model for a wide range of embedded accelerator memory models that OpenVX is targeting. This is why the image object in OpenVX is *opaque*, meaning that a user has no direct access to pixels other than through dedicated OpenVX functions. The same design principle is applied to all OpenVX data objects. This allows an implementation of OpenVX to change data layout and to move data between the CPU memory, called *host memory* throughout the OpenVX spec, and the accelerator memory. The access to data is provided by a pair of Map/Unmap functions defined for each object, which create a mapping between object data and a region in host memory. For example, the functions for accessing image pixels are called `vxMapImagePatch` and `vxUnmapImagePatch`.

1.3.2 Object attributes

Each object, in addition to the data it holds, has parameters that define its contents. For example, an image is characterized by width and height, as well as its format (the number of color planes, color format, etc.). These parameters are called *attributes* throughout the spec. Some of the attributes have to be specified when an object is being created and cannot be changed by a user during the object lifetime. Such attributes are referred to as "Read-only" in the spec. Attributes that can be changed are marked as "Read-write." Values of object attributes can be retrieved with a "query" function, usually named `vxQuery[Object]`, for example, `vxQueryImage` for the image object. The read-write attributes can be changed with a "set" function, usually named `vxSet[Object]Attribute`, for example, `vxSetImageAttribute` for the image object. Appendix A contains the list of all OpenVX data objects along with their attributes.

1.4 Graph API

As we discussed before, data objects in OpenVX can be stored in the host memory and accelerator memory. However, moving image data between devices can be time consuming. If we are to run a single image filtering operation, then a GPU may be faster to do the job than a CPU, but the overhead of moving image data between the host and GPU memory may negate all the speedup. Making such decisions requires knowledge about the platform. If we intend to execute an OpenVX-based algorithm on a wide variety of platforms (such as Android phones), all kinds of accelerators available on these platforms, as well as memory and data transfer between accelerators, need to be taken into account. It is practically impossible to build this level of decision making into the code. It is more realistic to expect a manufacturer of a specific hardware compute platform to take into account all this special knowledge in an efficient OpenVX implementation. This is why an OpenVX implementation manages where and when specific functions are going to be executed, and a user has practically no control over it. As a result, OpenVX provides an abstraction level that allows us to write code once and execute it efficiently on many different embedded platforms where the API is implemented.

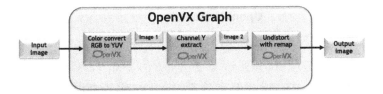

Figure 1.1 *An example of an OpenVX graph.* Graph nodes represent functions, and the directed links define input and output data.

Since an OpenVX implementation has to make decisions on how to execute each function, we need to provide it with some context in advance, so that efficient data management can be planned before the execution. Letting an implementation know a sequence of functions that we want to call on an input image will allow it to make an informed decision on where to keep image data and when to move it to/from an accelerator. A graph model is used in OpenVX to represent this information.

The idea of using graphs to express sequences of image processing functions has been around for a long time (see, e.g., [16]). A program is represented by a Directed Acyclic Graph (DAG), with nodes corresponding to functions and oriented links between nodes setting the input and output data, as well as the order of execution. An example of a graph is given in Fig. 1.1. The input color image in the RGB format is converted into the YUV format by the first (leftmost) node, then a Y (intensity) channel is extracted by the second node, and, finally, the camera lens distortion correction is done on the Y channel. If a function has parameters, then they are specified by *node attributes*, similar to data object attributes.

An OpenVX graph is set up in advance, before execution. Once all the nodes and links are set up, the graph is *verified*, either automatically before execution or with a manual function call. During graph verification time, the OpenVX implementation may prepare for execution, make decisions about which accelerator to use for executing each node, and check for errors in the graph. For some platforms such as FPGA, it can also compile a graph into binary code and upload it to an FPGA chip. Once the verification is complete, the graph is ready to be executed. Note that the same graph can be executed multiple times on different data without reverification. Changes in a graph such as insertion/deletion of nodes or links can trigger reverification. Changes in some node attributes may also require reverification before the next execution. A list of OpenVX graph nodes representing computer vision functions, along with the references to spe-

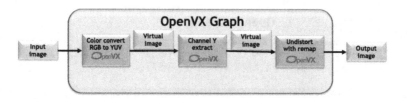

Figure 1.2 *An example of an OpenVX graph with virtual images.* Graph links with virtual images define a sequence of calls, but a user has no access to that data at any time.

cific chapters where these functions are discussed and to the code samples, is given in Appendix B.

Obviously, not every possible computer vision function can be predefined by OpenVX. Users can implement a C function and add it to a graph as a *user node*. A user node will be executed on a CPU, but it does not prevent using accelerators for user nodes. For instance, Chapter 13 discusses how a user node can be implemented with OpenCL, so that code get executed on a GPU/FPGA/DSP. The concept of user nodes allows a developer to go well beyond the set of computer vision functions that are included in the OpenVX standard.

1.5 Virtual objects

To provide an OpenVX implementation more opportunities for optimization, a user has no access to data during graph execution (other than from user nodes). In the example of Fig. 1.1, once the graph execution is finished, access to all four images (input image, image 1, image 2, and output image) is possible. However, in many cases a user does not need to access temporary data (images 1 and 2), whereas generating it may cause an additional speed and memory overhead. For example, if we did not need images 1 and 2, all three operations could happen in place, pixel by pixel, providing a lot of speedup on platforms with slow memory bus by minimizing the data flow. Examples of such operations include combining subsequent per-pixel image arithmetic operations and applying several linear filters to an image at the same time (so-called filter stacking). If a user does not need specific images, then he can create them as *virtual* (see Fig. 1.2). Virtual images, like regular data objects, connect two graph nodes, but an implementation is not obliged to actually generate data for these images. OpenVX does not require a user to provide image dimensions when creating a virtual image; zeroes can be used instead (see vxCreateVirtualImage in Chapter 6). It may be useful when you have a large graph with many images of different sizes (e.g., when using pyramids, see Chapter 8), but the authors recommend to use actual image sizes where possible, as it is less error prone.

All other OpenVX data objects, such as pyramids and histograms, can also be virtual. It is reasonable to expect that Map/Unmap function calls on virtual objects fail, but OpenVX requires this only outside of graph execution. If Map/Unmap are called inside a graph (from a user node), then the calls will be successful. So, a user of OpenVX has to be aware that inserting a user node in a sequence of nodes connected with virtual images may prevent certain optimizations.

1.6 Deep neural networks

Deep neural networks have recently become the standard tool for solving a variety of computer vision problems. Whereas training a neural network is outside the OpenVX scope, importing a pretrained network and running inference on it is an important part of the OpenVX functionality. The concept of the Graph API of nodes representing functions and links representing data is very convenient for implementing deep neural networks with OpenVX. In fact, each neural network unit can be represented as a graph node. OpenVX has a special data type representing tensors to provide data exchange between these nodes, and the nodes themselves are implemented in the *OpenVX Neural Network Extension* [17]. Another way to import a neural network into OpenVX is by using the *OpenVX Kernel Import Extension* [18]. The Kernel Import Extension can take a pretrained network model and load it into OpenVX as a single node. One of the data formats that can be used is *Neural Network Exchange Format* (NNEF) [20], the standard also developed by the Khronos Group. See Chapter 10 for details on how to import a pretrained neural network into OpenVX.

1.7 Immediate mode API

There are cases where the Graph API in its existing form does not provide an efficient implementation of a computer vision algorithm. For example, a sequence of quick custom operations on small blocks of pixels intermittent with standard computer vision functions, defined with a Graph API, will require a user node for each custom operation. Each user node will have to map and unmap an image to/from host memory, causing a significant overhead. This is why OpenVX, on top of the Graph API, also has the *Immediate Mode API*. Each immediate mode function replicates a graph node, with a few exceptions. The behavior of an immediate mode function is defined by the corresponding single node graph. Each immediate mode function name is prefixed with "vxu", to distinguish them from Graph API functions, prefixed with "vx". An immediate mode API allows us to write a computer vision algorithm without a graph and has small overhead for custom data processing.

1.8 OpenVX vs. OpenCV and OpenCL

OpenVX is not the first framework optimized for computer vision. OpenCV (Open Source Computer Vision Library) [21] is the de facto standard in this area. It provides a lot of useful functions, and many of them are optimized for specific platforms, including x86, ARM CPUs, and selected GPUs. Also, OpenCL [12], a generic programming framework, can be used to develop computer vision algorithms that can run on discrete GPUs. So why do we need another computer vision platform?

OpenCV is developed and maintained by the community, with the primary focus on providing necessary computer vision functionality. Many functions are optimized for a subset of platforms, and hardware vendors provide their own optimizations for their platforms (see, e.g., [22–24]). However, the wide scope of the library makes the optimization of all the functions for multiple embedded platforms next to impossible. Also, OpenCV uses algorithmic tests to check for function correctness, so the results across platforms may be different (although functionally correct). In contrast, OpenVX has a much smaller scope, making it possible to optimize for a wide range of platforms. Also, OpenVX conformance tests make sure the results to be similar across different platforms. In fact, these frameworks are complimentary: we can use the OpenVX graph for functions that are defined by OpenVX and then add more functionality as user nodes, based on OpenCV. A full comparison between OpenCV and OpenVX is given in the Table 1.1.

OpenCL is a general-purpose programming language that allows us to write code for heterogeneous systems. OpenCL existing requirement for full IEEE 754 floating point standard compliance[2] and its explicit memory

---

[2] This requirement may be relaxed in future.

Table 1.1 OpenVX vs. OpenCV*.

	OpenCV	OpenVX
Implementation	Community-driven open-source library	Callable API implemented, optimized, and shipped by hardware vendors
Scope	100s of imaging and vision functions, multiple camera APIs/interfaces	Tight focus on dozens of core hardware-accelerated functions plus extensions and accelerated custom nodes uses external camera drivers
Conformance	Extensive OpenCV Test Suite but no formal Adopters program	Implementations must pass Khronos Conformance Test Suite to use trademark
IP Protection	None. Source code licensed under BSD. Some modules require royalties/licensing	Protected under Khronos IP Framework – Khronos members agree not to assert patents against API when used in Conformant implementations
Acceleration	OpenCV 3.0 Transparent API (or T-API) enables function offload to OpenCL devices	Implementation free to use any underlying API such as OpenCL. Can use OpenCL for Custom Nodes
Efficiency	OpenCV 4.0 G-API graph model for some filters, arithmetic/binary operations, and well-defined geometrical transformations	Graph-based execution of all Nodes. Optimizable computation and data transfer
Inferencing	Deep Neural Network module to construct networks from layers for forward pass computations only. Import from ONNX, TensorFlow, Torch, Caffe	Neural Network layers and operations represented directly in the OpenVX Graph. NNEF direct import, ONNX through NNEF convertor

* *Courtesy of Neil Trevett, Khronos Group*

model prevent OpenVX to be implemented only using OpenCL. However, OpenCL can be used to efficiently implement a user node to run on a GPU (see Chapter 13 for more information). Also, OpenCV T-API can be used to run a computer vision algorithm implemented in OpenVX on an accelerator through OpenCL. A full comparison between OpenCL and OpenVX is given in the Table 1.2.

Table 1.2 OpenVX vs. OpenCL*.

	OpenCL	OpenVX
Use case	General heterogeneous programming	Domain targeted vision processing
Ease of use	General-purpose math libraries with no built-in vision functions	Fully implemented vision operators and framework "out of the box"
Architecture	Language-based – needs online compilation	Library-based – no online compiler required
Target hardware	"Exposed" architected memory model – can impact performance portability	Abstracted node and memory model – diverse implementations can be optimized for power and performance
Precision	Full IEEE floating point mandated	Minimal floating point requirements – optimized for vision operators

* *Courtesy of Neil Trevett, Khronos Group*

1.9 OpenVX versions

This revision of the book was mostly written for OpenVX version 1.2. Version 1.3 was released in September 2019, and Chapter 15 provides information on the new features introduced in OpenVX 1.3.

1.10 Prerequisites

We expect a reader to be familiar with the C programming language, as the API and all of the examples are in C. Also, we assume that a reader has experience with computer vision, and so we will not go into explanations about what a specific algorithm does or how it works. Here are some useful references on the subject [13, 25, 26, 27]. Having experience with OpenCV [21,28] can also be useful.

1.11 Code samples

Throughout the book, we often make use of code samples that show how to work with specific OpenVX functions. The samples are available for download from https://github.com/rgiduthuri/openvx_tutorial [29] under MIT license. The input data for them is located at https://www.dropbox.com/sh/urzzs64a85tqf3d/AADxdIEer_tjHFGzBifZWhsLa. The samples have been tested against the OpenVX sample implementation [30] available for download from https://github.com/KhronosGroup/OpenVX-sample-impl. See the beginning of Chapter 2 for the details on how to build and run the samples.

CHAPTER 2

Build your first OpenVX program

Contents

2.1 First things first

If you are going to build an OpenVX program, you will need a few things:

- A computer. In this first chapter, we assume that you are using a Linux-based machine; in general, this is the easiest option, and what you read in this chapter has been tested on a machine running Ubuntu 16.04.
- A text editor to write your program. You probably have a favorite, whether it is something simple like Vi, Nano, or Scite, or more complex like Emacs or Eclipse.
- A toolchain. For the examples, we assume GCC and give code in C99 (ISO/IEC 9899:1999, ref TBD). This should be a suitably low common denominator. You will also need CMake to build the examples.
- Some examples depend on 3rd party libraries: OpenCV [21], vxa [31], OpenVX-SC-Plus [32], and LAPACK [33].
- Our examples, downloaded from https://github.com/rgiduthuri/openvx_tutorial [29].
- Input data for the examples, downloaded from https://www.dropbox.com/sh/urzzs64a85tqf3d/AADxdIEer_tjHFGzBifZWhsLa.

Copyright © 2020 Elsevier Inc.
All rights reserved.
15

- Last but not least, a copy of OpenVX. We use the sample implementation from Khronos, but of course you may have another implementation from your favorite IP supplier.

2.1.1 How to get the OpenVX sample implementation

Both the OpenVX Specification and a sample implementation may be obtained from https://www.khronos.org/registry/OpenVX/. The sample implementation of OpenVX V1.2 is a tar.bz2 file, which should be unarchived to a suitable folder, for example, your home folder, and then built using the instructions in the file "README". If you opt to install OpenVX on a Linux system, then the libraries will be available in /usr/lib/, and the include file path for building the examples in this book will be ~/OpenVX_sample/include, assuming that you unzipped the archive into your home folder.

2.1.2 Building the examples

Assuming that you unzipped the sample implementation into your home folder, then built and installed it, the following commands should be sufficient to build the examples for this chapter. Note that the first three examples need the immediate-mode library (vxu) in addition to the OpenVX library.

```
$ mkdir build && cd build
$ gcc ../book_sample/example1/example1.c -I ~/OpenVX_sample/include -l
    OpenVX -l vxu -o example1
$ gcc ../book_sample/example2/example2.c -I ~/OpenVX_sample/include -l
    OpenVX -l vxu -o example2
$ gcc ../book_sample/example3/example3.c -I ~/OpenVX_sample/include -l
    OpenVX -l vxu -o example3
$ gcc ../book_sample/example4/example4.c -I ~/OpenVX_sample/include -l
    OpenVX -o example4
$ gcc ../book_sample/example4/example4a.c
    ../book_samples/ppm-io/writeImage.c -I ~/OpenVX_sample/include -I
    ../book_samples/ppm-io/ -l OpenVX -o example4a
$ gcc ../book_sample/example4/changeImage.c
    ../book_samples/ppm-io/readImage.c
    ../book_samples/ppm-io/writeImage.c -I ~/OpenVX_sample/include -I
    ../book_samples/ppm-io/ -l OpenVX -o changeImage
```

To build all examples, you will need to first install the prerequisites (OpenCV, vxa, and LAPACK) and then use CMake to build the examples.

The following commands assume that your current directory is the folder "book_samples" with the samples:

```
$ cd ../
$ mkdir build
$ cd build
$ cmake -G "Unix Makefiles" ../book_samples
$ make
```

2.2 Immediate mode

There are two ways to use OpenVX, "immediate mode" and "graph mode". The immediate mode is pretty straightforward, and is there really only for quick prototyping with the OpenVX functions, so that people who are used to using traditional APIs like OpenCV can get a quick flavor of the sort of functionality that is available in OpenVX. But the real power is in the "graph mode", because this allows implementations to do a lot of optimization. The graph mode is intended to address the main use case of OpenVX, which is when you want to apply the same processing repeatedly to different data, for example, a camera feed.

The immediate mode does what you might expect—you call a function and immediately get the results. For example, you can do a pixel-by-pixel multiplication of two images and get the result in a third image simply by calling one function. We will use the immediate mode for our first example.

2.2.1 Our first very simple example in immediate mode

The code for this example is in example1/example1.c. In outline, what it does is:
- Create an OpenVX context
- Create an image that is a white rectangle on a black background
- Locate the corners in the image, using the Fast Corners algorithm with and without nonmaximum suppression
- Display the results
  The first thing we have in the main() function is the line

```
vx_context context = vxCreateContext();
```

This line creates the OpenVX context, which is the first thing we have to do in any OpenVX program. Without this, there is nothing else we can do with OpenVX. Similarly, when we have finished with OpenVX, we release the context—in our example, this is at the end of main():

```
vxReleaseContext(&context);
```

This tells the OpenVX infrastructure that we have finished with the context, and it can go ahead and destroy it, together with anything else inside it that we have not already destroyed.

The second thing we do after calling vxCreateContext is checking that the context is OK and there were no any errors. In general, you can check any type of vx_reference by calling the function vxGetStatus() on it; if the result is VX_SUCCESS then it is OK to use it in further functions. If the result is not equal to this value, then probably it is a good time to stop. We have made a useful function errorCheck() that bails out with exit(1) if the status is nonzero—note that VX_SUCCESS is defined as being zero:

```
void errorCheck(vx_context *context_p, vx_status status, const char
    *message)
{
    if (status)
    {
    puts("ERROR! ");
    puts(message);
    vxReleaseContext(context_p);
    exit(1);
    }
}
```

We use this in the main function right after creating the context:

```
errorCheck(&context, vxGetStatus((vx_reference)context), "Could not
    create a vx_context\n");
```

Let us take a look at the second function we have defined to create our white rectangle on a black background:

```
vx_image makeInputImage(vx_context context)
{
  vx_image image = vxCreateImage(context, 1024U, 768U, VX_DF_IMAGE_U8);
  vx_rectangle_t rect = {
    .start_x = 256, .start_y = 192, .end_x=768, .end_y = 576
  };
```

```
if (VX_SUCCESS == vxGetStatus((vx_reference)image))
{
  vx_image roi = vxCreateImageFromROI(image, &rect);
  vx_pixel_value_t pixel_white, pixel_black;
  pixel_white.U8 = 255;
  pixel_black.U8 = 0;
  if (VX_SUCCESS == vxGetStatus((vx_reference)roi) &&
     VX_SUCCESS == vxSetImagePixelValues(image, &pixel_black) &&
     VX_SUCCESS == vxSetImagePixelValues(roi, &pixel_white))
    vxReleaseImage(&roi);
  else
    vxReleaseImage(&image);
}
return image;
}
```

We make our black background by filling all of the image and then a white rectangle by filling an ROI (region of interest) in this background. When we have finished with the ROI, we release it as we need not it any more. Note that we do not touch the image or the ROI further if we get an error on creating them, and if we fail to create the ROI or copy the data, then we release the image and return a NULL pointer.

Back in the main() function, we have to test the image after we have created it:

```
vx_image image1 = makeInputImage(context);
errorCheck(&context, vxGetStatus((vx_reference)image1), "Could not
    create image");
```

Now we still need some other parameter declarations before we can call the vxu functions to find the corners. You will find descriptions of the parameters for vxuFastCorners in the documentation for OpenVX. We also allocate some host memory for an array of key points as we will need somewhere to get our results back from OpenVX so that we can display them:

```
vx_float32 strength_thresh_value = 128.0;
vx_scalar strength_thresh = vxCreateScalar(context, VX_TYPE_FLOAT32,
    &strength_thresh_value);
vx_array corners = vxCreateArray(context, VX_TYPE_KEYPOINT, 100);
vx_array corners1 = vxCreateArray(context, VX_TYPE_KEYPOINT, 100);
vx_size num_corners_value = 0;
```

```
vx_scalar num_corners = vxCreateScalar(context, VX_TYPE_SIZE,
    &num_corners_value);
vx_scalar num_corners1 = vxCreateScalar(context, VX_TYPE_SIZE,
    &num_corners_value);
vx_keypoint_t *kp = calloc( 100, sizeof(vx_keypoint_t));
```

Now we have to check that everything has been created OK, including kp, which should not be NULL:

```
errorCheck(&context,
        kp == NULL ||
        vxGetStatus((vx_reference)strength_thresh) ||
        vxGetStatus((vx_reference)corners) ||
        vxGetStatus((vx_reference)num_corners) ||
        vxGetStatus((vx_reference)corners1) ||
        vxGetStatus((vx_reference)num_corners1),
        "Could not create parameters for FastCorners");
```

Then we can call the functions to do the actual work, once with non-maximum suppression and once without:

```
errorCheck(&context, vxuFastCorners(context, image1, strength_thresh,
    vx_true_e, corners, num_corners), "Fast Corners function failed");
errorCheck(&context, vxuFastCorners(context, image1, strength_thresh,
    vx_false_e, corners1, num_corners1), "Fast Corners function
    failed");
```

The last part of the example reads the output arrays and shows the results. You can clearly see the effect of nonmaximum suppression; in the following examples, we will use nonmaximum suppression, so that we see just the corners we expect.

In example 2, we use vxuWarpAffine to rotate our input image through 90 degrees and then vxuOr to logically OR the two images together, creating a white cross on a black background, and of course we see 12 corners. The affine transform is a rotation where each output x and y pixel is taken from pixels at addresses given by a linear combination of the input addresses; if the input address is not integral, then interpolation is performed as specified. The coefficients given in the code as the matrix_values simply swap x and y with no translation (no offset); then this is a 90-degree rotation.

Extracts from example2/example2.c:

```
vx_matrix warp_matrix = vxCreateMatrix(context, VX_TYPE_FLOAT32, 2U,
    3U);
```

```
vx_float32 matrix_values[3][2] = { /* Rotate through 90 degrees */
    {0.0, 1.0},    /* x coefficients */
    {1.0, 0.0},    /* y coefficients */
    {0.0, 0.0}     /* offsets */
};
errorCheck(&context, vxCopyMatrix(warp_matrix, matrix_values,
    VX_WRITE_ONLY, VX_MEMORY_TYPE_HOST), "Could not initialize the
    matrix");
errorCheck(&context, /* Now image2 set to image 1 rotated */
        vxuWarpAffine(context, image1, warp_matrix,
            VX_INTERPOLATION_NEAREST_NEIGHBOR, image2) ||
        /* image3 set to logical OR of images 1 and 2 */
        vxuOr(context, image1, image2, image3) ||
        /*And now count the corners */
        vxuFastCorners(context, image3, strength_thresh, vx_true_e,
            corners, num_corners),
        "Image functions failed");
```

In example 3, we take this further, using the Sobel, Magnitude, and Dilate filters to replace the white cross with the outline of a white cross, and the corner count doubles as both internal and external corners are counted. The Sobel filter is an edge detection filter, and applying it to the cross gives us two output images, the gradient in the x direction and the gradient in the y direction. Taking the magnitude of the x and y images gives us a solid line of single pixels outlining the cross. Note that the vxuMagnitude function takes two 16-bit signed images that are the output of vxuSobel and produces a 16-bit signed image as output. However, most other OpenVX functions only operate on 8-bit unsigned images, so we use the vxuConvertDepth function to produce such an image, with VX_CONVERT_POLICY_SATURATE specifying that values below zero should be set to zero, and values above 255 should be set to 255. Finally, the vxuDilate3x3 function applies a dilation filter, making the thin outline more substantial. So far, we have imagined how the output will actually look, but if you would like a sneak preview, then look at Fig. 2.2 later in the chapter.

From example3/example3.c:

```
/* Now image2 set to image 1 rotated */
vx_status status = vxuWarpAffine(context, image1, warp_matrix,
    VX_INTERPOLATION_NEAREST_NEIGHBOR, image2);
/* image3 set to logical OR of images 1 and 2 and then processed as
    described above */
```

```
errorCheck(&context, vxuOr(context, image1, image2, image3) ||
vxuSobel3x3(context, image3, grad_x, grad_y) ||
vxuMagnitude(context, grad_x, grad_y, magnitude) ||
vxuConvertDepth(context, magnitude, converted,
    VX_CONVERT_POLICY_SATURATE, 1) ||
vxuDilate3x3(context, converted, dilated) ||
/* And now count the corners */
vxuFastCorners(context, dilated, strength_thresh, vx_true_e, corners,
    num_corners),
"Image functions failed");
```

In example 3, you see that we are using a lot of images! In fact, most of these images really need not be retained, since we are not interested in the intermediate data. The only image of any interest is actually the input image that we create. After that, we only use the output from the final corner detector.

2.3 Graph mode

Let us now have a look at graph mode. Example 4 is a graph-mode version of example 3, and comparing the two will help us see how it works. To make it easier to understand the various things going on, example 4 (see the file example4/example4.c) introduces a number of changes:

- The function makeInputImage() now takes two more parameters, the half-width and half-height of the rectangle in the image, so it is easy to make different images.
- A new function makeTestGraph() creates a graph that implements the functionality of the vxu functions that were called in main() in example 3.
- Similarly, a new function showResults() runs the graph with an image and displays the results.
- A new function getGraphParameter() is a simple wrapper to make some of the OpenVX library functions more accessible.
- The new main() is a lot simpler, and it runs the graph with two different images.

Now let us look at things in more detail.

2.3.1 Creating the graph

In the function makeTestGraph(), we make extensive use of virtual images— these are images where we do not want either to read or write the data, and we do not care really how the framework decides to implement them. We use them to connect together processing nodes in the graph, just to inform the framework about the topology. Note that is does not matter in which order nodes are added to the graph (here we do it backward), because the topology is totally defined by the connecting edges, that is, the data objects.

The graph constructed in `makeTestGraph()` can be visualized as in Fig. 2.1. For clarity, some parameters (edges) of the graph are excluded, but all the processing nodes are there. As you can see, there is opportunity for parallel execution. Since the data objects are virtual, the implementation is free to perform optimization by merging nodes together.

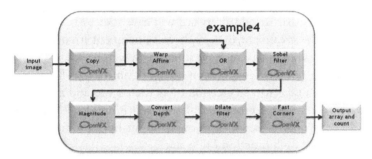

Figure 2.1 *Illustration of the graph created in example 4.* Graph nodes represent functions, and the directed links define input and output data.

The input image we create is not virtual, but like the virtual images and the other interim objects, and even those objects containing the output data, we release our reference to it before exiting the function. How then do we introduce an input or see the results?

The answer is that we use *graph parameters*. Graph parameters in OpenVX give you a simple mechanism for changing input or output objects in a graph once it has been made, and it is a mechanism that allows the actual content of the graph (the nodes and edges) to remain hidden. A graph parameter is associated with the input or output of one node only, so if you want an object to be an input for several nodes, then you can use a Copy node to isolate the input graph parameter. Copy nodes simply copy their input to their output; this is of course a logical or conceptual operation, and the implementation will just "optimize away" the Copy node if its output is a virtual object, so there is no actual overhead when executing the graph.

Note that our input image in example 3 was an input to two vxu functions, `vxuWarpAffine()` and `vxuOr()`, and similarly when we create a graph implementing this same functionality, we feed the same input image into two nodes. It is inconvenient to parameterize two images in this way; we would like just the one input to go to two places. So we introduce the useful Copy node; the output of this feeds both vxWarpAffineNode() and vxOrNode(), and we are able to create just one graph parameter associated with the input of the Copy node:

```
vxAddParameterToGraph(graph, vxGetParameterByIndex(vxCopyNode(graph,
    (vx_reference)input, (vx_reference)imagesU8[0]), 0));
```

It is important to note that graph parameters are added in order; since we added this one first, it will be identified with an index value of zero, and the output parameters that we add afterward will have indices 1 and 2. The assumption is that the creator of the graph will document it correctly so that anyone using it will know which parameter is which.

Note that we do not have much error checking in the graph creation function. This is because errors in creation of all the objects and nodes will be caught when the graph is processed; if we need more detail, then we can turn on logging and see some diagnostic output from the framework without having to test each function call result.

2.3.2 Connecting to parameters and running the graph

So, have a look at main() in the file example4/example4.c; it is also re-produced later in this section. Here we create the graph by calling the makeTestGraph() function and a couple of images, just rectangles of differing sizes, so we can illustrate calling the graph with a different input parameter. Running the graph and displaying the results is the work of our new function showResults(), which takes a vx_graph and a vx_image as parameters. It sets the image as the input parameter to the graph, which as you will remember was given the index 0 by adding it to the graph first:

```
vxSetGraphParameterByIndex(graph, 0, (vx_reference)image);
```

Next, we run the graph using the function vxProcessGraph(). The first time it is run, vxVerifyGraph() will be called internally, and this is the point at which any errors will be picked up. At this point the implementation may do any other processing it deems necessary. Some implementations may aggressively optimize the graph, taking advantage of any virtual objects so that kernels can be coalesced and data movement reduced to a minimum. At the present time the Khronos Sample Implementation does not do this, but implementations from hardware vendors will do so.

The second and third graph parameters are the array of corners and number of corners. These are extracted from the graph using our handy function `getGraphParameter()` and then processed just as in the previous example 3. It is worth having a little look at `getGraphParameter()` as it illustrates a use of one of the `vxQueryXXX()` functions.

2.3.3 Running example 4

Example 4 gives two sets of output. The first should be the same as for example 3, that is, 24 corners, as the image is identical. The second set of results should give just 8 corners, since the input image is a square, which when rotated 90 degrees and superimposed upon itself is still a square, so you will see 8 corners, 4 external and 4 internal.

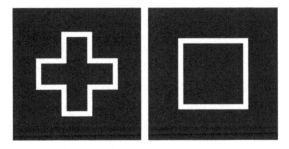

Figure 2.2 *The output images from example 4a.* The images were created using the same graph with different input images.

2.3.4 Code for example 4

```
void errorCheck(vx_context *context_p, vx_status status, const char
    *message)
{
    if (status)
    {
        puts("ERROR! ");
        puts(message);
        vxReleaseContext(context_p);
        exit(1);
    }
}

vx_image makeInputImage(vx_context context, vx_uint32 width, vx_uint32
    height)
```

```
{
    vx_image image = vxCreateImage(context, 100U, 100U,
        VX_DF_IMAGE_U8);
    if (width > 48)
    width = 48;
    if (height > 48)
    height = 48;
    vx_rectangle_t rect = {
        .start_x = 50 - width, .start_y = 50 - height, .end_x = 50 +
            width, .end_y = 50 + height
    };

    if (VX_SUCCESS == vxGetStatus((vx_reference)image))
    {
        vx_image roi = vxCreateImageFromROI(image, &rect);
        vx_pixel_value_t pixel_white, pixel_black;
        pixel_white.U8 = 255;
        pixel_black.U8 = 0;
        if (VX_SUCCESS == vxGetStatus((vx_reference)roi) &&
        VX_SUCCESS == vxSetImagePixelValues(image, &pixel_black) &&
        VX_SUCCESS == vxSetImagePixelValues(roi, &pixel_white))
        vxReleaseImage(&roi);
        else
        vxReleaseImage(&image);
    }
    return image;
}

vx_graph makeTestGraph(vx_context context)
{
    vx_graph graph = vxCreateGraph(context);
    int i;
    vx_image imagesU8[5], imagesS16[3];
    vx_image input = vxCreateImage(context, 100U, 100U,
        VX_DF_IMAGE_U8);

    for (i = 0; i < 5; ++i)
    imagesU8[i] = vxCreateVirtualImage(graph, 100, 100,
        VX_DF_IMAGE_U8);
    for (i = 0; i < 3; ++i)
    imagesS16[i] = vxCreateVirtualImage(graph, 0, 0, VX_DF_IMAGE_VIRT);
```

```
vx_matrix warp_matrix = vxCreateMatrix(context, VX_TYPE_FLOAT32,
    2U, 3U);
vx_float32 matrix_values[6] = {0.0, 1.0, 1.0, 0.0, 0.0, 0.0 }; /*
    Rotate through 90 degrees */
vx_float32 strength_thresh_value = 128.0;
vx_scalar strength_thresh = vxCreateScalar(context,
    VX_TYPE_FLOAT32, &strength_thresh_value);
vx_array corners = vxCreateArray(context, VX_TYPE_KEYPOINT, 100);
vx_size num_corners_value = 0;
vx_int32 shift_value = 1;
vx_scalar num_corners = vxCreateScalar(context, VX_TYPE_SIZE,
    &num_corners_value);
vx_scalar shift = vxCreateScalar(context, VX_TYPE_INT32,
    &shift_value);

vxCopyMatrix(warp_matrix, matrix_values, VX_WRITE_ONLY,
    VX_MEMORY_TYPE_HOST);

/* Create the nodes to do the processing, order of creation is not
    important */
vx_node last_node = vxFastCornersNode(graph, imagesU8[4],
    strength_thresh, vx_true_e, corners, num_corners);
vxDilate3x3Node(graph, imagesU8[3], imagesU8[4]);
vxConvertDepthNode(graph, imagesS16[2], imagesU8[3],
    VX_CONVERT_POLICY_SATURATE, shift);
vxMagnitudeNode(graph, imagesS16[0], imagesS16[1], imagesS16[2]);
vxSobel3x3Node(graph, imagesU8[2], imagesS16[0], imagesS16[1]);
vxOrNode(graph, imagesU8[0], imagesU8[1], imagesU8[2]);
vxWarpAffineNode(graph, imagesU8[0], warp_matrix,
    VX_INTERPOLATION_NEAREST_NEIGHBOR, imagesU8[1]);

/* Setup input parameter using a Copy node */
vxAddParameterToGraph(graph,
    vxGetParameterByIndex(vxCopyNode(graph, (vx_reference)input,
    (vx_reference)imagesU8[0]), 0));

/* Setup the output parameters from the last node */
vxAddParameterToGraph(graph, vxGetParameterByIndex(last_node, 3));
    /* array of corners */
vxAddParameterToGraph(graph, vxGetParameterByIndex(last_node, 4));
    /* number of corners */
```

```
        /* Release resources */
        vxReleaseImage(&input);
        for (i = 0; i < 5; ++i)
        vxReleaseImage(&imagesU8[i]);
        for (i = 0; i < 3; ++i)
        vxReleaseImage(&imagesS16[i]);
        vxReleaseMatrix(&warp_matrix);
        vxReleaseScalar(&strength_thresh);
        vxReleaseScalar(&num_corners);
        vxReleaseScalar(&shift);
        vxReleaseArray(&corners);

        return graph;
}

vx_reference getGraphParameter(vx_graph graph, vx_uint32 index)
{
        vx_parameter p = vxGetGraphParameterByIndex(graph, index);
        vx_reference ref = NULL;
        vxQueryParameter(p, VX_PARAMETER_REF, &ref, sizeof(ref));
        vxReleaseParameter(&p);
        return ref;
}

void showResults(vx_graph graph, vx_image image, const char * message)
{
        vx_context context = vxGetContext((vx_reference)graph);
        puts(message);
        vxSetGraphParameterByIndex(graph, 0, (vx_reference)image);
        if (VX_SUCCESS == vxProcessGraph(graph))
        {
                vx_size num_corners_value = 0;
                vx_keypoint_t *kp = calloc( 100, sizeof(vx_keypoint_t));
                errorCheck(&context,
                    vxCopyScalar((vx_scalar)getGraphParameter(graph, 2),
                    &num_corners_value,
                VX_READ_ONLY, VX_MEMORY_TYPE_HOST), "vxCopyScalar failed");
                printf("Found %zu corners with non-max suppression\n",
                    num_corners_value);

                /* Array can only hold 100 values */
                if (num_corners_value > 100)
```

```
            num_corners_value = 100;

            errorCheck(&context,
                vxCopyArrayRange((vx_array)getGraphParameter(graph, 1),
                0,
            num_corners_value, sizeof(vx_keypoint_t), kp,
            VX_READ_ONLY, VX_MEMORY_TYPE_HOST), "vxCopyArrayRange
                failed");
            for (int i=0; i<num_corners_value; ++i)
            {
                printf("Entry %3d: x = %d, y = %d\n", i, kp[i].x,
                    kp[i].y);
            }

            free(kp);
    }
    else
    {
        printf("Graph processing failed!");
    }
}


int main(void)
{
    vx_context context = vxCreateContext();
    errorCheck(&context, vxGetStatus((vx_reference)context), "Could
        not create a vx_context\n");

    vx_graph graph = makeTestGraph(context);

    vx_image image1 = makeInputImage(context, 30, 10);
    vx_image image2 = makeInputImage(context, 25, 25);

    showResults(graph, image1, "Results for Image 1");
    showResults(graph, image2, "Results for Image 2");

    vxReleaseContext(&context);
    return 0;
}
```

2.4 Image input and output

In the example code, a simple library is included, which provides input and output of portable pixelmap (.ppm) and portable greyscale map (.pgm) files. This may be found in the files ppm-io/readImage.h, ppm-io/readImage.c, ppm-io/writeImage.h, and ppm-io/writeImage.c, for you to statically link with the examples. You can see these in action; example4/example4a.c is just the same as example4/example4.c except that it adds another output parameter to the graph, the image that has its corners counted, and writes this to a .pgm file so that you can see the image created.

The `main()` function looks like this:

```
int main(void)
{
    vx_context context = vxCreateContext();
    errorCheck(&context, vxGetStatus((vx_reference)context), "Could not
        create a vx_context\n");
    vx_graph graph = makeTestGraph(context);
    vx_image image1 = makeInputImage(context, 30, 10);
    vx_image image2 = makeInputImage(context, 25, 25);
    showResults(graph, image1, "Results for Image 1");
    writeImage((vx_image)getGraphParameter(graph, 3), "example4-1.pgm");
    showResults(graph, image2, "Results for Image 2");
    writeImage((vx_image)getGraphParameter(graph, 3), "example4-2.pgm");
    vxReleaseContext(&context);
    return 0;
}
```

2.4.1 Converting to and from portable pixmap format

Portable pixmaps may be viewed under Linux using standard image viewers and on Windows using "Irfanview". There are a variety of tools that may be used to convert other formats to portable pixmap format, for example, on Linux, you can convert a portable pixmap to jpeg simply by

```
$ convert image.ppm image.jpg
```

Similarly, a conversion the other way is just as easy:

```
$ convert image.jpg image.ppm
```

The "convert" command is part of the "imagemagick" package and supports very many formats. If it is not on your system, then try the following command:

```
$ sudo apt-get install imagemagick
```

On Windows, Irfanview can read and write a wide variety of image formats, and after opening in one format, an image may be saved in another format. This conversion may also be done on the command line using the "/convert" option. For more information, see www.irfanview.com.

2.4.2 Other libraries for input and output of images

There are many other libraries useful for reading and writing images, perhaps most notably OpenCV. Other useful and less heavyweight libraries are libpng (see http://www.libpng.org/pub/png/libpng.html), libjpeg (see http://libjpeg.sourceforge.net/), and of course imagemagick; see http://www.imagemagick.org.

2.4.3 Image processing exercises

Another example, "example4/changeImage.c", is a framework that reads in an RGB (.ppm) image and processes it before outputting it again. It uses a Canny edge detector to find edges in the intensity and adds these back in to the image as black outlines. The graph is constructed in the function "makeTestGraph", and the processing follows the flow shown in Fig. 2.3.

Here we are using the Canny Edge Detect filter to find edges in an image. This is a more complex and more sophisticated algorithm than the method we used to detect edges in the previous examples (i.e., the Sobel filter followed by magnitude calculation) and is more suitable for use with greyscale images. A description of the Canny detector (and many other things!) may be found on the University of Edinburgh School of Informatics homepages [34].

The image we are operating on is the Y (luma) channel of an image that has been converted from RGB. We recombine the Y, U, and V planes back into a single image before converting it back to RGB to output again. An example of the results are shown in Fig. 2.4.

We leave it for the reader to experiment:

1. What are the effects of changing the hysteresis values in the Canny edge detector?
2. Why use the intensity for finding edges—what about changes in color?

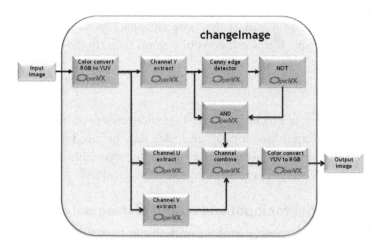

Figure 2.3 *Visualization of the graph in the "changeImage" example.* Graph nodes represent functions, and the directed links define input and output data.

3. I want thicker lines in my outlines.
4. I want to recolor this using just five colors.
5. I want a color-free "halo" around the lines.
6. I want to run this graph on several different images.

Figure 2.4 *Example of input and output images for the "changeImage" example.* An example image (left) and corresponding output with edges added (right).

2.4.4 Answers, or at least hints, for the exercises

1. Setting the upper tracking threshold too low increases the number of undesirable edge fragments appearing in the output; setting the lower tracking threshold too high will cause noisy edges to break up, so set

upper_value quite high and lower_value quite low; the original values are not the best!

2. Try using the other extracted channels (U, V, or both) to find edges and then place them on the Y plane as black lines.

3. Dilate the lines before adding them.

4. Use a look-up table or two convert depth operations back-to-back to reduce the number of colors.

5. Create two sets of lines, one dilated more than the other. The wider ones can be used to remove color and increase intensity on the Y plane before ANDing the thinner ones as black lines.

6. Add parameters to the graph—you will need no any Copy nodes as the input image goes only to one node.

CHAPTER 3

Building an OpenVX graph

Contents

To build an OpenVX graph, we start by creating all the data objects we will use in the graph. Once all the data objects we need are created, we can create the graph object itself and all the nodes that will do the actual computations using our data objects as parameters to the node-creation functions. As we create the nodes, we insert them into the graph and link together via the node parameters. Finally, we validate and execute the graph. Once the graph has been built and validated, we can execute it many times with different input data.

In this chapter, we illustrate this with a simple background subtraction example. Suppose we want to identify all the "foreground" pixels in a scene. We have an image of the "background" (we will talk about how to create such a background image in a later chapter) and a current image of the same scene that might have some foreground objects in it. For our purposes, foreground just means "not background." One way to get an idea of where the foreground objects are located is to simply subtract the background image from the current image, take the absolute value of all the pixel differences, and apply some threshold to these differences. In other words, if a pixel in the current image is sufficiently different from the background, we call it a foreground pixel. Now there are a number of problems with this simple approach, for example, a small camera movement or lighting change can make everything become "foreground," but we will ignore that for the purposes of this simple example.

Let us see how this looks in OpenVX. We need image data objects for the background image, current image, difference image, and final (binary) foreground image. The code at the top of the next page creates these.

Copyright © 2020 Elsevier Inc.
All rights reserved.

```
vx_image bg_image = vxCreateImage(ctxt, 640, 480, VX_DF_IMAGE_U8);
vx_image curr_image = vxCreateImage(ctxt, 640, 480, VX_DF_IMAGE_U8);
vx_image diff_image = vxCreateImage(ctxt, 640, 480, VX_DF_IMAGE_U8);
vx_image fg_image = vxCreateImage(ctxt, 640, 480, VX_DF_IMAGE_U8);
```

In a real production code, we should check that all the data objects were created successfully, but we leave this out of this sample code for simplicity. In this example, we also need to create a threshold object and set it to some initial value:

```
vx_threshold threshold =
  vxCreateThresholdForImage(ctxt, VX_THRESHOLD_TYPE_BINARY,
                    VX_DF_IMAGE_U8, VX_DF_IMAGE_U8);
vx_status status;
vx_uint8 threshval = 10;
status = vxCopyThresholdValue(threshold, &threshval,
                    VX_WRITE_ONLY, VX_MEMORY_TYPE_HOST);
```

In this example, we use 10 as the threshold, so if the grayscale value of the current image is different from the background by more than 10, then we call it a foreground pixel. We use the default values for the threshold outputs, so the foreground pixels will be set to 255 (0xFF), and the rest will be set to zero. Now that we have the necessary data objects, we can build a simple graph and link it up.

3.1 Linking nodes

In OpenVX, nodes are linked via the parameters to the node creation functions. If an output parameter of one node is the same OpenVX data object as the input parameter of another node, then the nodes are linked via this data object. There is no separate explicit "link" call. This enables OpenVX code to look very similar to traditional non-graph code. For our background subtraction example, we just have two nodes, an absolute difference (or absdiff) node and a threshold node (thresh). Here is the code to create the graph and insert the nodes:

```
vx_graph g = vxCreateGraph(ctxt);
vx_node absdiff = vxAbsDiffNode(g, bg_image, curr_image, diff_image);
vx_node thresh = vxThresholdNode(g, diff_image, threshold, fg_image);
```

The first line creates the graph object g within our OpenVX context. The next two lines create the absdiff and threshold nodes, respectively.

They are inserted into the graph as they are created by having the graph object g as the first parameter to the node creation functions. The inputs to the absdiff node are the background and current images (bg_image and curr_image, respectively). The output of the absdiff node is diff_image, and diff_image is also an input to the threshold node. In this way the two nodes are linked via the diff_image object. The output of the threshold node is fg_image. A pictorial representation of this graph is given in Fig. 3.1.

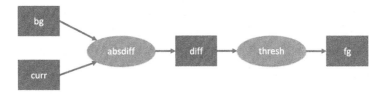

Figure 3.1 The background subtraction graph g.

The code that creates the nodes looks very much like traditional non-graph code. In fact, we can use the OpenVX utility library to create non-graph or "immediate mode" code that does the same image processing:

```
vxuAbsDiff(ctxt, bg_image, curr_image, diff_image);
vxuThreshold(ctxt, diff_image, threshold, fg_image);
```

Although this code looks similar to the graph code, and we can often think of the graph code as being similar to the traditional code, the graph code actually behaves very differently, and we need to keep these differences in mind when writing OpenVX programs. In the traditional immediate-mode code, when we call the vxuAbsDiff function, the image processing happens during this function. After the vxuAbsDiff function returns, the diff_image object is filled with the result pixels. However, with the graph code, no image processing is performed by the vxAbsDiffNode function—we are simply setting up the graph. The image processing occurs later when we execute the graph. We will see how this is done in a later section of this chapter.

3.2 Virtual images

Although our graph code above will work, we can make a significant performance improvement by changing the way we declare the diff_image object that links the two nodes. We created the `diff_image` object using the `vxCreateImage` function, which creates a "real" image that can have its pixels examined after the graph is executed. But in this case, we are not really interested in the `diff_image` pixels, only in the thresholded binary version of them in `fg_image`. The `diff_image` object is just an intermediate result. But since we declared `diff_image` as a "real" image, the OpenVX implementation has to allocate space for it somewhere and fill this space with the computed pixels in case we later ask to examine them via a call to the `vxMapImagePatch` function. This can waste a lot of time and space if we are not really interested in this intermediate result. Fortunately, we can inform the OpenVX implementation that we are never going to try to map the pixels of `diff_image` by declaring it as a *virtual* image. Let us see how that works.

Whereas "real" images exist in the OpenVX context, so that they can be queried and mapped outside graphs and be shared between different graphs, virtual images are local to the graph that contains them. They can only be used in this one graph. Therefore the first parameter of `vxCreateVirtualImage` is `vx_graph`, not `vx_context`. In our example the code that implements the `diff_image` object as a virtual image is as follows:

```
vx_graph g = vxCreateGraph(ctxt);
vx_image diff_image = vxCreateVirtualImage(g, 640, 480, VX_DF_IMAGE_U8);
vx_node absdiff = vxAbsDiffNode(g, bg_image, curr_image, diff_image);
vx_node thresh = vxThresholdNode(g, diff_image, threshold, fg_image);
```

Note that most of the code here is identical to the previous version of the graph construction code. The only difference is how we create the `diff_image` object. Since the virtual image is inside the graph, we need to create the graph itself before creating the virtual images it will contain. Then we need to provide the graph object as the first argument to the vxCreateVirtualImage function, as shown before. The other three lines of code are identical to the previous version. The resulting graph can be depicted pictorially as in Fig. 3.2.

In this version of the figure, there is no separate block shown for the `diff_image`; it is just shown as the name of the link between the two nodes. The `diff_image` object is just used a placeholder in the graph-construction code to indicate that the output of one node is the input of another.

Declaring the intermediate results of a graph as virtual objects enables the OpenVX implementation to "optimize away" the intermediate images. OpenVX no longer has to reserve a location in memory for all of the pixels,

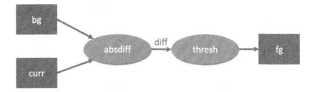

Figure 3.2 An optimized background subtraction graph.

just in case we ask to see them later. It can effectively merge the two nodes into a single operation that computes the difference and thresholds it in some internal register before storing the thresholded result. The OpenVX implementation is not *required* to do this, but building the graph and correctly using virtual objects *enables* this optimization, which is not possible with a traditional "immediate mode" API.

Unless you have an actual use for the intermediate objects in a graph, it is a good practice to always make them virtual to enable an optimized implementation of OpenVX to execute your graph more efficiently. When you do this, the objects are not necessarily data objects at all; they are just "links" between nodes, internal to the graph.

3.3 Graph verification and execution

As we mentioned before, the graph construction code does not actually do any image or vision processing. All we have really done is create a data structure that describes the computation we want to perform. This representation is a high-level abstract description of the algorithm that needs to be customized for the target hardware before execution. This is done via the vxVerifyGraph function, which typically does a lot more than just verifying the graph for correct construction. We call vxVerifyGraph and check its return value very simply:

```
status = vxVerifyGraph(g);
if (status != VX_SUCCESS) { /* Something went wrong */ }
else { /* We're ready to execute */ }
```

The call to vxVerifyGraph verifies that the graph is correctly constructed according to the rules of OpenVX. These rules include checks that are familiar from non-graph programming, such as making sure that the data types of the parameters match what the function expects. It also includes some rules that are more specific to graph programming. Two important rules to keep in mind when constructing an OpenVX graph are that a data object can only be written into one time within a given graph, and that the graph cannot contain any cycles. We call these the *single-writer* rule and the *no-cycles* rule.

The single-writer rule is needed to avoid ambiguous results when executing the graph. Recall that the nodes are not executed when you create them; they are just inserted into the graph. The order in which you create the nodes may not be the same order in which they are executed in the graph. The graph execution must respect the data dependencies, which means that the input data for every node needs to be available before the node executes and creates its output data. Other than that, the nodes can be executed in any order, which may not be the order in which you created them. Consider the snippet of code that creates an illegal(!) graph with two nodes that have the same input and output images:

```
vx_node thresh = vxThresholdNode(g, input, threshold, output);
vx_node box = vxBox3x3Node(g, input, output);
```

The ambiguity comes in determining the contents of the output image after the graph is executed. Will it be the thresholded version of the input image or the box-filtered version of the input image? You might think that the threshold would execute first, and the box filter would execute second, because that is the order you created them in, which would leave a box-filtered result in the output. But you would be wrong. That is what would happen in immediate-mode programming, but not in a graph. The illegal graph looks like that in Fig. 3.3.

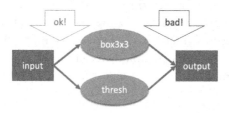

Figure 3.3 An illegal graph with multiple writers to the same output.

The two nodes get their inputs from the same image, which is fine, but they also put their outputs into the same image, which is not fine. The OpenVX implementation is free to execute the nodes in any order as long as the data dependencies are satisfied. Since the input image is available for both nodes, either one can execute first, so it is not defined as to which result finally ends up in the output. In fact, the OpenVX implementation might execute both nodes *at the same time*, so the contents of the output image might be a jumbled mixture of results. OpenVX gets around this by simply making such graphs illegal. When you try to verify a graph in which two nodes write to the same output, the verification will fail. Always check your verification result; if it is not VX_SUCCESS, then you have a problem in your graph.

The potential benefits of using the graph become clearer in the legal version of this graph in Fig. 3.4, in which separate images are used for the outputs of the two nodes. The OpenVX implementation can execute these two nodes in any order, or execute them at the same time, enabling a speed-up via parallelism.

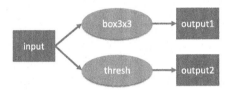

Figure 3.4 A legal graph with potential for parallelism.

The OpenVX implementation can also optimize memory transfers by noticing that the inputs of the two nodes are the same, so the input image only needs to be loaded into internal memory once, and then both nodes can use it. These are just a couple of optimizations that can be done via graphs, which is why we bother with graphs and put up with the "single-writer" restriction.

The other restriction to be aware of is the "no-cycles" rule. The OpenVX graph you construct must be a directed acyclic graph or "DAG" for short. It is directed because the execution flows directionally from the inputs to the outputs. It is acyclic because there are no "cycles." A cycle in a graph is where if you can follow the arrows from some point in the graph and end up back where you started, and it is not allowed in an OpenVX graph.

The reason for this restriction is that the OpenVX implementation would not know where to start executing in the cycle. When the graph is executed, the OpenVX implementation has to figure out where to start. It looks for nodes for which all the inputs are not the output of some other node in the graph. These nodes are ready to execute, and they can be executed in any order, in parallel, interleaved, and so on. The nodes that have inputs written by other nodes in a graph are *not* ready to execute—they cannot be executed until their inputs are written. This is what "respect the data dependencies" in the graph means. Nodes have to wait until their inputs are valid before they can execute. In our simple background subtraction example above, the `absdiff` node is able to execute immediately, because its inputs are not written by any node in the graph. The `thresh` node is *not* able to execute immediately, because its input is written by the `absdiff` node, which is in the same graph. As outputs are written, additional nodes become ready to execute as their inputs get written. This continues until all the nodes in the graph have been executed exactly once.

If you have a cycle in the graph, then every node in the cycle has an input written by another node in the graph. There is no obvious place to start. Even if you designated one node as the "start" node, then there would be no obvious place to stop—the execution would go in a cycle forever. Rather than try to come up with a bunch of rules to handle cycles, OpenVX just prohibits them. If you try to verify a graph with a cycle in it, then it will fail. If you want to do something more than once, then just execute the graph multiple times.

There is one special case that we just mention here but describe in detail in a later chapter, which is for `vx_delay` objects. It is legal to create something that looks like a cycle in a graph if the object involved in the cycles is a `vx_delay` object. The `vx_delay` object is considered an "advanced" object, and there are a fair number of rules about how to use them and how they behave, which we will discuss later. For now, just follow the no-cycles rule and make sure your graph is a DAG. If you try to verify a graph with no `vx_delay` objects that is not a DAG, then it will fail.

As described before, graph verification will check whether your graph is legal, but it can do much more. Graph verification, specifically, the `vxVerifyGraph` function, is an opportunity for the OpenVX implementation to analyze the graph, which is an abstract representation of the computation you want to perform, and figure out how to efficiently execute it on the hardware the implementation supports. If the hardware has a memory hierarchy with some large but relatively slow memory and some small fast memory (and all modern compute hardware is like this), then the OpenVX implementation can figure out how to efficiently move the data, preloading caches, setting up DMA transfers if the hardware supports it, tiling large images into smaller pieces that can fit in the small fast memories, and so on. If the hardware has multiple processing elements, then the OpenVX implementation can distribute the work among these processors to achieve data parallelism and/or functional parallelism.

When we described the graph execution, we described a naïve version of how it works, in which an entire output image gets written before it can be used as an input to a subsequent node. In fact, the implementation can do optimization tricks where nodes in a sequence are all run in parallel as soon as only a portion of their inputs are computed. The implementation just has to make sure that the results after the graph executes are the same *as if* they were computed in the naïve way.

Doing all this analysis and optimization can take some time, depending on the implementation, the hardware it supports, and the level of optimization being done. In some ways, it can be like running a compiler. This can make it a fairly heavyweight operation in terms of time and resources. You want to construct your OpenVX program so that you call vxVerifyGraph very infrequently, preferably only once at startup for each graph in your program (or even offline if your implementation supports the import/export extension—more on that later).

Once your graph is verified, you can think of it as having been transformed from an abstract description of your algorithm to an optimized executable program for your specific hardware. To extend the compiler analogy, an unverified graph is a source code, and the verified graph is an executable. You can run this executable as many times as you want over different data. Your program may have a simple structure like the following code snippet:

```
/* create graph ... */
status = vxVerifyGraph(g);
if (status != VX_SUCCESS) exit(1);
while (more_images_to_process()) {
  /* grab input images ... */
  status = vxProcessGraph(g);
  if (status != VX_SUCCESS) exit(1);
  /* display results ... */
}
```

3.4 Parameter validation

As part of the graph verification process, the parameters to each node are validated to ensure they are compatible with the requirements of the node.

These parameters are opaque OpenVX objects that can have a complex underlying structure and set of attributes. The C compiler you use to compile your OpenVX program will check that the basic object type (e.g., vx_image or vx_scalar) matches the requirements of the function, but it will not check the details of the attributes of objects for consistency. This is done by the implementation when you execute your program during vxVerifyGraph.

For example, when you add two images via vxAddNode, the dimensions of the input and output images all have to match up. You cannot add a VGA image to an HD image—they have to be of the same size for the result to be well-defined. If you add two VGA images, then the result has to be another VGA image. Also, according to the OpenVX specification, the only underlying pixel data types that must be supported by vxAddNode are unsigned 8-bit (VX_DF_IMAGE_U8) and signed 16-bit (VX_DF_IMAGE_S16). If the images are of some other type, then the implementation may not support them for vxAddNode, so these date types need to be checked. The vxVerifyGraph function needs to check that the image sizes match up and the pixel data types provided are supported by the implementation. Other checks of attribute values may be done during vxVerifyGraph—consult the OpenVX specification and/or your implementation's user documentation for details.

3.5 What can be changed at runtime?

Once you have verified your graph, it becomes a compiled executable. If you change your graph, then you should have to re-verify and compile it again. However, as we said before, you would like to avoid repeatedly doing the heavyweight verification process, so you really want to avoid changing your graph. If you have two slightly different things you want to do with a graph and to alternate between them, rather than modifying a single graph each time, then you are usually better off creating two versions of the graph and alternating between the two graphs, even if the two graphs are mostly the same.

The OpenVX specification says (in the graph "state transition diagram") that if you modify the graph, then it is "optional" whether the graph stays verified. Whether your modification to the graph causes it to become unverified depends on the change you make and the implementation you use. In some implementations, even the slightest change may cause the graph to become unverified. Other implementations may try to patch up the verified graph for some changes rather than requiring a complete reverification. You will need to consult your implementation documentation (or experiment with it) to determine whether your change requires a reverification. You can check directly whether your change caused the graph to become unverified using the function `vxIsGraphVerified`.

The OpenVX standard enables you to write *functionally* portable code, meaning that if you run the same code on different implementations, then you will get the same results. (Within reasonable limits—some functions are bit-accurate, and some have an error tolerance.) The graph-programming features of OpenVX also make it possible to write *performance* portable code. Being performance-portable does not mean you get the same performance on every platform—some hardware innately does certain things faster than other hardware. Being performance-portable means that you will get pretty good performance on multiple platforms with the same code. In other words, you do not have to write different code for different platforms to get good performance. The performance you observe will depend more on the underlying hardware itself and the optimizations done by the OpenVX implementation than on any platform-specific specializations you make in your application code. This is a great feature of OpenVX.

The fact that re-verification is "optional" after making graph changes can reduce performance portability if you are not careful. If you make a small change to a graph in your video-processing loop, then some implementations may happily adjust without re-verification, and others may impose a big re-verification overhead on every frame. The behavior required by the OpenVX specification is that if the graph is not verified when you call `vxProcessGraph`, then the graph gets immediately verified. In other words, `vxVerifyGraph` gets called automatically inside `vxProcessGraph` without you explicitly asking for it. The result is that on the implementation where your changes do not trigger reverification, the performance of `vxProcessGraph` will be as expected, whereas on another implementation the overhead of verification will be included inside the `vxProcessGraph` function, possibly making it much longer. The same function call would have very different performance on the two systems, which is the opposite of performance portability. So, if you truly want performance portability, then do not change your graphs.

That said, some changes are more likely to cause issues than others. If you change the connectivity of the graph, for example, inserting or deleting nodes, then this is almost certainly going to trigger a re-verification. We advise against this—it is better to create a separate graph. Changing the size of data objects, for example, the dimensions of an input image, is also quite likely to cause a re-verification, since many of the optimizations done by

OpenVX implementations have to do with memory management. Changing the image sizes may trigger a different memory allocation and therefore a re-verification. Some implementations may be able to take this in stride, with little or no extra overhead. Changing the value of an attribute that is unrelated to memory management is usually OK. For example, most implementations will allow you to change the value of a threshold without going through a re-verification cycle, so such a change is probably safe. It is not guaranteed in the spec though, so your mileage may vary. Check the documentation for your implementation.

3.6 Example

Here is the full code for the background subtraction example using a virtual image for the intermediate result, building and verifying the graph, and then executing the graph in a loop:

```
int main ()
{
  vx_status status;
  vx_uint8 threshval = 10;
  vx_image bg_image = vxCreateImage(ctxt, 640, 480, VX_DF_IMAGE_U8);
  vx_image curr_image = vxCreateImage(ctxt, 640, 480, VX_DF_IMAGE_U8);
  vx_image fg_image = vxCreateImage(ctxt, 640, 480, VX_DF_IMAGE_U8);
  vx_threshold threshold =
    vxCreateThresholdForImage(ctxt, VX_THRESHOLD_TYPE_BINARY,
                       VX_DF_IMAGE_U8, VX_DF_IMAGE_U8);
  status = vxCopyThresholdValue(threshold, &threshval,
                       VX_WRITE_ONLY, VX_MEMORY_TYPE_HOST);
  vx_graph g = vxCreateGraph(ctxt);
  vx_image diff_image = vxCreateVirtualImage(g, 640, 480, VX_DF_IMAGE_U8);
  vx_node absdiff = vxAbsDiffNode(g, bg_image, curr_image, diff_image);
  vx_node thresh = vxThresholdNode(g, diff_image, threshold, fg_image);
  status = vxVerifyGraph(g);
  if (status != VX_SUCCESS) exit(1);

  /* initialize bg_image ... */
  while (more_images_to_process()) {
    /* grab curr_image ... */
    status = vxProcessGraph(g);
    if (status != VX_SUCCESS) exit(1);
    /* display results and update bg_image ... */
  }
```

CHAPTER 4

Using the graph API to write efficient portable code

Contents

In this chapter, we talk about OpenVX graphs and how they make it possible to write performance-portable applications. By performance portable we mean near-optimal performance on any platform. This does not necessarily mean the same execution time on all platforms, since the capabilities of different hardware differ due to various factors, based on the engineering trade-offs made when designing that particular hardware to meet specific customer requirements.

First, let us start with few concepts of OpenVX graphs, and how to build graphs using the node-creation APIs, node parameters, and graph parameters. Then we will talk about an execution model and asynchronous execution and explain how the OpenVX graphs make it possible for hardware vendors to provide OpenVX implementations that give applications the best possible performance on their hardware. We will describe how the code can be performance portable across multiple platforms.

Some advanced topics in OpenVX include control flow and custom kernels. Custom kernels can provide application-specific functionality, which can be included as a node in a graph.

OpenVX Programming Guide
https://doi.org/10.1016/B978-0-12-816425-9.00010-3
Copyright © 2020 Elsevier Inc.
All rights reserved.
47

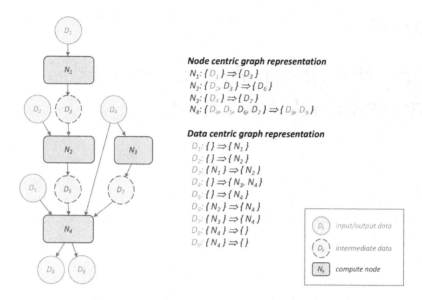

Node centric graph representation
$N_1: \{D_1\} \Rightarrow \{D_3\}$
$N_2: \{D_2, D_3\} \Rightarrow \{D_6\}$
$N_3: \{D_4\} \Rightarrow \{D_7\}$
$N_4: \{D_4, D_5, D_6, D_7\} \Rightarrow \{D_8, D_9\}$

Data centric graph representation
$D_1: \{\} \Rightarrow \{N_1\}$
$D_2: \{\} \Rightarrow \{N_2\}$
$D_3: \{N_1\} \Rightarrow \{N_2\}$
$D_4: \{\} \Rightarrow \{N_3, N_4\}$
$D_5: \{\} \Rightarrow \{N_4\}$
$D_6: \{N_2\} \Rightarrow \{N_4\}$
$D_7: \{N_3\} \Rightarrow \{N_4\}$
$D_8: \{N_4\} \Rightarrow \{\}$
$D_9: \{N_4\} \Rightarrow \{\}$

D_j input/output data

D_k intermediate data

N_k compute node

Figure 4.1 Bipartite DAG representing an OpenVX graph.

4.1 OpenVX graph

In OpenVX a program is represented by a graph with compute nodes that correspond to functions and connection between compute nodes and data objects that correspond a dataflow, which in turn imply the order of execution. An OpenVX graph can be built by creating a graph object using vxCreateGraph() and connecting nodes and data objects together. Prior to execution, a graph needs to be verified, using vxVerifyGraph(), to check for consistency, correctness, and other conditions, such as memory availability and so on. The graph verification stage is used by vendors to optimize a graph to hardware platforms, so that graph execution incurs no any additional costs.

4.1.1 OpenVX graph is a bipartite DAG

An OpenVX graph can be formally defined as a bipartite Directed Acyclic Graph (DAG) that can be represented as a tuple (N, D, C), where N is a set of compute nodes, D is a set of data objects, and C is a set of unidirectional connections between compute nodes and data objects.

Fig. 4.1 explains a few concepts used in this chapter. Node-centric and data–centric graph representations can be used for connections between compute nodes and data objects. The OpenVX node API uses a node-centric graph representation. Each node creation API call instantiates a compute node into an OpenVX graph. The node-creation APIs take input parameters and output parameters as arguments as depicted in Fig. 4.1. The same graph can be looked at in a data-centric manner. The data-centric graph representation helps identify most common graph input and output parameters. All the graph inputs will have an empty set of compute nodes as inputs in the data-centric graph representation. Similarly, all the graph outputs will have an empty set of compute nodes as outputs in the data-centric graph representation. From the data-centric representation in Fig. 4.1 it is obvious that D_1, D_2, D_4, and D_5 are graph inputs and D_8 and D_9 are graph outputs. Also note that a data object can be written by at most one compute node in the graph. In other words, a data object should not appear twice in a node–centric graph representation as output.

4.1.2 Intermediate results as virtual data objects

In most scenarios, the set of intermediate data objects, that is, $\{D_3, D_6, D_7\}$ in Fig. 4.1, will not be accessed by the application. In such case the application can mark these data objects as *virtual* data objects, indicating that application will *not* access these objects for read or write. Virtual data objects must appear once as output and at least once as input in a node-centric graph representation.

A virtual data object is scoped within the graph in which it is created. In other words, a virtual data object, created using one of `vxCreateVirtualXXXX()` functions with a `vx_graph` object, will not be valid once the graph object is destroyed.

Use of the virtual data objects enable several optimizations that are portable across hardware platforms.
- reuse memory across multiple virtual data objects
- use local memory for intermediate results without allocating main memory
- fuse nodes to accelerate overall computation
- remove computation for unused data
- etc.

4.1.3 A graph example

Let us start with an example of the OpenVX node creation API that performs *Harris Corner Detector* on an 8-bit image producing list of corners into an array as shown in Fig. 4.2.

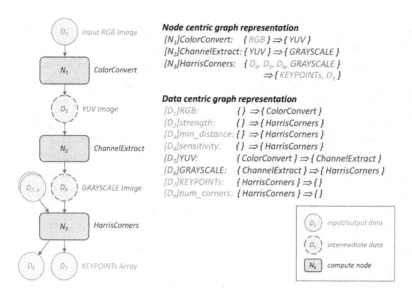

Figure 4.2 Bipartite DAG for Harris Corners Detection.

The node centric graph representation in Fig. 4.2 has compute nodes N_1 through N_3, each of which has the corresponding node creation APIs in OpenVX, namely, *vxColorConvertNode()*, *vxChannelExtractNode()*, and *vxHarrisCornersNode()*. This will force an application to create all node parameters prior to calling a node creation API. See *step-4* in the following code snippet for use of node creation APIs to build the graph in Fig. 4.2:

```
// application configuration parameters
vx_uint32 width = 640;
vx_uint32 height = 480;
vx_size keypoint_count = 10000;
vx_float32 strength_init = 0.0005f;
vx_float32 min_distance_init = 5.0f;
vx_float32 sensitivity_init = 0.04f;
vx_int32 gradient_size = 3;
vx_int32 block_size = 3;
...
// [step-1] create input data objects
vx_image rgb_image = vxCreateImage(context, width, height,
    VX_DF_IMAGE_RGB);
vx_scalar strength = vxCreateScalar(context, VX_TYPE_FLOAT32,
    &strength_init);
```

```
vx_scalar min_distance =
          vxCreateScalar(context, VX_TYPE_FLOAT32, &min_distance_init);
vx_scalar sensitivity =
          vxCreateScalar(context, VX_TYPE_FLOAT32, &sensitivity_init);
// [step-2] create output data objects
vx_size zero = 0;
vx_array keypoints = vxCreateArray(context, VX_TYPE_KEYPOINT,
    keypoint_count);
vx_scalar num_corners = vxCreateScalar(context, VX_TYPE_SIZE, &zero);
...
// [step-3] create intermediate data objects. Note the image dimensions
// are set as ZEROs. This asks the OpenVX to automatically calculate
// the intermediate image dimensions based on the graph.
vx_image yuv = vxCreateVirtualImage(graph, 0, 0, VX_DF_IMAGE_YUV);
vx_image gray = vxCreateVirtualImage(graph, 0, 0, VX_DF_IMAGE_U8);

// [step-4] build the graph using node create APIs
vx_node node_convert = vxColorConvert(graph, rgb_image, yuv);
vx_node node_extract = vxChannelExtract(graph, yuv, VX_CHANNEL_Y, gray);
vx_node node_harris = vxHarrisCornersNode(graph, gray,
        strength, min_distance, sensitivity,
        gradient_size, block_size,
        keypoints, num_corners);
vxVerifyGraph(graph);
...
```

Let us examine an optimization opportunity provided by the virtual image objects used in the previous example. Since the virtual image objects yuv and gray are not required to be allocated in memory, a vendor can directly produce the gray image from rgb_image and even not generate the U & V planes in the yuv image. This will reduce the overall memory requirement by the space required for the yuv image and reduce overall execution time by omitting the U & V plane computation and the memory transfer for the yuv image. It is also possible for a vendor to avoid memory allocation for gray image by performing RGB to GRAY scale conversion into local memory and use GRAY scale pixels directly by *Harris Corner Detector*.

Few additional optimization opportunities include:
- splitting *Harris Corner Detector* execution across the whole system
- execute pixel-processing in *Harris Corner Detector* at tile granularity
- etc.

4.2 Node parameters

A node creation API takes a *graph* as its first argument, followed by all the node parameters. Each node parameter is identified by its index in the corresponding node creation APIs. For example, the *Harris Corner Detector* API has EIGHT node parameters:

```
vx_node vxHarrisCornersNode(vx_graph graph,
           vx_image input,        // input parameter #0
           vx_scalar strength_thresh, // input parameter #1
           vx_scalar min_distance, // input parameter #2
           vx_scalar sensitivity,  // input parameter #3
           vx_int32 gradient_size, // configuration parameter #4
           vx_int32 block_size,   // configuration parameter #5
           vx_array corners,      // output parameter #6
           vx_scalar num_corners); // output parameter #7 [optional]
```

The input *GRAYSCALE image* parameter index is 0, and the *num_corners* parameter index is 7. The data object type of a node parameter is specified in the node creation API. For adjustable scalar parameters, such as the floating-point *sensitivity*, vx_scalar objects are used. If the value of a scalar parameter is required during the graph compilation, such as *gradient_size* and *block_size*, then the node creation APIs take them as *constant values* instead of vx_scalar objects. Optional node parameters such as *num_corners* can be NULL when an application does not need access to the output parameter. In addition, optional input parameters are not used by nodes when they are NULL, for example, the third input tensor of vxTensorMatrixMultiplyNode().

When a node parameter is a valid data object, its value can be accessed by an application. The application has to be careful not to access a data object while a graph accessing the same data object is executing.

```
// [step-5] set the graph inputs
vxCopyImagePatch(rgb_image, ..., input_rgb, VX_WRITE_ONLY,
     VX_MEMORY_TYPE_HOST);
// [step-6] execute the graph
vxProcessGraph(graph);
// [step-7] access the graph outputs
vx_size num_corners_value;
vxCopyScalarWithSize(num_corners, sizeof(num_corners_value),
     &num_corners_value, VX_READ_ONLY, VX_MEMORY_TYPE_HOST);
vxCopyArrayRange(corners, 0, num_corners_value, sizeof(vx_keypoint_t),
```

```
            corners_buffer_ptr, VX_READ_ONLY, VX_MEMORY_TYPE_HOST);
...
```

Applications can change node parameters at a later time using *vxSetParameterByIndex()* API. For example, in the previous example, the application changes input from SD camera to HD camera:

```
// [step-7] replace input image by HD image
vxSetParameterByIndex(node_convert, 0, (vx_reference)rgb_image_HD);
```

In certain scenarios, these changes can result in graph reverification during the next call to vxProcessGraph(), depending on underlying vendor's OpenVX implementation.

4.3 Graph parameters

It is natural for most applications to separate graph building and graph execution. In such cases, graph execution may not have access and/or knowledge of the graph internal nodes and node parameters. In such cases, it comes handy to create an interface to the graph, such that graph parameters can automatically propagate to node parameters.

Now let us look at the data centric graph representation example in Fig. 4.3. All the data objects that are not produced by any compute nodes are inputs to the bipartite DAG, that is, D_1, D_2, D_3, and D_4 are inputs to the corresponding OpenVX graph. Similarly, all the data objects that have not consumed any compute node, that is, D_7 and D_8, are outputs of the OpenVX graph. Any node parameter can be a graph parameter, except for virtual data objects.

OpenVX supports two APIs to create a graph parameter from a node parameter, vxGetParameterByIndex() and vxAddParameterToGraph().

```
// [step-4] build the graph and create graph interface
//  parameter[0]: rgb_image
//  parameter[1]: strength
//  parameter[2]: min_distance
//  parameter[3]: sensitivity
//  parameter[4]: corners
//  parameter[5]: num_corners
vx_node node_convert = vxColorConvert(graph, rgb_image, yuv);
vx_node node_extract = vxChannelExtract(graph, yuv, VX_CHANNEL_Y, gray);
vx_node node_harris = vxHarrisCornersNode(graph, gray,
```

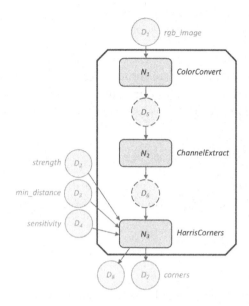

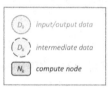

Figure 4.3 Graph Interface for Harris Corners Detection.

```
        strength, distance, sensitiv,
        gradient_size, block_size,
        keypoints, num_corners);
vx_parameter params[6] = {
    vxGetParameterByIndex(node_convert, 0),
    vxGetParameterByIndex(node_harris, 1),
    vxGetParameterByIndex(node_harris, 2),
    vxGetParameterByIndex(node_harris, 3),
    vxGetParameterByIndex(node_harris, 6),
    vxGetParameterByIndex(node_harris, 7)
  };
vxAddParameterToGraph(graph, params[0]);
vxAddParameterToGraph(graph, params[1]);
vxAddParameterToGraph(graph, params[2]);
vxAddParameterToGraph(graph, params[3]);
vxAddParameterToGraph(graph, params[4]);
vxAddParameterToGraph(graph, params[5]);
vxVerifyGraph(graph);
```

Use the vxGetGraphParameterByIndex() API to access graph parameters as shown below:

```
// get current graph parameters
vx_image rgb_image = (vx_image) vxGetParameterByIndex(graph, 0);
vx_scalar strength = (vx_scalar) vxGetParameterByIndex(graph, 1);
vx_scalar min_distance = (vx_scalar) vxGetParameterByIndex(graph, 2);
vx_scalar sensitivity = (vx_scalar) vxGetParameterByIndex(graph, 3);
vx_array corners = (vx_array) vxGetParameterByIndex(graph, 4);
vx_scalar num_corners = (vx_scalar) vxGetParameterByIndex(graph, 5);
...
```

Use the `vxSetGraphParameterByIndex()` API to change graph parameters as shown below:

```
// replace input image to another camera
vxSetGraphParameterByIndex(graph, 0,
    (vx_reference)rgb_image_back_camera);
```

4.4 Execution model

The execution model specifies how work takes place inside OpenVX.

A graph has to be verified once prior to scheduling for execution. As shown in Fig. 4.4, at any given time the graph will be one of the following states:

- `VX_GRAPH_STATE_UNVERIFIED`: created/modified, should be verified to execute
- `VX_GRAPH_STATE_VERIFIED`: verified, is ready to schedule for execution
- `VX_GRAPH_STATE_RUNNING`: scheduled, not completed or is being executed
- `VX_GRAPH_STATE_ABANDONED`: execution abandoned
- `VX_GRAPH_STATE_COMPLETED`: execution is completed and ready to schedule again

During the graph verification, an OpenVX implementation optimizes the graph execution for the underlying acceleration hardware. OpenVX enables graphs to be optimized for several modes of execution:

- *Synchronous blocking execution mode*
- *Asynchronous single-issue-per-reference execution mode*

4.4.1 Synchronous execution

A graph can be executed in *Synchronous blocking execution mode* using `vxProcessGraph()` that blocks until the graph execution has completed. The graph inputs have to be written prior to calling the `vxProcessGraph()`, and graph outputs can be read if `VX_SUCCESS` is returned.

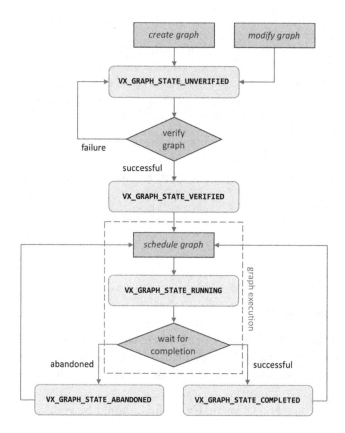

Figure 4.4 OpenVX Graph State Transitions.

This mode guarantees that the host scheduling thread will be automatically in sync with the OpenVX run-time:

```
...
while(/* more_data_available() */)
{
  /* prepare_input_data(); */
  /* write_input_data_to_input_data_objects(); */

  status = vxProcessGraph(graph);
  if(status != VX_SUCCESS) {
    break;
  }

  /* read_output_data_from_output_data_objects(); */
```

```
/* process_output_data(); */
}
...
```

4.4.2 Asynchronous execution

The *Asynchronous single-issue-per-reference execution mode* is more flexible and allows scheduling of a graph multiple times using vxScheduleGraph() and vxWaitGraph() APIs. When pipelining is enabled, this mode can further be used to schedule multiple initiations with different inputs and output, as specified by the OpenVX pipelining extension.

An application thread can schedule a graph for execution using vxScheduleGraph() and continue working on host until it needs the results from graph execution. Before accessing the outputs from the graph, the application has to call vxWaitGraph() API:

```
...
while(/* there_are_more_things_to_do() */)
{
  /* write_input_data_to_input_data_objects(); */

  status = vxScheduleGraph(graph);
  if(status != VX_SUCCESS) {
    break;
  }

  /* process_output_data_from_previous_iteration(); */
  /* prepare_input_data_for_next_iteration(); */

  status = vxWaitGraph(graph);
  if(status != VX_SUCCESS) {
    break;
  }

  /* read_output_data_from_output_data_objects(); */
}
...
```

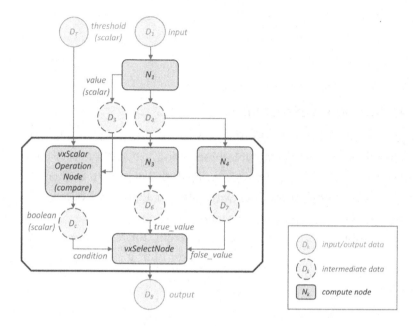

Figure 4.5 Conditional Execution.

4.5 Control flow

Some applications require different portions of a graph to be executed depending on a condition computed within the graph or passed as an argument. To support these use cases, OpenVX has a predicated execution model, which uses scalar operations and a conditional data object copy function.

Fig. 4.5 shows a graph that uses vxSelectNode() to predicate the execution of N_3 and N_4 based on the value of D_c. If D_6 and D_7 are virtual data objects, then the conditional part of the OpenVX graph execution can be represented using the following pseudocode:

- execute $D_8 = N_3(D_4)$, *if compare(D_3,D_c) == true*
- execute $D_8 = N_4(D_4)$, *otherwise*

4.6 User kernels and nodes

Some applications use their own compute functions in the middle of vision pipelines. To schedule such functions outside the OpenVX context, the vision pipeline has to be built using multiple graphs and manually schedule

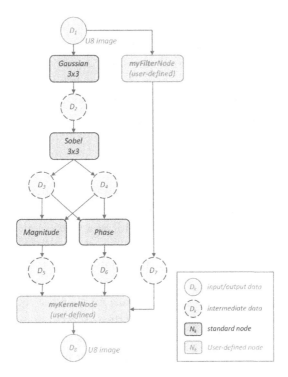

Figure 4.6 Graph with User-defined Kernel nodes.

these graphs along with the custom functions. This may not be efficient because the vision pipeline is scheduled at smaller granularity.

To improve efficiency with such custom compute functions, OpenVX supports the concept of user-defined functions that will be executed as nodes from inside the graph. The purpose of this paradigm is to:

- Further exploit independent operation of nodes within the OpenVX platform
- Allow componentized functions to be reused elsewhere in OpenVX
- Formalize strict verification requirements (i.e., Contract Programming)

Fig. 4.6 shows a graph that contains two user-defined kernel nodes as part of the graph. This allows custom functions to be executed in an independent fashion with respect to independent base nodes within OpenVX. This allows OpenVX to further minimize execution time if supported by the hardware.

The OpenVX user-defined kernels will be registered into the OpenVX context immediately after creation of the context using the vxAddUserKernel()

API. Each kernel in the OpenVX context will be identified by unique a kernel enumeration and a kernel name. The user-defined kernels will be implemented using callback functions vx_kernel_f, vx_kernel_validate_f, vx_kernel_initialize_f, and vx_kernel_deinitialize_f. In addition, the kernel signature will be set to indicate the number of kernel arguments and type of each parameter.

4.7 The OpenVX pipelining extension

The OpenVX graph API as defined in the main standard contains a potential inefficiency when executing a graph on parallel hardware that can work on multiple images at the same time. If you process a video sequence, then you do not necessarily have to fully process a given frame before you start working on the next frame. If you only have one processor, then it does not matter—the processor can only do one thing at a time. However, if you have two processors and the next frame is available, then the second processor can start work on the next frame before the first processor completes work on the current frame. If you have 10 processors, or 1000, then you can work on as many frames as are available until your processing capacity is fully utilized.

The main OpenVX API *does* enable parallel execution *within* a graph, so, for example, you can have multiple processors executing different nodes in graph at the same time or multiple processors working on different parts of an image within a given node. However, it does not enable parallel execution *across* executions of the same graph. Even if you use the asynchronous vxScheduleGraph() and vxWaitGraph() APIs, although your host processor can schedule a graph execution and go off and do something else for a while, then it cannot push more data through the same graph while it is executing. The OpenVX Graph Pipelining, Streaming, and Batch Processing Extension solves this problem and closes this potential efficiency gap.

The pipelining extension spec is available on the Khronos registry (https://www.khronos.org/registry/OpenVX). A direct link to the latest version (1.1) as of the time if this writing is https://www.khronos.org/registry/OpenVX/extensions/vx_khr_pipelining/1.1/html/vx_khr_pipelining_1_1_0.html. It contains an extensive discussion of the motivation for it and several examples that we will not try to reproduce here. The purpose of this section is giving you a high-level idea of what is in the extension and what it is good for, so that you can know whether to use it in your application or perhaps urge the vendor of the OpenVX implementation you use to implement this extension.

The basic idea of the graph pipelining is that there are queues of objects at the inputs and outputs of the graph. You can put things into the queues and the graph will either consume them (if it is an input) or fill them up (if it is an output). The basic idea is illustrated in Fig. 4.7. The diagram shows an arbitrary graph with one input on the left and one output on the right. The application feeds data to the graph by enqueuing data objects to be processed (e.g., images) via the function `vxGraphParameterEnqueueReadyRef()`. (Technically, what gets enqueued is `vx_reference`, since a graph parameter can be any OpenVX object type.)

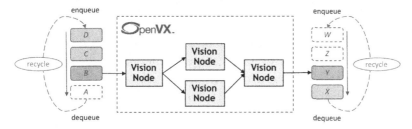

Figure 4.7 Illustration of a pipelined graph.

When the graph runs, it "consumes" an object, or reference, from the input queue. The entire graph has not necessarily executed yet, but enough has been done that the graph does not need the reference any more. The application can check to see whether the graph has consumed the input data using the function `vxGraphParameterCheckDoneRef()`, or just call `vxGraphParameterDequeueDoneRef()`, which will block until an item in the queue has been consumed and can be dequeued.

Something similar happens on the output side, except that the applications enqueues "empty" references and dequeues object references that have been "filled" by the executing graph. Once the application has dequeued the output object, it can do whatever it wants with the graph results as usual.

On both the input and output sides of the graph, used objects can be "recycled." At the input, an object that has been consumed by the graph can be "refilled" by the application and enqueued again at the graph input. At the output, once the application is done doing whatever it wants with the results of the graph, the object can be reenqueued at the graph output as an "empty" object to be overwritten by the graph with another result. This recycling is indicated by the dashed arrows in the diagram.

When you first start processing, you will enqueue and dequeue a few times at the input before you will dequeue anything at the output. This is because the first few objects that are consumed will only get partway through the graph before the graph is ready to consume another input. This will continue until the graph pipeline is full. This is called the "pipe-up" phase in the extension spec, and it ends when the graph eventually produces its first results at the output. Once the pipeline is full, it reaches a steady-state "pipeline" phase, where an output is produced for every input. At the end of processing the sequence of inputs, there will be a "pipe-down" phase while the graph completes processing of the partial results still inside the graph and the pipeline is emptied.

The spec also describes "batch" processing, in which a whole set, or batch, of inputs is provided to the graph for execution at once. A batch of inputs is consumed to produce a batch of outputs. There are no any special functions specific to batch processing; the enqueue and dequeue functions (vxGraphParameterEnqueueReadyRef and vxGraphParameterDequeueDoneRef) can take an array containing an entire batch of inputs or outputs at once. The spec provides an example of this.

We have not yet said what triggers the graph to start executing. The spec defines three different "schedule modes," which can be set using the vxSetGraphScheduleConfig() function: AUTO, MANUAL, and NORMAL. In VX_GRAPH_SCHEDULE_MODE_QUEUE_AUTO, once enough data is enqueued at the inputs for the graph to be able to start, it just starts automatically. The application does not need to call vxScheduleGraph() or vxProcessGraph() at all—it happens automatically when the graph has sufficient input data. In VX_GRAPH_SCHEDULE_MODE_QUEUE_MANUAL the application *does* need to call vxScheduleGraph() to trigger the graph to execute, which provides the application more control at the expense of additional code and opportunities for bugs. The VX_GRAPH_SCHEDULE_MODE_NORMAL option is just a backward compatibility mode that makes the graph operate just like a nonpipelined graph that does not use this extension.

The pipelining extension offers a means to abstract the details of queuing and execution even further with the "streaming" functions. In this case, you create "source" and "sink" user nodes for the inputs and outputs, respectively; the extension spec gives examples of these. You connect the sources to the inputs of your graph and the sinks to the outputs and then enable streaming via the vxEnableGraphStreaming() function. This function takes two parameters, the graph you want to stream and a node within the graph to be identified as the "trigger" node. When this trigger node completes, the graph automatically executes again. Then you just call `vxStartGraphStreaming()` to get things going and `vxStopGraphStreaming()` whenever you are done.

The last feature in the streaming spec that we will talk about here is event handling. When you start using the more abstract features of this extension, the graph is pretty much off executing by itself. You have to set up all the streaming so that the data automatically flow through the graph and the main application executes asynchronously from the graph. The application may want to know when certain things happen in the graph, so that it can react accordingly. It does this by "registering" events on the graph using the `vxRegisterEvent()` function so that when these events happen, the application can find out about them by calling the `vxWaitEvent()` function. The application can register events for when a graph parameter is consumed, a graph or node completes execution, or when a node generates an error. There is also an option for the application to create and be notified of "user" events.

Events are enabled and disabled globally for the entire OpenVX context using the `vxEnableEvents()` and `vxDisableEvents()` functions. So the sequence executing an event-handling application is to:

- Create your graph (`vxCreateGraph`)
- Create your parameter queues (e.g., `vxCreateImage`)
- Set your graph to run in AUTO mode (`vxSetGraphScheduleConfig`)
- Register the events you are interested in (`vxRegisterEvent`)
- Enable events (`vxEnableEvents`)
- Wait for events in a loop and react accordingly (`vxWaitEvent`)

The pipelining spec gives an example of an event handling application with all the gory details. If your OpenVX implementation supports this extension, then you can use it with streaming and event handling to squeeze the most performance out of your parallel hardware in an elegant and portable manner.

CHAPTER 5

Deploying an OpenVX graph to a target platform

Contents

In this chapter, we discuss how to deploy an OpenVX graph to a target platform. The reason for this chapter is based upon two key assumptions: that you use a graph not necessarily in the same place that the graph was created and that once you have made a graph, you are going to use it many times without modification. Typically, a graph is created to be used in some product or inside another application. This can be done for several reasons:

- Code reuse. A graph to fulfill a required function is taken from another project or from a library.
- IP protection. A graph implements a proprietary algorithm that the providers wish to hide.
- Code minimization. A product is cleaner and smaller without the code required to create the graph.
- Secure field updates. A graph can be stored as data so that it may be replaced in a fielded application, with data integrity checks.

The acknowledgment of these use cases is very important and one of the major raisons d'être for OpenVX graphs.

Using the OpenVX API, there are actually several ways that you can deploy a graph to a target platform, and these are appropriate in different

Copyright © 2020 Elsevier Inc.
All rights reserved.

cases. We discuss these different methods in the separate sections that follow using the "ChangeImage" example from Chapter 2.

5.1 Graph factories

Graph factories provide a mechanism where a complete OpenVX graph may be packaged as a function that returns a graph, which may be verified, processed, and then destroyed. Note that the graph must be created, processed, and destroyed all in the same OpenVX context.

Graphs created in this way can use graph parameters as a handy way of customizing the graph by allowing different objects to be used as inputs and outputs to the same graph. As long as metadata (e.g., the dimensions of an image) do not change on those parameters, the graph will not need reverification before processing with new parameters attached.

5.1.1 An example of a graph factory

If we look at the file "graphFactory.c," then we can see the example from changeImage.c, or at least something similar, repackaged as a function that just returns a graph. The code is reproduced below for easy reference:

Note the following in the listing:

- Great care is taken to release unwanted references such as those to nodes, which otherwise could stay in the context until it is destroyed, even if the graph is destroyed.
- The structure of the graph is completely hidden if the function is supplied as a precompiled object module, perhaps in a library.
- The interface to the graph (i.e., the graph parameters) must be clearly documented elsewhere and known to the users for the graph to be used

We use the function releaseNode to wrap our calls to the node creation functions. This function creates a stack object and then calls vxReleaseNode on it, so it is just an alternative to assigning the value to a variable and releasing it explicitly, but it does provide a common place where the node may be tested for validity. Skip past the listing below to see the discussion on how it is used in the next subsection.

```
/*
graphFactory.c
Create a test graph in the context
*/
#include <VX/vx.h>
```

```
#include <stdio.h>
#include <stdlib.h>

void releaseNode(vx_node node)
{
    vx_status status = vxGetStatus((vx_reference) node);
    if (VX_SUCCESS != vx_status)
    {
        printf("Error %d creating node\n", status);
    }
    else
    {
        vxReleaseNode(&node);
    }
}


vx_graph makeTestGraph(vx_context context, vx_image image, vx_image
    output)
{
    /* creates a graph with one input image and one output image.
    The input and output images can be provided through the mechanism of
        graph parameters,
    it is assumed that the input and output images are RGB.
    Replace the default processing with what you like!
    */
    enum {
        numvyuv = 2,  /* Number of virtual YUV images we need */
        numv16 = 3,   /* Number of virtual S16 images we need */
        numv8 = 8     /* Number of virtual U8 images we need */
    };
    vx_graph graph = vxCreateGraph(context);
    vx_image virtsyuv[numvyuv], virts8[numv8], virts16[numv16];

    int i;

    for (i = 0; i < numvyuv; ++i)
        virtsyuv[i] = vxCreateVirtualImage(graph, 0, 0, VX_DF_IMAGE_NV12);
    for (i = 0; i < numv8; ++i)
        virts8[i] = vxCreateVirtualImage(graph, 0, 0, VX_DF_IMAGE_U8);
    for (i = 0; i < numv16; ++i)
        virts16[i] = vxCreateVirtualImage(graph, 0, 0, VX_DF_IMAGE_S16);
```

```
/* Do some arbitrary processing on the input image */
/* First, make a true greyscale image. We do this by converting to YUV
and extracting the Y. */
vx_node node = vxColorConvertNode(graph, image, virtsyuv[0]);

/* Get the parameter that will be the input and add it to the graph */
vx_parameter parameter = vxGetParameterByIndex(node, 0);
vxReleaseNode(&node);
vxAddParameterToGraph(graph, parameter);
vxReleaseParameter(&parameter);

/* Extract the Y */
releaseNode(vxChannelExtractNode(graph, virtsyuv[0], VX_CHANNEL_Y,
    virts8[0]));

/* Use Sobel plus magnitude to find edges on the greyscale image */
releaseNode(vxSobel3x3Node(graph, virts8[0], virts16[0], virts16[1]));
/* Note that we have to use specifically U8 and S16 images to satisfy
    the convert depth node */
releaseNode(vxMagnitudeNode(graph, virts16[0], virts16[1],
    virts16[2]));
vx_int32 shift = 1;
vx_scalar shift_scalar = vxCreateScalar(context, VX_TYPE_INT32,
    &shift);
releaseNode(vxConvertDepthNode(graph, virts16[2], virts8[1],
    VX_CONVERT_POLICY_WRAP, shift_scalar));
vxReleaseScalar(&shift_scalar);

/* Make the edges wider, then black and AND the edges back with the Y
    value so as to superimpose a black background */
releaseNode(vxDilate3x3Node(graph, virts8[1], virts8[2]));
releaseNode(vxDilate3x3Node(graph, virts8[2], virts8[3]));
releaseNode(vxNotNode(graph, virts8[3], virts8[4]));
releaseNode(vxAndNode(graph, virts8[0], virts8[4], virts8[5]));

/* Get the U and V channels as well.. */
releaseNode(vxChannelExtractNode(graph, virtsyuv[0], VX_CHANNEL_U,
    virts8[6]));
releaseNode(vxChannelExtractNode(graph, virtsyuv[0], VX_CHANNEL_V,
    virts8[7]));

/* Combine the color channels to give a YUV output image */
```

```
releaseNode(vxChannelCombineNode(graph, virts8[5], virts8[6],
    virts8[7], NULL, virtsyuv[1]));

/* Convert the YUV to RGB output */
node = vxColorConvertNode(graph, virtsyuv[1], output);

/* Now get the parameter that will be the output and add it to the
    graph */
parameter = vxGetParameterByIndex(node, 1);
vxReleaseNode(&node);
vxAddParameterToGraph(graph, parameter);
vxReleaseParameter(&parameter);

/* Give the graph a name */
vxSetReferenceName((vx_reference)graph, "Test Graph");

for (i =0; i < numv16; ++i)
    vxReleaseImage(&virts16[i]);
for (i =0; i < numvyuv; ++i)
    vxReleaseImage(&virtsyuv[i]);
for (i =0; i < numv8; ++i)
    vxReleaseImage(&virts8[i]);
return graph;
}
```

5.1.2 Using a graph factory

The previous example graph factory can be compiled into either statically linkable object code (either just as a stand-alone object file or part of a static library) or placed in a dynamically loaded library (shared object file) and then linked with code designed to use it. In this way a previously tested graph may be deployed into a variety of applications without the details being known; if the graph is in a dynamically loaded library, then this can be updated in the field without changing the main program.

The file "graphFactoryTest.c," reproduced further, demonstrates how this can be done.

```
/*
graphFactoryTest.c
Read an image, change it, write it out.
*/
#include <VX/vx.h>
```

```c
#include <stdio.h>
#include <stdlib.h>
#include "readImage.h"
#include "writeImage.h"

extern vx_graph makeTestGraph(vx_context context, vx_image image,
    vx_image output);

void main(int argc, void **argv)
{
    if (argc != 3)
    {
        printf("Change an image\n"
        "%s <input> <output>\n", (char *)argv[0]);
    }
    else
    {
        struct read_image_attributes attr;
        vx_context context = vxCreateContext();
        vx_image image = createImageFromFile(context, (const char
            *)argv[1], &attr);
        vx_image output = vxCreateImage(context, attr.width,
            attr.height, attr.format);
        vx_graph graph = makeTestGraph(context, image, output);
        if (vxGetStatus((vx_reference)image))
            printf("Could not create input image\n");
        else if (vxProcessGraph(graph))
            printf("Error processing graph\n");
        else if (writeImage(output, (const char *)argv[2]))
            printf("Problem writing the output image\n");
        vxReleaseContext(&context);
    }
}
```

If you have all the examples and associated files, this program can be compiled and linked with the command

```
gcc -o factory graphFactoryTest.c readImage.c writeImage.c
    graphFactory.c -lopenvx -I ~/openvx/include/
```

5.1.3 When to use a graph factory for deployment

The graph factory can be used for deployment, typically in a shared object library when either there is access to the source code or the library provided is built specifically for the target system. For example, an IP provider can supply an OpenVX implementation for a certain hardware, complete with a set of useful graphs in a library, or a third party can be contracted to provide and support an OpenVX graph for a particular system.

Even if a third party is not used, the graph factory concept provides a neat packaging by which functionality can be separated into distinct deliverables and well-defined projects. For example, a specification for a graph factory may be produced that specifies the following:

- Signature of the graph factory function, that is, a name and any configuration parameters extra to the context, that must be passed.
- The number and types of the graph parameters (these should be the only interfaces)
- The resources allowed, for example, no more than so much data memory, or the utilization rate of processing elements and maximum time for the graph to run
- A description of the processing to be performed by the graph
- Acceptance tests corresponding to all of the above

5.1.4 Graph factory pros and cons

Pros:
- Simple to understand, requires no special OpenVX extensions
- Easy way of packaging code and defining projects
- Adaptable – can be used generally as a way of developing OpenVX applications and for specifically deploying to a target
- If the graph factory is written using only the standard OpenVX API, then it is portable between conformant implementations from different vendors
- It is efficient in terms of storage and memory usage compared to, for example, the XML extension.
- It is possible to create a graph where all the virtual images do not have their sizes specified, so changing the input and output images to those of different sizes and reverifying the graph is possible.
Cons:
- As this is an object code, it must be built for a specific platform and is in general not portable between platforms

• It is possible to easily reverse engineer the graph factory with an instrumented version of the OpenVX library (that anyone with access to the OpenVX standard could create), so it is not a good way to protect IP by obfuscation; the usual legal remedies used for source code are required.

5.2 The XML extension

The XML extension allows the complete context to be exported as an XML file. For example, a small program can be used to create a single graph in the context and then output this as XML. It can be convenient to use the graph factory to create the graph. This XML description is then read into the target system context, and the graph is recreated for use there.

An example code for this (using the graph factory for convenience) may be found in "XML-example.c," and is also given further. You can download this code from the link given in Chapter 2 and compile and link it according to the instructions given there or with this command:

```
gcc -o XML-example XML-Example.c readImage.c writeImage.c graphFactory.c
    -lopenvx -I ~/openvx/include/
```

When you run "XML-example," for example, providing "cup.ppm" as the first parameter, you will then be able to see the XML output in the file "ExampleXMLGraph.xml." Note that the virtual graphs near the end of the file have no size. If you change the line that creates the graph in the listing (see the return statement in createXMLGraph() below) to also verify the graph, then you will see this information added. Because the XML export is made just as is, without any verification, it can be a useful tool to find out why your graphs fail verification.

```
#include <VX/vx.h>
#include <stdio.h>
#include <stdlib.h>
#include "readImage.h"
#include "writeImage.h"
#include <VX/vx_khr_xml.h>

vx_char xmlFilename[] = "ExampleXMLGraph.xml";

extern vx_graph makeTestGraph(vx_context context, vx_image image,
    vx_image output);
```

```
vx_status createXMLGraph(vx_uint32 width, vx_uint32 height, vx_char
    xmlfile[])
{
   vx_context context = vxCreateContext();
   return vxGetStatus((vx_reference)makeTestGraph(context,
                                   vxCreateImage(context, width,
                                       height, VX_DF_IMAGE_RGB),
                                   vxCreateImage(context, width,
                                       height, VX_DF_IMAGE_RGB))) ||
         vxExportToXML(context, xmlfile) ||
         vxReleaseContext(&context);
}


void main(int argc, char **argv)
{
   if (argc != 3)
      printf("Change an image\n%s <input> <output>\n", argv[0]);
      /* We create the XML graph here but in practice it will be done by
          a different application */
      /* Note also our example must specify the width and height up
          front, if the images are a different size
      then the graph will fail to verify later */
   else if (createXMLGraph(640, 480, xmlFilename))
      printf("Failed to export the context\n");
   else
   {
      struct read_image_attributes attr;
      vx_context context = vxCreateContext();
      vx_image image = createImageFromFile(context, argv[1], &attr);
      vx_image output = vxCreateImage(context, attr.width, attr.height,
          attr.format);
      vx_import import = vxImportFromXML(context, xmlFilename);
      if (vxGetStatus((vx_reference)import))
         printf("Failed to import the XML\n");
      else
      {
         vx_graph graph = (vx_graph)vxGetImportReferenceByName(import,
             "Test Graph");
         if (vxGetStatus((vx_reference)graph))
            printf("Failed to find the test graph\n");
         else if (vxSetGraphParameterByIndex(graph, 0,
             (vx_reference)image) ||
```

```
                vxSetGraphParameterByIndex(graph, 1,
                    (vx_reference)output))
            printf("Error setting the graph parameters\n");
        else if (vxProcessGraph(graph))
            printf("Error processing the graph\n");
        else if (writeImage(output, argv[2]))
            printf("Problem writing the output image\n");
        }
    vxReleaseContext(&context);
    }
}
```

[Hint: try changing the createXMLGraph() function as follows and see the XML change. The processing remains the same, since the graph is verified again upon input.]

```
vx_status createXMLGraph(vx_uint32 width, vx_uint32 height, vx_char
    xmlfile[])
{
    vx_context context = vxCreateContext();
    return vxVerifyGraph(makeTestGraph(context,
                            vxCreateImage(context, width, height,
                                VX_DF_IMAGE_RGB),
                            vxCreateImage(context, width, height,
                                VX_DF_IMAGE_RGB))) ||
        vxExportToXML(context, xmlfile) ||
        vxReleaseContext(&context);
}
```

5.2.1 Pros and cons of the XML extension

Pros:
- Completely platform independent and portable between implementations that support the extension
- May be used as an interface to other tools, for example, XML graph descriptions could be output by a design tool requiring no code to be written
- Could be used as input for a documentation or visualization tool
- Simple text format
- Simple to use: one function exports all the context to a text file, and one function imports all XMLs to the context.

- Graph may be handled as data during deployment to a target system
- All the objects imported are in full detail, so, for example, graphs may be modified to use images of different sizes and reverified before use. Cons:
- Very bulky, nonoptimal format, especially bad for data. It is suggested that XML descriptions are always compressed.
- Completely transparent, no hiding of IP at all
- Probably not very fast and more resource-hungry in comparison to other methods.

5.2.2 When to use the XML extension for deployment

Basically, the only reason to use the XML extension for deployment is when IP protection is not an issue, portability between different OpenVX implementations is required, or if graphical design tools are available that can directly generate XML.

5.3 The export and import extension

The export and import extension is also part of the OpenVX SC specification and has been designed to allow efficient import of objects on a deployed target system. We will give an example that will be referenced and built upon in the chapter on safety-critical use of OpenVX. In contrast to the XML extension, which exports all the context, the export and import extension is designed to operate only upon specifically named objects. Also, in contrast to the XML extension, the format is completely undefined and left up to the implementation, allowing the possibility of tailoring to specific hardware or the use of custom IP to create efficient implementations.

5.3.1 Exporting a graph with the export and import extension

Exporting a graph using the export and import extension is more complex than with the XML extension and at the same time more controlled. It is necessary to specify which objects are to be exported in the current context and how it is to be done. Defining the object to be exported is done by passing an array of object references to the export function and how each object is to be exported (and imported later) by passing a corresponding array of values defined with specific meaning. Objects may be exported in one of three ways:

- Complete along with all their data (use the value VX_IX_USE_EXPORT_ VALUES)
- Export metadata only; after import, the importing application will set the data (use the value VX_IX_USE_NO_EXPORT_VALUES)
- Export sufficient data just to check that an object supplied by the importing application is compatible (use the value VX_IX_USE_APPLICATION_ CREATE)

You can think of these three enumerations actually describing more how the object will be *imported*, and the implementation will export whatever is necessary to achieve that goal. With this in mind, the implementation should do the following on *import* in each case:

- VX_IX_USE_EXPORT_VALUES: The implementation will create the object in its entirety, assigning the value(s) it had at the time of export
- VX_USE__NO_EXPORT_VALUES: The implementation will create the object, but assign no data to it. In this case the application must supply the data, for example the pixel values of am image.
- VX_IX_USE_APPLICATION_CREATE: The implementation expects that the application will have already created the object and will check that it is valid. In this case, upon import the application must supply a reference to a valid object; data may be assigned to the object either before or after the import operation.

Which types of object may actually be exported and whether you can use a specific type of export depend upon the object. There are some objects that cannot be exported: the vx_context, vx_parameter, vx_node and vx_kernel objects. When a graph is exported, all the other objects necessary to recreate the graph are also exported, and the export method (or "use") is ignored. Note that if a graph has parameters, then the data objects used for the parameters must be explicitly listed in the list of references, even if they are going to be replaced when the graph is later imported.

Any data objects that have been made by the application rather than the framework (e.g., images created from handle) must be exported with VX_IX_USE_APPLICATION_CREATE, because the framework will not know how to create them when they are imported.

In contrast to the XML extension, objects are exported to a memory "blob" of length given by the framework, not to a text file, and the format is completely undefined and left up to the OpenVX implementers to determine. The following code illustrates how to export just the graph created by our graph factory. Note that we must get the references for the graph parameters and include them in the export, so it is more convenient to pass the image objects to the graph factory, rather than just the image dimensions. To allow for a simple alternative to using the graph parameters, we also note that these images will be created by the importing application, and in our later import example, we will use both methods of replacing the graph parameters. Note that, for clarity, we omit many of the xvReleaseXXX function calls; in practice, vxReleaseContext() should release the resources used by all the objects in the context.

```c
/*
export_graph.c
Create a graph and export it using the export and import extension
The memory "blob" is written to a file so it may be later read and
    imported
*/
#include <VX/vx.h>
#include <stdio.h>
#include <stdlib.h>
#include <VX/vx_khr_ix.h>

extern vx_graph makeTestGraph(vx_context context, vx_image image,
    vx_image output);

void main(int argc, void **argv)
{
    vx_context context = vxCreateContext();
    vx_image input = vxCreateImage(context, 640, 480, VX_DF_IMAGE_RGB);
    vx_image output = vxCreateImage(context, 640, 480, VX_DF_IMAGE_RGB);
    vx_graph graph = makeTestGraph(context, input, output);
    vx_reference refs[3] = {
       (vx_reference)graph,
       (vx_reference)input,
       (vx_reference)output
    };
    vx_enum uses[3] = {
       VX_IX_USE_EXPORT_VALUES,
       VX_IX_USE_APPLICATION_CREATE,
       VX_IX_USE_APPLICATION_CREATE
    };
    const vx_uint8 *blob = NULL;
    vx_size length;
    vx_status status = vxExportObjectsToMemory(context, 3, refs, uses,
        &blob, &length);
```

```
if ( VX_SUCCESS == status) {
    /* We have a valid export of length bytes at address blob. Do
        something with it like writing it
    to a file... */
    if (argc == 2) {
        const char * filename = argv[1];
        FILE *fp = fopen(filename, "wb");
        if (fp) {
            if ((fwrite(blob, length, 1, fp) == 1) && (fclose(fp) == 0))
                {
                printf("Wrote the exported graph to file '%s', total %zu
                    bytes\n", filename, length);
            } else {
                fclose(fp);
                printf("Error writing to file '%s'\n", filename);
            }
        } else {
            printf("Could not open '%s' for writing\n", filename);
        }
    } else {
        printf("Expected a valid filename: %s <file>\n", (char
            *)argv[0]);
    }
} else {
    /* There was an error creating the export, report to the user... */
    printf("Got error %d when exporting the graph. No file was
        written.\n", status);
}
/* now release the export blob memory, now we have copied it
    somewhere */
vxReleaseExportedMemory(context, &blob);
/* Release the context and all other resources */
vxReleaseContext(&context);
}
```

5.3.2 Importing a graph with export and import extension

To import our saved graph, written to the output file using our "export_graph" program, we have created a handy function loadObjectsFromFile, which has almost the same signature as vxImportObjectsFromMemory but deals in files rather than memory blobs. If it is unsuccessful in reading the file, then it returns NULL rather than an import object, so we have to be careful about using the import object in the main program. Note that as soon as we have imported objects into the context, we can free the memory used for the "blob." Our loadObjectsFromFile function returns the import object, but in fact we do not need it, since we have the reference to the graph we want in the array refs, which was passed to and filled in by the vxImportObjectsFromMemory function, so we could have made a void function or one that returned a status. Alternatively, we could use the import object to find references using vxGetImportReferenceByName as we did for the XML example. In our import example, we demonstrate two ways in which objects attached to the graph are replaced, firstly by using the VX_IX_USE_APPLICATION_CREATE import flag and then by setting the graph parameters and executing the graph again. Note that to correctly import the graph and other objects, you must know what objects have been exported and by what method (application create, or with or without values); this is in contrast to the XML extension, where the contents of the import may be enumerated and discovered. However, the actual internal structure of graphs in the "blob" is entirely hidden.

```
/*
processGraph.c
Read an image, change it using a saved graph, write it out.
*/
#include <VX/vx.h>
#include <VX/vx_khr_ix.h>
#include <stdio.h>
#include <stdlib.h>
#include <sys/types.h>
#include <sys/stat.h>
#include "readImage.h"
#include "writeImage.h"

vx_import loadObjectsFromFile(vx_context context, vx_size num_refs,
    vx_reference *refs, vx_enum *uses, const char * fname)
{
    struct stat statbuf;
    int statres = stat(fname, &statbuf);
    FILE *fp = fopen(fname, "rb");
    vx_uint8 *blob = (vx_uint8 *)malloc(statbuf.st_size);
    vx_import import = NULL;
    if (fp && 0 == statres && blob) {
        if (fread(blob, statbuf.st_size, 1, fp) == 1) {
```

```
            printf("Read %zu bytes ok\n", (size_t)statbuf.st_size);
            import = vxImportObjectsFromMemory(context, num_refs, refs,
                uses, blob, statbuf.st_size);
        } else {
            printf("Failed to read the file '%s'\n", fname);
        }
    } else {
        printf("Problem opening '%s' for reading, or allocating %zu bytes
            of memory\n",
            fname, (size_t)statbuf.st_size);
    }
    fclose(fp);
    if (blob) {
        free(blob);
    }
    return import;
}


void main(int argc, void **argv)
{
    if (argc != 4) {
        printf("Change an image using a saved graph\n"
            "%s <exported graph> <input image> <output image>\n", (char
                *)argv[0]);
    } else {
        struct read_image_attributes attr;
        vx_context context = vxCreateContext();
        vx_image input = createImageFromFile(context, (const char
            *)argv[2], &attr);
        vx_image output = vxCreateImage(context, attr.width, attr.height,
            attr.format);
        vx_image final = vxCreateImage(context, attr.width, attr.height,
            attr.format);
        printf("Image Width = %d, height = %d\n", attr.width, attr.height);
        enum {num_refs = 3};
        vx_reference refs[num_refs] = {
            NULL,
            (vx_reference)input,
            (vx_reference)output
        };
        vx_enum uses[num_refs] = {
            VX_IX_USE_EXPORT_VALUES,
```

```
            VX_IX_USE_APPLICATION_CREATE,
            VX_IX_USE_APPLICATION_CREATE
        };
        vx_import import = loadObjectsFromFile(context, num_refs, refs,
            uses, (const char *)argv[1]);
        if (vxGetStatus((vx_reference)input) ||
            vxGetStatus((vx_reference)output) ||
            vxGetStatus((vx_reference)final)) {
          printf("Could not create input or output images\n");
        } else if (vxGetStatus(refs[0])) {
          printf("Problem with status of imported graph\n");
        } else {
          vx_graph graph = (vx_graph)refs[0];
          if (VX_SUCCESS != vxProcessGraph(graph)) {
            printf("Error processing graph\n");
          } else {
            printf("Graph was processed OK, about to set parameters and
                process again\n");
            if (VX_SUCCESS == vxSetGraphParameterByIndex(graph, 0,
                (vx_reference)output) &&
              VX_SUCCESS == vxSetGraphParameterByIndex(graph, 1,
                (vx_reference)final) &&
              VX_SUCCESS == vxProcessGraph(graph) ) {
              printf("Once again, successful, writing output image\n");
              if (writeImage(final, (const char *)argv[3])) {
                printf("Problem writing the output image\n");
              }
            } else {
              printf("Error setting parameters or processing graph\n");
            }
          }
        }
        vxReleaseImport(&import);
        vxReleaseContext(&context);
    }
}
```

5.3.3 Pros and cons of the export and import extension

Pros:
- Potentially offers the best IP protection (only those with intimate knowledge of the implementation format can reverse engineer)

- Implementations may even offer encryption via the use of hints, directives, or custom attributes.
- Potentially offers the fastest and least resource-hungry solution
- Most likely portable between platforms supported by an implementation from the same vendor
- In conjunction with the "feature sets" of OpenVX-SC, it offers the most complete separation between development and deployment
- The specification requires that the implementation provides a means of checking the integrity of the import
- The graph may be handled as data during deployment to a target system

Cons:

- Vendor-specific format not portable between different implementations
- Neither as easy to use as XML format nor as conceptually simple as graph factories
- Since imported graphs cannot be modified (they are effectively already verified), any attached objects that are replaced must have the same metadata (e.g., image sizes)

5.3.4 When to use the export and import extension

The export and import extension should be used whenever IP protection is needed, where in-field updates could be required, or when OpenVX is being used in safety-critical applications. For more information on the use of OpenVX-SC, see the chapter on safety-critical applications, where a C++ wrapper for the OpenVX API is described [32], and for reference, we include "processGraph.cpp," which is a version of the import example described before but in C++:

```
/*
processGraph.cpp
Read an image, change it using a saved graph, write it out.
Using a C++ API
*/
#include "openvx_deploy.hpp"
#include <stdio.h>
#include <stdlib.h>
#include <string>
#include <vector>
#include <string.h>
#include <iostream>
#include <sys/types.h>
```

```cpp
#include <sys/stat.h>

#include "readImage.h"
#include "writeImage.h"
using namespace openvx;
using namespace deployment;

VxImport loadObjectsFromFile(VxContext context, VxRefArray & refs, const
    char * fname)
{
    struct stat statbuf;
    auto statres { stat(fname, &statbuf) };
    auto fp { fopen(fname, "rb") };
    vx_uint8 blob[statbuf.st_size];
    if (!fp || statres || (fread(blob, statbuf.st_size, 1, fp) != 1) )
        std::cout << "Failed to read the file '" << fname << "'\n";
    fclose(fp);
    return context.importObjectsFromMemory(refs, blob, statbuf.st_size);
}

int main(int argc, char **argv)
{
    if (argc != 4) {
        std::cout << "Change an image using a saved graph\n" << argv[0] <<
            " <exported graph> <input image> <output image>\n";
    } else {
        struct read_image_attributes attr;
        VxContext context;
        VxImage input(createImageFromFile(context, argv[2], &attr));
        auto output { context.createImage(attr.width, attr.height,
            attr.format) };
        auto final_image { context.createImage(attr.width, attr.height,
            attr.format) };
        std::cout << "Image Width = " << attr.width << ", height = " <<
            attr.height << "\n";
        VxRefArray refs(3);
        refs.put(1, input, VX_IX_USE_APPLICATION_CREATE);
        refs.put(2, output, VX_IX_USE_APPLICATION_CREATE);
        auto graph { loadObjectsFromFile(context, refs,
            argv[1]).getReferenceByName<VxGraph>("Test Graph") };
        if (input.getStatus() || output.getStatus() ||
            final_image.getStatus()) {
```

```
        std::cout << "Could not create input or output images\n";
    } else if (graph.getStatus()) {
        std::cout << "Problem with status of imported graph\n";
    } else if (graph.processGraph()) {
        std::cout << "Error processing graph\n";
    } else {
        std::cout << "Graph was processed OK, about to set parameters
            and process again\n";
        if (VX_SUCCESS == graph.setGraphParameterByIndex(0, output) &&
           VX_SUCCESS == graph.setGraphParameterByIndex(1, final_image)
              &&
           VX_SUCCESS == graph.processGraph() ) {
           std::cout << "Once again, successful, writing output
                image\n";
           if (writeImage(final_image, argv[3])) {
               std::cout << "Problem writing the output image\n";
           }
        } else {
           std::cout << "Error setting parameters or processing
                graph\n";
        }
    }
  }
  return 0;
}
```

CHAPTER 6

Basic image transformations

Contents

At the time of writing this book, computer vision is developing with a very fast pace, so building an API to account for rapid changes in the field is an extremely challenging task. However, there is a pretty well-defined set of methods that many computer vision algorithms use, and being able to execute these methods efficiently is a core requirement for building a real-time embedded product. It is no surprise that basic image processing functions are a significant part of OpenVX. This chapter will go over the `vx_image` object, which encapsulates images, discuss image properties such as color space and region of interest, and talk about linear filtering border modes. We will then look at Hough transform, remapping and its application to fast undistorted transformation, as well as perspective transformations in OpenVX.

6.1 OpenVX image object

OpenVX is a computer vision API, and it is no surprise that an image object is a first-class citizen. As we observed in Chapter 2 (see Example 1), we need fairly limited information to create an image: a context, width, height, and color space. For example:

OpenVX Programming Guide
https://doi.org/10.1016/B978-0-12-816425-9.00012-7

Copyright © 2020 Elsevier Inc.
All rights reserved.

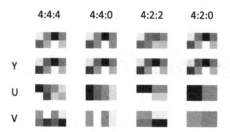

Figure 6.1 An illustration of chroma subsampling.

```
vx_context context = vxCreateContext();
vx_image image = vxCreateImage(context, 640, 480, VX_DF_IMAGE_U8);
```

Whereas the first three arguments of vxCreateImage are straightforward, the fourth one that encodes color space is less trivial. There is a range of color space options supported by OpenVX, both grayscale and color. Most functions in OpenVX support grayscale 8-bit images, but a few functions will have 16- and 32-bit images as input and/or output. Here is a list of grayscale image types:

- VX_DF_IMAGE_U8: a single plane of unsigned 8-bit pixels (pixel intensity varies from 0 to 255)
- VX_DF_IMAGE_U16: a single plane of unsigned 16-bit pixels (pixel intensity varies from 0 to 65535)
- VX_DF_IMAGE_S16: a single plane of signed 16-bit pixels (pixel intensity varies from −32768 to 32767)
- VX_DF_IMAGE_U32: a single plane of unsigned 32-bit pixels
- VX_DF_IMAGE_S32: a single plane of signed 32-bit pixels

There are a few OpenVX functions that can work with color images, but this is not the only reason color images are supported by the standard. Cameras will often produce images in various formats that OpenVX has to support to avoid expensive copying or transforming pixel data for each frame. Many of these images come in the YUV format, which uses a different number of bits to encode the intensity Y and the chroma channels U and V. Usually this subsampling is described by three numbers A:B:C, for example, 4:2:2. Here the first number means the block of Ax2 pixels (A columns and 2 rows). B describes the number of pixels used to encode chroma channels for the first row, and C for the second row. This is illustrated by Fig. 6.1. 4:4:4 encodes chroma for a 4×2 block of pixels using 8 values for U and V channels, 4:4:0 is using 4 values, so that pixels in each column have the same color, and `4:2:0` is using only two values. OpenVX supports a range of color formats:

- `VX_DF_IMAGE_RGB`: standard RGB color space in 3 separate planes
- `VX_DF_IMAGE_RGBX`: RGB color space with alpha channel in 4 separate planes
- `VX_DF_IMAGE_NV12`: a YUV color space with 2 planes: a Y plane and an interleaved UV plane at 4:2:0 sampling
- `VX_DF_IMAGE_NV21`: a YUV color space with 2 planes: a Y plane and an interleaved VU plane at 4:2:0 sampling
- `VX_DF_IMAGE_UYVY`: a YUV color space with 4:2:2 sampling, organized into a single interleaved plane of 32-bit macropixels of U0, Y0, V0, Y1 bytes
- `VX_DF_IMAGE_YUYV`: a YUV color space with 4:2:2 sampling, organized into a single interleaved plane of 32-bit macropixels of Y0, U0, Y1, V1 bytes
- `VX_DF_IMAGE_IYUV`: a YUV color space with 4:2:0 sampling in 3 separate planes
- `VX_DF_IMAGE_YUV4`: a YUV color space with 4:4:4 sampling in 3 separate planes

6.2 Image filtering

6.2.1 Simple image filtering example

One of the most primitive image transformations in computer vision is Gaussian filtering. A 3×3 linear filter is independently applied to each color channel. We will create an OpenVX program that takes a color image and smoothes it with the Gaussian filter using the function `vxGaussian3x3Node`. We will use the graph API, and the resulting code will be similar to "changeImage.c," which was discussed in Chapter 2. `vxGaussian3x3Node` works only with greyscale images, so we will need to split a color input image into channels, run the filter on each of the channels, and then combine the channels into an output color image. To make the result more noticeable, we run filtering several times. The corresponding graph is shown in Fig. 6.2.

You can find the source code in "filter/filterGaussImage.c". The graph is constructed in the `makeFilterGraph` function. After creating the graph and allocating images, we add the nodes that extract individual channels from an input image:

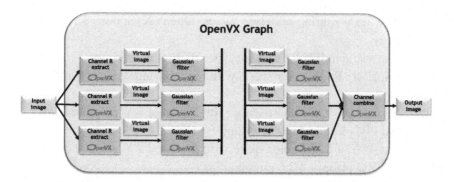

Figure 6.2 OpenVX graph for the Gaussian filter example.

```
vxChannelExtractNode(graph, input, VX_CHANNEL_R, virtu8[0]);
vxChannelExtractNode(graph, input, VX_CHANNEL_G, virtu8[1]);
vxChannelExtractNode(graph, input, VX_CHANNEL_B, virtu8[2]);
```

Then we add the Gaussian filter nodes for each of the channels:

```
for(i = 0; i < numv8 - 3; i++)
    vxGaussian3x3Node(graph, virtu8[i], virtu8[i + 3]);
```

With numv8=18, this adds five Gaussian filters for each channel. For example, the images corresponding to the red color channel are transformed into the following sequence: $virtu8[0] \rightarrow virtu8[3] \rightarrow virtu8[6] \rightarrow virtu8[9] \rightarrow virtu8[15]$.

Finally, we combine the filtered images into an output color image:

```
vxChannelCombineNode(graph,
virtu8[numv8 - 3], virtu8[numv8 - 2],
    virtu8[numv8 - 1], NULL, output)
```

The rest of the code, including main() with image read/write, looks very much like "changeImage.c," which was already discussed. Note that all virtu8[i] images are virtual. This means that an OpenVX implementation that has a Gaussian filter that works on color images could just run it, skipping channel extract/combine operations. Also, if an implementation supports Gaussian filter stacking, then it can use it instead of executing five filters one by one, resulting in a code generating much less memory traffic.

To compile "filterGaussImage.c," you can use either CMake or the following command:

```
$ gcc ../book_samples/filter/filterGaussImage.c
    ../book_samples/ppm-io/readImage.c
    ../book_samples/ppm-io/writeImage.c -I ~/OpenVX_sample/include -I
    ../book_samples/ppm-io -l OpenVX -o filterGaussImage
```

You can run the sample on "cup.ppm":

```
$ ./filterGaussImage ../../book_samples_data/cup.ppm output.ppm
```

Fig. 6.3 shows the input and the output images.

Input image   Output image

Figure 6.3 Gaussian image filtering: input and output.

6.2.2 Custom convolution

Now let us see how we can apply an arbitrary linear filter to an image. OpenVX has a special object for linear image filters called vx_convolution. We will need to create this object, set filter coefficients, and then apply the convolution to each of the image channels. You can find the source code in "filter/filterImage.c," which is very similar to "filterGaussImage," which we discussed in the previous section. We begin by defining the filter coefficients. In this example, we will use a Scharr 3×3 filter:

```
vx_int16 scharr_coeffs[3][3] = {
    {3, 0, -3},
    {10, 0, -10},
    {3, 0, -3}
};
```

Now we create a vx_convolution object and assign our convolution coefficients to it:

```
vx_convolution scharr = vxCreateConvolution(context, 3, 3);
vxCopyConvolutionCoefficients(scharr, (vx_int16*)scharr_coeffs,
    VX_WRITE_ONLY,
     VX_MEMORY_TYPE_HOST);
```

Apart from coefficients, there is one more attribute of our convolution object that we need to take care of. Convolutions used on a VX_DF_IMAGE_U8 image can result in pixel values outside of the 0-255 range. Because OpenVX needs to be efficient on embedded platforms that may not have full support for floating point arithmetics, the output of a convolution is either a VX_DF_IMAGE_U8 or a VX_DF_IMAGE_S16 image. The policy used for convolution is VX_CONVERT_POLICY_SATURATE, which means that if the output pixel value is above the maximum, then it is clamped to the maximum value. To make it possible to use VX_DF_IMAGE_U8 in a reasonable number of cases, vx_convolution has a parameter called "scale," which, together with the saturation policy, gives the output intensity $output(x, y)$ in the pixel with coordinates (x, y) for 8-bit unsigned images defined as follows:

$$output(x, y) = \begin{cases} 0 \text{ if } sum(x, y) < 0, \\ 255 \text{ if } sum(x, y)/scale > 255, \\ sum(x, y)/scale \text{ otherwise,} \end{cases} \quad (6.1)$$

where $sum(x, y)$ is the result of a convolution applied to an image patch of the same size as the convolution with a center in coordinates (x, y). To set the convolution scale, we will use the attribute set function:

```
vx_uint32 scale = 2;
vxSetConvolutionAttribute(scharr, VX_CONVOLUTION_SCALE, &scale,
    sizeof(scale));
```

Note that for the reasons of efficiency, the scale can be only a power of two (up to 2^{31}) for OpenVX 1.x. Now that we have the vx_convolution object set up, we construct a graph. First, we add nodes for splitting the color input image into three grayscale images:

```
vxChannelExtractNode(graph, input, VX_CHANNEL_R, virtu8[0]);
vxChannelExtractNode(graph, input, VX_CHANNEL_G, virtu8[1]);
vxChannelExtractNode(graph, input, VX_CHANNEL_B, virtu8[2]);
```

Then we add a convolution node for each channel:

```
for(i = 0; i < 3; i++)
        vxConvolveNode(graph, virtu8[i], scharr, virtu8[i + 3]);
```

Note that you can use different convolutions on different channels here. However, if you change the convolution coefficients in between graph executions, then the graph will need to be reverified each time. This allows OpenVX to check the filter coefficients and the sequence of filters in a graph and see if any optimizations can be applied for a specific hardware platform. Finally, we combine the grayscale images into a color one:

```
vxChannelCombineNode(graph, virtu8[3], virtu8[4], virtu8[5], NULL,
    output);
```

"filterImage.c" can be compiled similarly to the "filterGaussImage.c" in the previous section. Fig. 6.4 shows the input and the output images for the "filterImage.c" executed on "cup.ppm".

Input image   Output image

Figure 6.4 Scharr image filtering: input and output.

6.3 Regions of interest

6.3.1 Reading from regions of interest

A standard operation in computer vision is preprocessing an image and selecting a rectangular area (region of interest, ROI) containing an object of interest for further processing. An ROI in OpenVX is an image that can be created using the vxCreateImageFromROI function. The ROI image is a part of a parent image, so, for instance, if a pixel value in an ROI image is updated, then this change will be reflected in a parent image. We will demonstrate the use of ROI with a slightly modified version of the Scharr filtering graph discussed in the previous section. You can find the full source code in "filter/filterImageROI.c". The first change is that we need to define an output image in the "main" function with the size of the ROI rather than the size of the input image:

```
vx_rectangle_t rect;
rect.start_x = 48;
rect.start_y = 98;
rect.end_x = 258;
rect.end_y = 202;
int width = rect.end_x - rect.start_x;
int height = rect.end_y - rect.start_y;


vx_image output = vxCreateImage(context, width, height, VX_DF_IMAGE_RGB);
```

Then we pass the "rect" structure to the "makeFilterGraph" function, where we make the following change to the "vxChannelExtractNode" calls:

```
/* create ROI image */
vx_image roi = vxCreateImageFromROI(input, rect);

/* Do scharr filtering on the input image */
/* First, extract R, G, and B channels to individual virtual images */
vxChannelExtractNode(graph, roi, VX_CHANNEL_R, virtu8[0]);
vxChannelExtractNode(graph, roi, VX_CHANNEL_G, virtu8[1]);
vxChannelExtractNode(graph, roi, VX_CHANNEL_B, virtu8[2]);
```

Now the convolution node will take the channels of the ROI image as an input. The sample can be compiled similarly to "filterGaussImage.c" in Section 6.2.1. Fig. 6.5 shows the input and output images for the "filterImageROI.c" executed on "cup.ppm".

6.3.2 Writing to regions of interest

A less frequent use of ROI is modifying a part of an image. We will take an object on a cup and enhance its edges. We will use a Canny edge detector to find edges and binary operations to change the corresponding part of an input image. However, it will be challenging to do with the graph API. We will need to write both to an output image (to copy the pixels outside of the ROI) and to an ROI image within it. This means that two nodes will write to the same data object. Such a topology will cause a graph verification failure "VX_ERROR_MULTIPLE_WRITERS". So, to write to a region of interest, we will use the immediate mode API. You can find the source code in "filter/filterImageROIvxu.c". First, we will create an ROI image:

Input image   Output image

Figure 6.5 Scharr ROI image filtering: input and output.

```
vx_rectangle_t rect;
rect.start_x = 48;
rect.start_y = 98;
rect.end_x = 258;
rect.end_y = 202;
vx_image roi = vxCreateImageFromROI(input, &rect);
```

Then we create temporary images for running the Canny edge detector and working with edge images:

```
int width = rect.end_x - rect.start_x;
int height = rect.end_y - rect.start_y;

/* create temporary images for working with edge images */
vx_image copy_channel[3], roi_channel[3], edges, edges_inv;
edges = vxCreateImage(context, width, height, VX_DF_IMAGE_U8);
edges_inv = vxCreateImage(context, width, height, VX_DF_IMAGE_U8);
```

Since we will run a Canny edge detector, we need to create a threshold object:

```
/* set the threshold value */
vx_pixel_value_t lower, higher;
lower.U32 = 50;
higher.U32 = 100;

/* create a threshold object */
vx_threshold threshold = vxCreateThresholdForImage(context,
    VX_THRESHOLD_TYPE_RANGE, VX_DF_IMAGE_U8, VX_DF_IMAGE_U8);
```

```
if(vxGetStatus(threshold) != VX_SUCCESS)
{
    printf("Threshold creation failed\n");
}


/* set threshold values */
vxCopyThresholdRange(threshold, &lower, &higher, VX_WRITE_ONLY,
    VX_MEMORY_TYPE_HOST);
```

Finally, we iterate through channels of our color image, compute a canny edge detector for each of them (stored in `edges`), invert it, and then use a bitwise "and" to make the corresponding pixels in the input image black:

```
enum vx_channel_e channels[] = {VX_CHANNEL_R, VX_CHANNEL_G,
    VX_CHANNEL_B};
for(int i = 0; i < 3; i++)
{
        roi_channel[i] = vxCreateImage(context, width, height,
            VX_DF_IMAGE_U8);
        copy_channel[i] = vxCreateImage(context, width, height,
            VX_DF_IMAGE_U8);
        vxuChannelExtract(context, roi, channels[i], roi_channel[i]);

        vxuCannyEdgeDetector(context, roi_channel[i], threshold, 3,
            VX_NORM_L2, edges);

        vxuNot(context, edges, edges_inv);
        vxuAnd(context, roi_channel[i], edges_inv, copy_channel[i]);
}
```

Finally, we combine all the modified channels in the input image and save it to disk. Note that we combine channels in the `roi` image and then save the `input` image: our changes in the former have a direct impact on the latter:

```
vxuChannelCombine(context, copy\_channel[0], copy\_channel[1],
    copy\_channel[2], NULL, roi);
if(writeImage(input, \"cup\_roi.ppm\"))
        printf("Problem writing the output image\\n\");
```

The sample code can be compiled similarly to the "filterGaussImage.c" in Section 6.2.1. Fig. 6.6 shows the input and output images for the "filterImageROIvxu.c" code executed on "cup.ppm."

Input image   Output image

Figure 6.6 Canny edge effect on an ROI: input and output.

6.4 Feature extraction

6.4.1 Hough transform

Now let us see how we can use OpenVX to extract some meaningful information about the scene. One of the important functions in computer vision is extracting lines from an image. OpenVX has the function `vxHoughLinesPNode`, an implementation of the probabilistic Hough transform algorithm [35]. This function takes a binary image as an input and returns a set of lines. A single line in OpenVX is represented by a data structure `vx_line2d_t`:

```
typedef struct _vx_line2d_t {
  vx_float32
  vx_float32
  vx_float32
  vx_float32
} vx_line2d_t;
```

A collection of lines is represented by an array object `vx_array`. Being a graph API object, `vx_array` is opaque, just like `vx_image`. The `vxCopyArrayRange` function can be used to map the contents of the array into host memory for both reading and writing. Let us start with a simple example of the probabilistic hough transform, applied to an image of a road taken from a car. Our goal is to find the road lines. To do that, we will binarize an input image by computing a Sobel filter magnitude and applying a threshold and then running a hough transform on the resulting binary image. The scheme of the OpenVX graph that we will use is shown in Fig. 6.7. You can find the source code in the file "hough/houghLines.c."

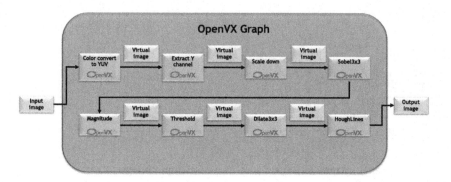

Figure 6.7 OpenVX graph for the Hough transform example.

We start by reading the input image with the function vxa_read_image from the vxa library, and finding its dimensions in the main function:

```
const char* input_filename = argv[1];
const char* binary_filename = argv[2];
const char* lines_filename = argv[3];

vx_context context = vxCreateContext();
vx_image image, binary;
vxa_read_image((const char *)input_filename, context, &image);

vx_uint32 width, height;
vxQueryImage(image, VX_IMAGE_WIDTH, &width, sizeof(vx_uint32));
vxQueryImage(image, VX_IMAGE_HEIGHT, &height, sizeof(vx_uint32));
```

Then we create the lines array, create a graph (we will review this function in detail further), register log callback function, and initiate graph processing:

```
/* create an array for storing hough lines output */
const vx_size max_num_lines = 2000;
lines = vxCreateArray(context, VX_TYPE_LINE_2D, max_num_lines);
vx_graph graph = makeHoughLinesGraph(context, image, &binary, &lines);

vxRegisterLogCallback(context, log_callback, vx_true_e);

vxProcessGraph(graph);
```

Note that the `binary` image is passed to the graph creation function as a pointer; it will be created inside the graph processing function as we do not know its dimensions here. Finally, we save the binary image, draw the detected lines on top of it, and also save the result:

```
vxa_write_image(binary, binary_filename);

// draw the lines
vx_pixel_value_t color;
color.RGB[0] = 0;
color.RGB[1] = 255;
color.RGB[2] = 0;
vx_image image_lines;
vx_size _num_lines;
// query the number of lines in the lines array
vxQueryArray(lines, VX_ARRAY_NUMITEMS, &_num_lines, sizeof(_num_lines));
draw_lines(context, binary, lines, _num_lines,
      &color, 2, &image_lines);
vxa_write_image(image_lines, lines_filename);
```

Now let us review the function that creates the graph. It starts by querying the dimensions of the image and defining the dimensions of the binary image that we will use for line detection, since the input image resolution is too high:

```
vx_graph makeHoughLinesGraph(vx_context context, vx_image input,
  vx_image* binary, vx_array lines)
{
    vx_uint32 width, height;
    vxQueryImage(input, VX_IMAGE_WIDTH, &width, sizeof(vx_uint32));
    vxQueryImage(input, VX_IMAGE_HEIGHT, &height, sizeof(vx_uint32));

    int widthr = width/4;
    int heightr = height/4;
```

Then we create a graph and allocate all images that we need:

```
vx_graph graph = vxCreateGraph(context);

#define nums16 (3)
vx_image virt_s16[nums16];

/* create virtual images */
```

```
vx_image virt_nv12 = vxCreateVirtualImage(graph, 0, 0, VX_DF_IMAGE_NV12);
vx_image virt_y = vxCreateVirtualImage(graph, 0, 0, VX_DF_IMAGE_U8);
vx_image virt_yr = vxCreateVirtualImage(graph, widthr, heightr,
    VX_DF_IMAGE_U8);
vx_image binary_thresh = vxCreateVirtualImage(graph, 0, 0,
    VX_DF_IMAGE_U8);

for(int i = 0; i < nums16; i++)
{
    virt_s16[i] = vxCreateVirtualImage(graph, 0, 0, VX_DF_IMAGE_S16);
}

*binary = vxCreateImage(context, widthr, heightr, VX_DF_IMAGE_U8);
```

Now we proceed with adding the graph nodes. First, we convert the input RGB image into the YUV color format, extract the Y channel, and resize it down:

```
/* extract grayscale channel */
vxColorConvertNode(graph, input, virt_nv12);
vxChannelExtractNode(graph, virt_nv12, VX_CHANNEL_Y, virt_y);

/* resize down */
vxScaleImageNode(graph, virt_y, virt_yr, VX_INTERPOLATION_BILINEAR);
```

Then we compute image gradient magnitude with a Sobel filter:

```
vxSobel3x3Node(graph, virt_yr, virt_s16[0], virt_s16[1]);
vxMagnitudeNode(graph, virt_s16[0], virt_s16[1], virt_s16[2]);
```

Now we apply a threshold to the resulting greyscale image. Choosing a threshold value can be a complex task, but for simplicity, here we will use a constant value. As we discussed earlier, we need to create a threshold object, set its value, and only then add a thresholding graph node:

```
vx_threshold thresh = vxCreateThresholdForImage(context,
    VX_THRESHOLD_TYPE_BINARY, VX_DF_IMAGE_S16, VX_DF_IMAGE_U8);
vx_pixel_value_t pixel_value;
pixel_value.S16 = 256;
vxCopyThresholdValue(thresh, &pixel_value, VX_WRITE_ONLY,
    VX_MEMORY_TYPE_HOST);
vx_node thresh_node = vxThresholdNode(graph, virt_s16[2], thresh,
        binary_thresh);
```

There are some filters you can run on the resulting binary image to improve line detection. We will use a 3 × 3 dilate filter:

```
vxDilate3x3Node(graph, binary_thresh, *binary);
```

Finally, we are ready to run a Hough transform function on the binary image. It is important to choose right parameters for the Hough transform that are stored in the `vx_hough_lines_p_t` structure. The most important parameters are: `rho` is the size of a histogram bin for the distance from a line to the coordinate center, `theta` is the size of a histogram bin for the line orientation angle, and `threshold` is the minimum number of white pixels from the binary image that will lie on the detected line:

```
vx_hough_lines_p_t hough_params;
hough_params.rho = 1.0f;
hough_params.theta = 3.14f/180;
hough_params.threshold = 100;
hough_params.line_length = 100;
hough_params.line_gap = 10;
hough_params.theta_max = 3.14;
hough_params.theta_min = 0.0;


vx_scalar num_lines = vxCreateScalar(context, VX_TYPE_SIZE, NULL);
vxHoughLinesPNode(graph, *binary, &hough_params, lines, num_lines);
```

The results of executing the code on "IMG-7875.JPG" are given in Fig. 6.8. We can see that there are quite a few false alarms that should be filtered out. We will consider such a filtering in the next section.

Input image   Binary image with lines

Figure 6.8 Lines detected with Hough transform.

6.4.2 Postprocessing hough transform results

Usually, it is not enough to just find the lines in an image; there is information about scene or 3D geometry that can be extracted from the lines. Specifically, for the lane detection problem we considered in the previous section, it is often useful to find the vanishing point, the crossing of the parallel lines representing road markings. We will implement the OpenVX graph shown in Fig. 6.9. The code that solves this problem is located in the "hough/houghLinesEx.c" example. First, judging from Fig. 6.8, we have too many false positives that we need to filter out. To this end, we will create a user node. We already covered the concept of user nodes in Section 4.6, so here we will just briefly review the code for the user node that implements line filtering. The filtering algorithm is based on two assumptions: the lines should be oriented almost vertically, and they should be located in the lower part of the image. First, let us review the callback function implementing the user kernel. This function (which will be called during graph execution) takes an array of lines as an input and also returns an array of lines.

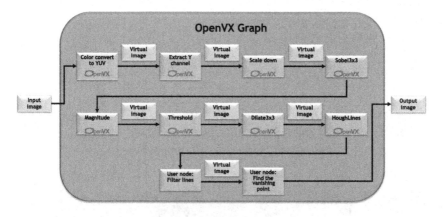

Figure 6.9 OpenVX graph for the Hough transform postprocessing example.

```
vx_status VX_CALLBACK filter_lines_calc_function( vx_node node, const
    vx_reference * refs, vx_uint32 num )
{
  vx_array lines = (vx_array) refs[0];
  vx_array lines_output = (vx_array) refs[1];
```

We start by extracting data from the input array of lines lines. First, we find the number of elements in the input array:

```
vx_size num_lines = -1;
ERROR_CHECK_STATUS(vxQueryArray(lines, VX_ARRAY_NUMITEMS,
    &num_lines, sizeof(num_lines)));
```

Note that we are using the macro ERROR_CHECK_STATUS and later ERROR_CHECK_OBJECT, which are handy for locating return value errors, as they will print both the error code, which you can look up in the OpenVX specification, and the line number of the function call generating this error. The macros are defined as follows:

```
#define ERROR_CHECK_STATUS( status ) { \
    vx_status status_ = (status); \
    if(status_ != VX_SUCCESS) { \
        printf("ERROR: failed with status = (%d) at " __FILE__ "#%d\n", \
            status_, __LINE__); \
        exit(1); \
    } \
}

#define ERROR_CHECK_OBJECT( obj ) { \
    vx_status status_ = vxGetStatus((vx_reference)(obj)); \
    if(status_ != VX_SUCCESS) { \
        printf("ERROR: failed with status = (%d) at " __FILE__ "#%d\n", \
            status_, __LINE__); \
        exit(1); \
    } \
}
```

We continue the filtering function by mapping the input array data into host memory:

```
char* __lines = NULL;
vx_map_id map_id;
vx_size stride = sizeof(vx_line2d_t);
vxMapArrayRange(lines, 0, num_lines, &map_id, &stride,
    (void**)&__lines,
        VX_READ_ONLY, VX_MEMORY_TYPE_HOST, 0);
```

Then we go through each line, and if it satisfies the filtering conditions, we copy it into specially allocated host memory _lines_filtered:

```
vx_line2d_t _lines_filtered[max_num_lines];
vx_size _num_lines_filtered = 0;
```

```
const float max_ratio = 0.1;
for(int i = 0; i < num_lines; i++, __lines += stride)
{
        vx_line2d_t* _line = (vx_line2d_t*)__lines;
        int dx = _line->end_x - _line->start_x;
        int dy = _line->end_y - _line->start_y;

        if(_line->start_y < heightr/2 || _line->end_y < heightr/2)
        {
                continue;
        }

        memcpy(&_lines_filtered[_num_lines_filtered++], _line,
                sizeof(vx_line2d_t));
}
```

Last, we unmap the input array and add all the copied data into the output array:

```
vxUnmapArrayRange(lines, map_id);

vxAddArrayItems(lines_output, _num_lines_filtered, _lines_filtered,
        sizeof(vx_line2d_t));

return(VX_SUCCESS);
}
```

To create a user node, we need a validator function, which will be called during the graph verification to check the correctness of input and output parameter types. In our case the validator enforces the input and output arrays to be of type VX_TYPE_LINE_2D:

```
vx_status VX_CALLBACK filter_lines_validator( vx_node node, const
    vx_reference parameters[], vx_uint32 num, vx_meta_format metas[] )
{
    // parameter #0 -- check array type
    vx_enum param_type;
    ERROR_CHECK_STATUS( vxQueryArray( ( vx_array )parameters[0],
        VX_ARRAY_ITEMTYPE, &param_type, sizeof( param_type ) ) );
    if(param_type != VX_TYPE_LINE_2D) // check that the array contains
        lines
    {
        return VX_ERROR_INVALID_TYPE;
```

```
}

// parameter #1 -- check array type
ERROR_CHECK_STATUS( vxQueryArray( ( vx_array )parameters[1],
    VX_ARRAY_ITEMTYPE, &param_type, sizeof( param_type ) ) );
if(param_type != VX_TYPE_LINE_2D)
{
    return VX_ERROR_INVALID_TYPE;
}

// set output metadata
ERROR_CHECK_STATUS( vxSetMetaFormatAttribute( metas[1],
    VX_ARRAY_ITEMTYPE, &param_type, sizeof( param_type ) ) );

return VX_SUCCESS;
}
```

We also need a function that registers the user kernel with OpenVX:

```
vx_status registerUserFilterLinesKernel( vx_context context )
{
    vx_kernel kernel = vxAddUserKernel( context,
                        "app.userkernels.filter_lines",
                        USER_KERNEL_FILTER_LINES,
                        filter_lines_calc_function,
                        2,  // numParams
                        filter_lines_validator,
                        NULL,
                        NULL );
    ERROR_CHECK_OBJECT( kernel );

    ERROR_CHECK_STATUS( vxAddParameterToKernel( kernel, 0, VX_INPUT,
        VX_TYPE_ARRAY, VX_PARAMETER_STATE_REQUIRED ) ); // input
    ERROR_CHECK_STATUS( vxAddParameterToKernel( kernel, 1, VX_OUTPUT,
        VX_TYPE_ARRAY, VX_PARAMETER_STATE_REQUIRED ) ); // output
    ERROR_CHECK_STATUS( vxFinalizeKernel( kernel ) );
    ERROR_CHECK_STATUS( vxReleaseKernel( &kernel ) );

    vxAddLogEntry( ( vx_reference ) context, VX_SUCCESS, "OK: registered
        user kernel app.userkernels.filter_lines\n" );
    return VX_SUCCESS;
}
```

Finally, we need a function that adds a user node to the graph:

```
vx_node userFilterLinesNode(vx_graph graph,
                     vx_array input,
                     vx_array output)
{
    vx_context context = vxGetContext( ( vx_reference ) graph );
    vx_kernel kernel = vxGetKernelByEnum( context,
        USER_KERNEL_FILTER_LINES);
    ERROR_CHECK_OBJECT( kernel );
    vx_node node  = vxCreateGenericNode( graph, kernel );
    ERROR_CHECK_OBJECT( node );

    ERROR_CHECK_STATUS( vxSetParameterByIndex( node, 0, ( vx_reference )
        input ) );
    ERROR_CHECK_STATUS( vxSetParameterByIndex( node, 1, ( vx_reference )
        output ) );

    ERROR_CHECK_STATUS( vxReleaseKernel( &kernel ) );

    return node;
}
```

At this point, we have everything we need to run line filtering as a user node in an OpenVX graph. Now let us add a function that finds the crossing point of all filtered lines. We will implement it as a user kernel, which will be executed right after the line filtering kernel. We will use the uniform coordinates (e.g., see [26]) for representing lines as they are very convenient for finding line crossings. Each line is represented by a three-dimensional vector l so that the equation describing the line can be represented as $(x, y, 1)^T l = 0$, where x, y are pixel coordinates. We start with the function that computes the coordinates of the cross point for two lines, each given by a three-dimensional vector. According to projective geometry [26], the cross point in the uniform coordinates will be given by the vector product of these vectors:

```
void find_cross_point(const float* line1, const float* line2,
  float* cross_point)
{
  cross_point[0] = line1[1]*line2[2] - line1[2]*line2[1];
  cross_point[1] = line1[2]*line2[0] - line1[0]*line2[2];
  cross_point[2] = line1[0]*line2[1] - line1[1]*line2[0];
}
```

Now let us see the implementation of the kernel that computes the cross point of the road lines. As with the line filtering kernel, it starts with mapping the input array to host memory:

```
vx_status VX_CALLBACK vanishing_point_calc_function( vx_node node, const
    vx_reference * refs, vx_uint32 num )
{
  vx_array lines = (vx_array)refs[0];
  vx_array vanishing_points = (vx_array)refs[1];

  vx_size num_lines = -1;
  ERROR_CHECK_STATUS(vxQueryArray(lines, VX_ARRAY_NUMITEMS, &num_lines,
      sizeof(num_lines)));

  char* __lines = 0;
  vx_size stride = sizeof(vx_line2d_t);
  vx_map_id map_id;

  vxMapArrayRange(lines, 0, num_lines, &map_id, &stride, (void**)&__lines,
    VX_READ_ONLY, VX_MEMORY_TYPE_HOST, 0);
```

Then we convert the lines into uniform coordinates:

```
      float lines_uniform[max_num_lines][3];
      for(int i = 0; i < num_lines; i++, __lines += stride)
      {
            vx_line2d_t* _line = (vx_line2d_t*)__lines;
            float x0 = _line->start_x;
            float y0 = _line->start_y;
            float dx = _line->end_x - _line->start_x;
            float dy = _line->end_y - _line->start_y;

            lines_uniform[i][0] = dy;
            lines_uniform[i][1] = -dx;
            lines_uniform[i][2] = -x0*dy + y0*dx;
      }

      vxUnmapArrayRange(lines, map_id);
```

Now we calculate the crossing point of each pair of lines and find the average. Obviously, this algorithm is sensitive to strong outliers, and there are many ways to make it more robust, but for brevity, we will stick with the simplest version. The final result is stored in the output vx_array object:

```
vx_coordinates2d_t avg_cross_point = {0.0, 0.0};
int count = 0;
for(int i = 0; i < num_lines; i++)
{
        for(int j = 0; j < num_lines; j++)
        {
                float cross_point[3];
                find_cross_point(lines_uniform[i], lines_uniform[j],
                    cross_point);
                if(fabs(cross_point[2]) < FLT_MIN)
                {
                        // filter the vanishing point
                        continue;
                }
                float cx = cross_point[0]/cross_point[2];
                float cy = cross_point[1]/cross_point[2];

                if(cx < 0 || cy < 0 || cx > widthr || cy > heightr)
                {
                        // we know the cross point lies inside an image,
                            so this is an outlier
                        continue;
                }

                avg_cross_point.x += (int)cx;
                avg_cross_point.y += (int)cy;
                count++;
        }
}

avg_cross_point.x /= count;
avg_cross_point.y /= count;

vxAddArrayItems(vanishing_points, 1, &avg_cross_point,
    sizeof(avg_cross_point));

return(VX_SUCCESS);
}
```

The node validation and registration functions and the function for adding
this node to a graph are similar to the line filtering node. The graph creation
function is almost the same as in the previous section, except for the last

part where the Hough transform is computed. The line filtering node and the node for finding the vanishing point are added:

```
vx_array _lines = vxCreateVirtualArray(graph, VX_TYPE_LINE_2D,
    max_num_lines);

vx_scalar num_lines = vxCreateScalar(context, VX_TYPE_SIZE, NULL);

/* run hough transform */
vx_hough_lines_p_t hough_params;
hough_params.rho = 1.0f;
hough_params.theta = 3.14f/180;
hough_params.threshold = 100;
hough_params.line_length = 100;
hough_params.line_gap = 10;
hough_params.theta_max = 3.14;
hough_params.theta_min = 0.0;

vxHoughLinesPNode(graph, *binary, &hough_params, _lines,
    num_lines);

userFilterLinesNode(graph, _lines, lines);
userFindVanishingPoint(graph, lines, vanishing_points);

return graph;
}
```

Note that the array _lines, which we use as an input to the userFilterLinesNode, is virtual. Nevertheless, the calls to vxMapArrayRange and vxUnmapArrayRange executed from the user node will be executed successfully, as they are called during graph execution. This is guaranteed by the OpenVX spec; see the subsection "Virtual Data Objects" in the chapter "Graph Concepts": "No calls to an Map/Unmap or Copy APIs will succeed given a reference to an object created through a virtual create function from a graph external perspective. Calls to Map/Unmap or Copy APIs from within client-defined node that belongs to the same graph as the virtual object will succeed as they are graph internal."

The main function is also very similar, and we add the drawing of a circle at the vanishing point:

```
// read the coordinates of the vanishing point
vx_coordinates2d_t coordinates;
```

```
vxCopyArrayRange(vanishing_points, 0, 1, sizeof(coordinates),
    &coordinates, VX_READ_ONLY, VX_MEMORY_TYPE_HOST);

// draw the circle around each vanishing point coordinate
vx_image image_final;
draw_circles(context, image_lines, vanishing_points, 1, 10, &color, 3,
    &image_final);
vxa_write_image(image_final, lines_filename);
```

The results of running "houghLinesEx.c" on "IMG-7875.JPG" are shown in Fig. 6.10.

Input image

Binary image with filtered lines and the vanishing point.

Figure 6.10 Lines detected with Hough transform.

6.5 Geometric image transformations

6.5.1 Undistortion implemented with remap

One of the essential geometric transformations of an image in computer vision is correcting for lens distortion, usually called "undistort." A typical effect of lens distortion is that a straight line in a three dimensional space is not straight in an image generated with a camera. Undistort transformation maps an image into another image as if the new image is generated with a perspective transformation, and straight lines in 3D are mapped to straight lines in the image. Undistort needs information about camera intrinsic parameters and lens distortion coefficients. OpenVX, being a library focused on runtime, has no way to compute this data (a process typically referred to as "camera calibration"). Also, OpenVX contains no any specific model for lens distortion. Since the undistort transformation, given camera and lens parameters, maps pixels only depending on their positions in images, undistort can be implemented with a remap. So, we first will use OpenCV offline to create a remap transformation.

The standard way to find lens parameters is calibrating a camera by making images of a known pattern like a checkerboard. OpenCV "calibration" sample is used to obtain camera intrinsic parameters and lens distortion coefficients. We refer to the OpenCV calibration tutorial [36] for details. Then we need to calculate the remap corresponding to the undistort mapping.

Remap is a very simple image transformation: for each pixel with coordinates (x_d, y_d) in the destination image, it specifies floating point coordinates in the source image $(x_s(x_d, y_d), y_s(x_d, y_d))$, so that the destination image intensity I_d is defined using the source image intensity I_s as

$$I_d(x_d, y_d) = I_s\left(x_s(x_d, y_d), y_s(x_d, y_d)\right). \qquad (6.2)$$

Since x_s, y_s are floating point and do not necessarily fall into a pixel center, I_s is interpolated from the intensities in the neighboring pixels of the source image. OpenCV and OpenVX specify several such interpolation methods.

The method for generating a remap transformation given camera parameters is implemented in the "undistort/undistortOpenCV.cpp" sample. It reads a file of camera parameters created by an OpenCV calibration procedure and then writes a file of undistortion remapping data suitable for use by OpenVX. First, it reads the camera parameters and image dimensions saved by the OpenCV calibration sample:

```
FileStorage fs(camera_file, FileStorage::READ);
Mat intrinsic_params, dist_coeffs;
fs["camera_matrix"] >> intrinsic_params;
fs["distortion_coefficients"] >> dist_coeffs;
int width, height;
fs["image_width"] >> width;
fs["image_height"] >> height;
```

Then we generate undistort remap transformation with

```
Mat map1, map2, new_camera;
initUndistortRectifyMap(intrinsic_params, dist_coeffs, Mat(),
    intrinsic_params, Size(width, height), CV_32FC2, map1, map2);
```

The result is stored in map1, whereas map2 is not used. Now we save the remap together with source and destination image dimensions required by OpenVX:

```
FileStorage fs1(map_fname, FileStorage::WRITE);
fs1 << "remap" << map1;
fs1 << "remap_src_width" << width;
fs1 << "remap_src_height" << height;
fs1 << "remap_dst_width" << width;
fs1 << "remap_dst_height" << height;
```

As a result of executing this sample, we get an xml or yml file with the remap transformation. Now let us import it into OpenVX.

A remap in OpenVX is encapsulated by a special object vx_remap. It is very similar to vx_image. Instead of width and height attributes, it has both source and destination image sizes:

```
enum vx_remap_attribute_e {
    VX_REMAP_SOURCE_WIDTH = VX_ATTRIBUTE_BASE(VX_ID_KHRONOS,
        VX_TYPE_REMAP) + 0x0,
  VX_REMAP_SOURCE_HEIGHT = VX_ATTRIBUTE_BASE(VX_ID_KHRONOS,
      VX_TYPE_REMAP) + 0x1,
  VX_REMAP_DESTINATION_WIDTH = VX_ATTRIBUTE_BASE(VX_ID_KHRONOS,
      VX_TYPE_REMAP) +
      0x2,
  VX_REMAP_DESTINATION_HEIGHT = VX_ATTRIBUTE_BASE(VX_ID_KHRONOS,
      VX_TYPE_REMAP) +
          0x3};
```

Similar to vx_image, data can be copied to/from a vx_remap object using the functions vxMapRemapPatch, vxUnmapRemapPatch, and vxCopyRemapPatch. As of OpenVX version 1.3, the only graph node that uses a remap is created with vxRemapNode. This node has one image as an input and one image as an output.

The image undistort transformation based on OpenVX is implemented in "undistort/undistort-remap.c." This sample uses the library "vxa" [31] (https://github.com/relrotciv/vxa) to read an input image from a jpeg file:

```
vx_image input_image;
if(vxa_read_image(image_filename, context, &input_image) != 1)
{
```

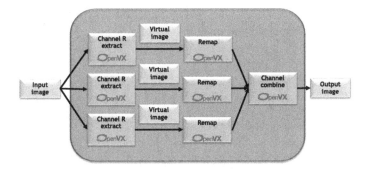

Figure 6.11 A remap transformation graph.

```
        printf("Error reading image 1\n");
        return(-1);
}
```

We use the same library to read a remap from a file created by OpenCV. The function that reads remap also returns us the width and height of the output image:

```
int width, height;
vx_remap remap;
if(vxa_import_opencv_remap(remap_filename, "remap", context, &remap,
    &width, &height) != 1)
{
        printf("Error reading remap1\n");
        return(-1);
}
```

Then we create an output color image using the dimensions provided to us by the remap:

```
vx_image output_image = vxCreateImage(context, width, height,
    VX_DF_IMAGE_RGB);
```

Now that all the data are in OpenVX, let us create a graph (see the makeRemapGraph function). Our graph is shown in Fig. 6.11. Since a remap node only accepts greyscale images, as usual, we will use virtual images to process remaps individually on each channel. A smart OpenVX implementation can figure this out and process all three channels together, saving on memory data transfer. The `makeRemapGraph` function starts by creating a graph object and the helper virtual images:

```
const int numu8 = 2;
vx_image virtu8[numu8][3];
int i, j;

vx_graph graph = vxCreateGraph(context);

for(i = 0; i < numu8; i++)
    for (j = 0; j < 3; j++)
        virtu8[i][j] = vxCreateVirtualImage(graph, 0, 0,
            VX_DF_IMAGE_U8);
```

Then we extract each channel from an input image and setup a remap node with a bilinear interpolation:

```
enum vx_channel_e channels[] = {VX_CHANNEL_R, VX_CHANNEL_G,
    VX_CHANNEL_B};
for(i = 0; i < 3; i++)
{
    vxChannelExtractNode(graph, input_image, channels[i],
        virtu8[0][i]);
    vxRemapNode(graph, virtu8[0][i], remap, VX_INTERPOLATION_BILINEAR,
        virtu8[1][i]);
}
```

Now we combine all the remapped images into a single-color image and release the virtual images:

```
vxChannelCombineNode(graph, virtu8[1][0], virtu8[1][1], virtu8[1][2],
    NULL, output_image);

for (i = 0; i < numu8; i++)
    for(j = 0; j < 3; j++)
        vxReleaseImage(&virtu8[i][j]);
```

The graph is set up, and we only need to run the graph processing and save the results to a file using the "vxa" library:

```
if((status = vxVerifyGraph(graph)))
{
    printf("Graph verification failed, error code %d, %d\n",
        (int)status, (int)VX_ERROR_NOT_SUFFICIENT);
```

```
}
else if (vxProcessGraph(graph))
        printf("Error processing graph\n");
else if (vxa_write_image(output_image, output_filename) != 1)
        printf("Problem writing the output image\n");
vxReleaseContext(&context);
```

Examples input and output images for two different cameras are shown in Figs. 6.12 and 6.13. Note that the GoPro undistorted image shows a small part of the original image. This is a common effect of the undistort function on a wide angle camera with a relatively strong distortion.

To generate remap xml files, use the "undistortOpenCV.cpp" on the "*camera.xml" files in the data folder. Assuming that the full path to the data folder is in \$BOOK_SAMPLES_DATA, run

```
$ ./undistortOpenCV $BOOK_SAMPLES_DATA/canon-camera.xml
    $BOOK_SAMPLES_DATA/canon-test.jpg output.jpg
    $BOOK_SAMPLES_DATA/canon-remap.xml
$ ./undistortOpenCV $BOOK_SAMPLES_DATA/gopro-camera.xml
    $BOOK_SAMPLES_DATA/gopro-test.png output.jpg
    $BOOK_SAMPLES_DATA/gopro-remap.xml
```

Run the "undistort.c" sample to reproduce the results in Figs. 6.12 and 6.13:

```
$ ./undistort $BOOK_SAMPLES_DATA/canon-remap.xml
    $BOOK_SAMPLES_DATA/canon-test.jpg output.jpg
$ ./undistort $BOOK_SAMPLES_DATA/gopro-remap.xml
    $BOOK_SAMPLES_DATA/gopro-test.png output.jpg
```

Input image   Output image

Figure 6.12 *Undistort image transformation: input and output.* Undistort image transformation: input and output, Canon EOS 100D, Sigma 18 mm.

Input image   Output image

Figure 6.13 *Undistort image transformation: input and output.* Undistort image transformation: input and output, GoPro HERO 3+, video 1080 p.

6.5.2 Perspective transformations

OpenVX supports two most commonly used image transformations in computer vision, affine and perspective. An affine transformation is given by a 2 × 3 matrix, which defines a pixel coordinate mapping from the output image to the input. Specifically:

$$x_0 = M_{1,1}x + M_{2,1}y + M_{3,1},$$
$$y_0 = M_{1,2}x + M_{2,2}y + M2, 3. \tag{6.3}$$

Here (x_0, y_0) and x, y are the coordinates of a pixel in the input and output images, respectively, and M is an affine matrix. An example of affine transformation has been given in Chapter 2, where it was used to rotate an image 90 degrees. So in this chapter, we focus on the perspective transformation. The API for both functions is very similar, and everything we learn here can be applied to the affine transformation too.

The homography or perspective transformation is defined by a 3 × 3 matrix that defines a mapping of pixel coordinates:

$$x_u = M_{1,1}x + M_{2,1}y + M_{3,1},$$
$$y_u = M_{1,2}x + M_{2,2}y + M_{2,3},$$
$$z_u = M_{1,3}x + M_{2,3}y + M_{3,3}. \tag{6.4}$$

Here x, y are pixel coordinates in the output image, and x_u, y_u, z_u are uniform pixel coordinates in the input image. The normal input pixel coordinates are given by

$$x_0 = x_u/z_u,$$
$$y_0 = y_u/z_u. \tag{6.5}$$

The OpenVX function that creates a perspective transformation graph node is specified as follows:

```
vx_node vxWarpPerspectiveNode(vx_graph graph, vx_image input, vx_matrix
    matrix, vx_enum type, vx_image output);
```

The algorithm implemented in this node computes the intensity in each output image pixel by mapping it to an input image using Eqs. (6.4)–(6.5). Since there usually is no one-to-one mapping between input and output pixels, the output pixel intensity is computed by interpolating the neighboring pixels intensity. The specific interpolation method is given by the "type" parameter. If the output pixel is mapped outside of the input image boundaries, then the border mode is used to compute the input pixel intensity. The perspective node supports BORDER_MODE_UNDEFINED and BORDER_MODE_CONSTANT. Note that the output image dimensions do not necessarily have to be equal to the input image dimensions. This puts a not too obvious restriction on the output image: its dimensions cannot be inferred from the input image dimensions, so the output image cannot be a virtual image without specified width and height. The same is true for the affine transformation. The dimensions of the output image for both vxWarpAffineNode and vxWarpPerspectiveNode must always be specified.

To illustrate the OpenVX perspective transformation, we will use the previously developed example of using the Hough transform to detect road lanes. Section 6.4.2 describes finding the vanishing point as a crossing of parallel lanes. We will extend this sample to generate a bird's eye view from a single image. The bird's eye view sample is implemented in "birds-eye/birdsEyeView.c," which is created by modifying "filter/hough-LinesEx.c." The result of the algorithm is shown in Fig. 6.14. To reproduce these results, run

```
./birdsEyeView $BOOK_SAMPLES_DATA/IMG-7875.JPG output.jpg
```

Since a road is flat, a change in camera position can be simulated with a perspective transformation (see [26]). So, we need to come up with a perspective transformation that sends the vanishing point to infinity, and this will make the road lines parallel to each other. Since a perspective transformation depends on the vanishing point, it will have to be generated during graph execution time, so we will need a user node for that. We will discuss how to do this a little later; for now, let us see how we can apply the perspective transformation to an image.

Input image   Bird's eye view

Figure 6.14 Results of the bird's eye view perspective transformation.

6.5.2.1 Applying a perspective transformation

The perspective transformation node is added to an OpenVX graph in the graph creation function "makeBirdsEyeViewGraph," which is almost the same as "the makeHoughLinesGraph" from "houghLinesEx.c." The scheme of the graph we will discuss in this section is shown in Fig. 6.15.

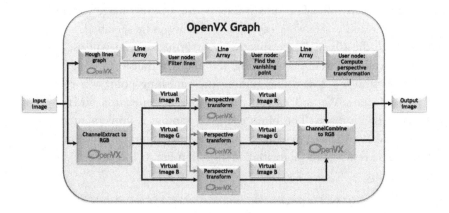

Figure 6.15 OpenVX graph for generating bird's eye view.

After adding the node that calculates a position of the vanishing point "userFindVanishingPoint," we add the user node that returns a perspective transformation:

```
userFindVanishingPoint(graph, lines, vanishing_points);
userComputeBirdsEyeTransform(graph, vanishing_points, input,
    perspective);
```

Then we apply the perspective transformation to the input image. Since "vxWarpPerspectiveNode" works with grayscale images only, we split the input image into three channels, process each of them, and then combine them back into the output image:

```
/* Create the same processing subgraph for each channel */
enum vx_channel_e channels[] = {VX_CHANNEL_R, VX_CHANNEL_G,
    VX_CHANNEL_B};

for(int i = 0; i < 3; i++)
{
    /* First, extract input and logo R, G, and B channels to individual
    virtual images */
    vxChannelExtractNode(graph, input, channels[i], virt_u8[i]);

    vx_node warp_node = vxWarpPerspectiveNode(graph, virt_u8[i],
        perspective, VX_INTERPOLATION_BILINEAR, virt_u8[i + 3]);
    ERROR_CHECK_OBJECT(warp_node);

    // set the border mode to constant with zero value
    vx_border_t border_mode;
    border_mode.mode = VX_BORDER_CONSTANT;
    border_mode.constant_value.U8 = 0;
    vxSetNodeAttribute(warp_node, VX_NODE_BORDER, &border_mode,
        sizeof(border_mode));

}
vxChannelCombineNode(graph, virt_u8[3], virt_u8[4], virt_u8[5], NULL,
    birds_eye);
```

Note that the matrix generated by the userComputeBirdsEyeTransform node is an input to the vxWarpPerspectiveNode. Since no object metadata change here, graph reverification will not be triggered for each graph execution.

There will be a substantial amount of pixels in the output image that will be mapped outside of the input image boundaries. We want them to be black, and so we set the border mode to VX_BORDER_CONSTANT with the pixel value equal to 0. Also, note that we use virtual images, so that an OpenVX implementation can execute this operation in a more optimal way, for example, running the perspective transformation on a color image in one pass. Since the vxWarpPerspectiveNode cannot figure out the size of the output image from the input image, the virtual images have to be ini-

tialized with specific values for width and height; see the beginning of the
`makeBirdsEyeViewGraph` implementation:

```
vx_uint32 width, height;
vxQueryImage(input, VX_IMAGE_WIDTH, &width, sizeof(vx_uint32));
vxQueryImage(input, VX_IMAGE_HEIGHT, &height, sizeof(vx_uint32));

/* create virtual images */
const int numu8 = 6;
vx_image virt_u8[numu8];

for(int i = 0; i < numu8; i++)
{
        virt_u8[i] = vxCreateVirtualImage(graph, width, height,
            VX_DF_IMAGE_U8);
}
```

Now let us see how we can create a perspective transformation during
graph execution time.

6.5.2.2 Generating a perspective transformation

We want to create a perspective transformation that sends the vanishing
point to infinity. This can be done by considering the mapping

$$H = KRK^{-1}, \tag{6.6}$$

where

$$K = \begin{pmatrix} f_x & 0 & c_x \\ f_y & 0 & c_y \\ 0 & 0 & 1 \end{pmatrix} \tag{6.7}$$

is the intrinsic camera matrix, and R is a rotation around x axis,

$$R = \begin{pmatrix} 1 & 0 & 0 \\ 0 & \cos(\phi) & \sin(\phi) \\ 0 & -\sin(\phi) & \cos(\phi) \end{pmatrix}. \tag{6.8}$$

The rotation angle ϕ is chosen so that the vanishing point maps to infinity.
Also, we need to keep the part of the road in front of the camera in the
view; otherwise, our output will be a black image. So, we will add an
additional pan and zoom transformation given by the matrix Z:

$$H_{\text{final}} = ZH. \tag{6.9}$$

Note that throughout this section, we will use the direct perspective transformation that maps an input image to an output image. OpenVX uses an inverse matrix that maps an output image to an input, and we will address this only in the end when we will generate the output `vx_matrix` object.

This algorithm is implemented in the `birdseye_transform_calc_function`. It has two input parameters: a `vx_array` with one element corresponding to the vanishing point and the input image, which is only needed to pass the required size of the output image. The output parameter is the perspective transformation in a `vx_matrix` object. First, we get the input/output parameters and image width/height:

```
vx_status VX_CALLBACK birdseye_transform_calc_function( vx_node node,
    const vx_reference * refs, vx_uint32 num )
{
  vx_array points = (vx_array)refs[0];
  vx_image image = (vx_image)refs[1];
  vx_matrix perspective = (vx_matrix)refs[2];

  // get image height
  vx_uint32 image_width, image_height;
  ERROR_CHECK_STATUS(vxQueryImage(image, VX_IMAGE_WIDTH, &image_width,
      sizeof(image_width)));
  ERROR_CHECK_STATUS(vxQueryImage(image, VX_IMAGE_HEIGHT, &image_height,
      sizeof(image_height)));
```

Then we initialize the intrinsics matrix and calculate its inverse (needed in (6.6)):

```
  // intrinsic parameters
  float _K[9] = {
    8.4026236186715255e+02*scale_factor, 0.,
        3.7724917600845038e+02*scale_factor,
    0., 8.3752885759166338e+02*scale_factor,
        4.6712164335800873e+02*scale_factor,
    0., 0., 1.
  };

  // calculate intrinsics inverse
  float _Kinv[9];
```

```
calc_inverse_3x3matrix(_K, _Kinv);
```

scale_factor = 4 is used here and further because several operations, including camera calibration and vanishing point detection, were done on an image resized down 4 times each dimension. calc_inverse_3x3matrix is implemented using the LAPACK library. Then we obtain the coordinates of the vanishing point from the input vx_array argument:

```
// obtain the vanishing point
const int num_points = 1;
vx_coordinates2d_t* _points = 0;
vx_size stride = sizeof(vx_coordinates2d_t);
vx_map_id map_id;
vxMapArrayRange(points, 0, num_points, &map_id, &stride,
    (void**)&_points,
  VX_READ_ONLY, VX_MEMORY_TYPE_HOST, 0);
```

Now we find the corresponding uniform coordinates of the vanishing point using the inverse intrinsic matrix:

```
// generate the vanishing point in uniform coordinates
float pv[] = {_points[0].x*scale_factor,
    _points[0].y*scale_factor};
float pvu[2];
calc_homography(_Kinv, pv, pvu);
float yv = pvu[1];
```

We are ready to find the angle ϕ from (6.8). Note that we do all matrix operations with floating point arrays, and we will use vx_matrix only for the output:

```
// generate a homography that sends the vanishing point to infinity
float phi = atan(1/yv);
float _rotate[9] = {
  1.0f, 0.0f, 0.0f,
  0.0f, -cos(phi), -sin(phi),
  0.0f, sin(phi), -cos(phi)
};
```

Once we know the rotation matrix, we are ready to generate a perspective transformation that sends the vanishing point to infinity:

```
// generate birds eye view homography
float _temp[9], _perspective[9];
```

```
mult_3x3matrices(_K, _rotate, _temp);
mult_3x3matrices(_temp, _Kinv, _perspective);
```

We also have to make sure that the important part of the image is visible after this transformation. We will use an affine transformation that maps parallel lines to parallel lines, but we cannot make it a separate node since if the image is empty after the perspective transformation node, then the output image will be empty too. For simplicity, we will construct this mapping as a pan and zoom transformation, making sure two control points in the input image map inside the output image. First, we generate the coordinates of the control points in the input image:

```
// now map two control points using the perspective matrix,
// to adjust scale and translation
float upper_boundary_factor = 1.2f;
float control1[2] = {pv[0], pv[1]*upper_boundary_factor};
float control2[2] = {pv[0], image_height};
```

Then we map them to the output image:

```
float control1_mapped[2], control2_mapped[2];
calc_homography(_perspective, control1, control1_mapped);
calc_homography(_perspective, control2, control2_mapped);

// find y coordinates of the mapped points from the uniform
   coordinates
float y1 = control1_mapped[1];
float y2 = control2_mapped[1];
```

Now we generate a pan and zoom transformation that maps these points to the upper and lower boundaries of the output image and multiply it to the left from the perspective transformation:

```
// now define additional translation and scale to have the control
   points
// mapped to the upper and lower boundary of the output image
float scale = ((float)y2 - y1)/image_height;
float _panzoom[] = {1.0f, 0.0f, image_width*scale/2 - pv[0],
                    0.0f, 1.0f, -y1,
                    0.0f, 0.0f, scale};

// now create the final perspective transformation by multiplying
// _perspective by _panzoom from the left
```

```
float _perspective_final[9];
mult_3x3matrices(_panzoom, _perspective, _perspective_final);
```

We have obtained the required perspective transformation. Note that OpenVX deals with the inverse transposed homography transformation (see (6.4)), so we invert and transpose the matrix before importing it:

```
// now we need to invert and transpose the homography for OpenVX
float _perspective_final_inv[9];
calc_inverse_3x3matrix(_perspective_final, _perspective_final_inv);
transpose(_perspective_final_inv);

vxCopyMatrix(perspective, _perspective_final_inv, VX_WRITE_ONLY,
    VX_MEMORY_TYPE_HOST);

return VX_SUCCESS;
```

The validation of this user node is implemented in the `birdseye_transform_validator` function. We check that the output matrix is 3×3 floating point and set the corresponding metadata:

```
// parameter #2 -- check that this is a floating point 3x3 matrix
ERROR_CHECK_STATUS( vxQueryMatrix( ( vx_matrix )parameters[2],
    VX_MATRIX_TYPE, &param_type, sizeof( param_type ) ) );
if(param_type != VX_TYPE_FLOAT32)
{
        return VX_ERROR_INVALID_TYPE;
}


vx_size rows, columns;
ERROR_CHECK_STATUS( vxQueryMatrix( ( vx_matrix )parameters[2],
    VX_MATRIX_ROWS, &rows, sizeof( rows ) ) );
if(rows != 3)
{
        return VX_ERROR_INVALID_DIMENSION;
}


ERROR_CHECK_STATUS( vxQueryMatrix( ( vx_matrix )parameters[2],
    VX_MATRIX_COLUMNS, &columns, sizeof( columns ) ) );
if(columns != 3)
{
        return VX_ERROR_INVALID_DIMENSION;
}
```

```
// set output metadata
ERROR_CHECK_STATUS( vxSetMetaFormatAttribute( metas[2], VX_MATRIX_TYPE,
    &param_type, sizeof( param_type ) ) );
ERROR_CHECK_STATUS( vxSetMetaFormatAttribute( metas[2], VX_MATRIX_ROWS,
    &rows, sizeof( rows ) ) );
ERROR_CHECK_STATUS( vxSetMetaFormatAttribute( metas[2],
    VX_MATRIX_COLUMNS, &columns, sizeof( columns ) ) );
```

CHAPTER 7

Background subtraction and object detection

Contents

7.1 A threshold-based object detector

A very simple method of object detection is to assume that everything at the beginning of a video sequence is just "background" and therefore not interesting, but if something changes, then it is due to the appearance of an object that we want to detect. This can be used, for example, to process a security camera video. Most security camera video is very boring—imagine a camera in a warehouse looking down an aisle of inventory. Perhaps most of the time no one is there, so the video is just a static scene. Usually, no one watches this video in real time; instead, it is recorded. A security video is only reviewed when something happens, for example, if something is stolen. The investigator may need to fast forward through hours of static video to find the interesting parts. We can help by automatically noticing when something happens in the video and saving timestamps of these interesting parts of the video. These timestamps can be used to index the video, enabling the reviewer to access them directly without searching. Background subtraction and object detection is one way to do this.

We will illustrate background subtraction using the technique introduced in Chapter 3, applied to a short video of a dog fetching a ball. Six frames from this video are shown in Figs. 7.1 and 7.2. The scene is an empty hallway at the beginning of the video. After a few seconds, a ball is thrown into the scene, and a dog runs in to fetch it. The dog retrieves the ball and exits the scene. The video was captured via a stationary cellphone camera, and the original is in vertically oriented HD video, 1920 pixels high by 1080 pixels wide, at 30 frames per second. The original video was saved in MP4 format, and a free software package (https://www.dvdvideosoft.com/products/dvd/Free-Video-to-JPG-Converter.htm) was used to extract the individual frames into JPEG files. Finally, IrfanView

Copyright © 2020 Elsevier Inc.
All rights reserved.

(https://www.irfanview.com/) was used to convert the color JPEG files to black-and-white PGM files, which can be easily read using utility functions in the OpenVX sample implementation.

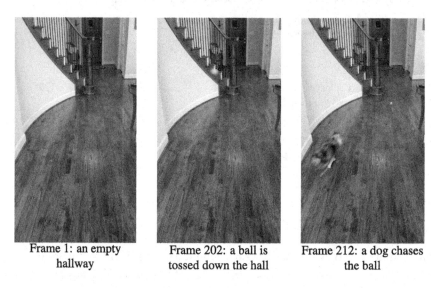

Frame 1: an empty
hallway

Frame 202: a ball is
tossed down the hall

Frame 212: a dog chases
the ball

Figure 7.1 Ball chase sequence.

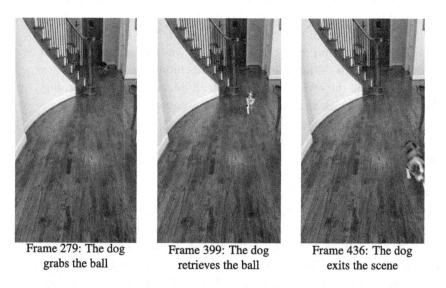

Frame 279: The dog
grabs the ball

Frame 399: The dog
retrieves the ball

Frame 436: The dog
exits the scene

Figure 7.2 Ball retrieval sequence.

The code below adds some set-up details to the example from Chapter 3. Some variables for the image sizes and the threshold are declared, and then the context, graph, and images are created. We omit the error checking of the return values for clarity—production code should check that all the OpenVX objects are successfully created.

Background subtraction requires no high-resolution images; in fact, lower-resolution processing is generally more robust. So the first node in our graph will significantly scale the image down. All the rest of the images are created at the lower resolution.

```
vx_uint32 w_in = 1080, h_in = 1920; // input image size
int scale = 4; // image size scale
int w = w_in/scale; // scaled image width
int h = h_in/scale; // scaled image height

vx_uint8 threshval = 10; // basic difference threshold value

vx_context context = vxCreateContext();
vx_graph graph = vxCreateGraph(context);

vx_image input_image = vxCreateImage(context, w_in, h_in,
    VX_DF_IMAGE_U8);
vx_image curr_image = vxCreateImage(context, w, h, VX_DF_IMAGE_U8);
vx_image diff_image = vxCreateVirtualImage(graph, w, h, VX_DF_IMAGE_U8);
vx_image bg_image = vxCreateImage(context, w, h, VX_DF_IMAGE_U8);
vx_image fg_image = vxCreateImage(context, w, h, VX_DF_IMAGE_U8);
```

Next, we create the threshold object and set its value, create the nodes in the graph, and verify the resulting graph. Again, the production code should check that the objects are successfully created and the graph was verified successfully. The scaling parameter is set to AREA interpolation rather than NEAREST_NEIGHBOR, which tends to introduce aliasing noise. A good implementation of AREA scaling will have less aliasing at strong diagonal edges:

```
vx_threshold threshold = vxCreateThresholdForImage(context,
    VX_THRESHOLD_TYPE_BINARY, VX_DF_IMAGE_U8, VX_DF_IMAGE_U8);
vxCopyThresholdValue(threshold, (vx_pixel_value_t*)&threshval,
    VX_WRITE_ONLY, VX_MEMORY_TYPE_HOST);

vx_node scale_node = vxScaleImageNode(graph, input_image, curr_image,
    VX_INTERPOLATION_AREA);
```

```
vx_node absdiff_node = vxAbsDiffNode(graph, bg_image, curr_image,
    diff_image);
vx_node thresh_node = vxThresholdNode(graph, diff_image, threshold,
    fg_image);

vxVerifyGraph(graph);
```

Now that we have constructed the graph, we can start feeding images into the graph's input and executing it. The main loop below uses utility functions to capture and display video frames, which in this case just read and write image files. The myCaptureImage and myDisplayImage functions construct the filenames to read or write from their arguments, and directory pathnames kept in global variables. Note that in this simple example the first image is taken to be the background model. An immediate-mode function is used to fill the bg_image by scaling it from the input the first time through the loop.

```
int framenum = 1;
while (myCaptureImage(context, input_image, framenum) == VX_SUCCESS) {

  if (framenum == 1) {
    vxuScaleImage(context, input_image, bg_image, VX_INTERPOLATION_AREA);
  }
  vxProcessGraph(graph);

  myDisplayImage(context, fg_image, "fg", framenum);
  framenum++;
}
```

When we look at the results on the left side of Fig. 7.3, the first thing we will notice is that the threshold is too low. There is enough noise in the camera input that there is quite a bit of "foreground" even where nothing is happening. The figure shows Frame 212 of the thresholded output. The pixels identified as "foreground" are white. We can see that even with AREA scaling, there is quite a bit of speckle noise. Just for comparison, we show the same frame with identical processing except for using NEAREST_NEIGHBOR scaling on the right side of Fig. 7.3, which is even worse. Our next step is raising the threshold, so some of this noise will go away, but it is better to start with cleaner data, so for the rest of the examples in this chapter, we will stick to AREA scaling.

Next we look at increasing the threshold to reduce the noise. Fig. 7.4 shows the results when raising the threshold from 10 to 60 in increments

AREA interpolation   NEAREST_NEIGHBOR interpolation

Figure 7.3 Frame 212 foreground with two different types of scaling interpolation.

of 10 gray levels. The first couple of increases reduce the noise, but beyond that, the detection sensitivity decreases significantly. At a threshold of 60, much of the dog is missing from the detected foreground. We'll use a threshold of 30 for now.

7.2 Adding alpha blending to the background model

Using a static background model taken from the first frame of the input works for a while, but subtle lighting changes and slight camera movement can cause some changes to be detected where there really is not anything interesting going on. In our sample video, frame 212 looks pretty clean, but just a few frames later, on frame 229, some noise starts to creep in. As can be seen in Fig. 7.5, a few spots along the bannister are starting to light up where there should not be anything detected.

One way to combat this is using *alpha blending* on the background model. Rather than simply using a single static background frame, the background model is continuously updated with the current image. The blending rate is referred to as "alpha." This technique has the benefit of ignoring some uninteresting changes caused by lighting effects, especially if these changes are gradual. OpenVX provides a function for updating a background model via alpha blending called `vxAccumulateWeightedImageNode`.

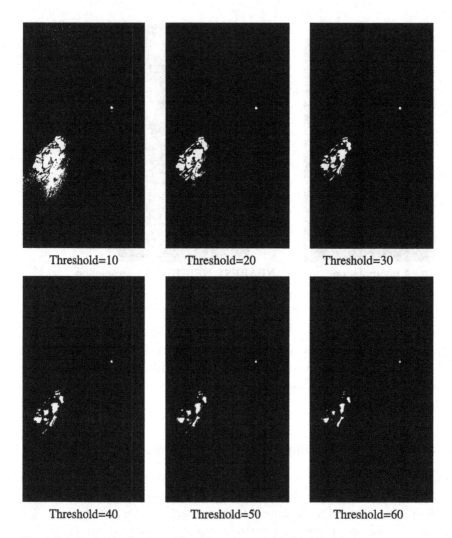

Threshold=10   Threshold=20   Threshold=30

Threshold=40   Threshold=50   Threshold=60

Figure 7.4 Frame 212 foreground with various gray level thresholds.

We can augment our graph to add this node to blend the current image into the background model at some rate we determine. We can add the following lines to the example code, just after creating the other graph nodes, but before verifying the graph:

```
vx_float32 alphaval = 0.1f;
vx_scalar alpha = vxCreateScalar(context, VX_TYPE_FLOAT32, &alphaval);
vx_node accum_node = vxAccumulateWeightedImageNode(graph, curr_image,
    alpha, bg_image);
```

Figure 7.5 Top portion of Frame 229 foreground with a static background model.

This code augments the graph to create the one below in Fig. 7.6. The background model is blended with 10% (`alphaval = 0.1f`) of the current image on each frame.

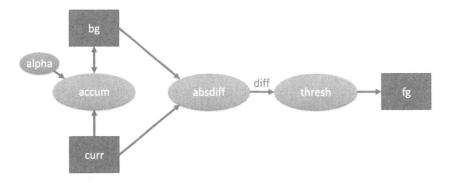

Figure 7.6 A background subtraction graph with alpha blending.

As a result, some of the noise caused by small lighting changes is suppressed. In our sample video on frame 229 the noise that started to appear with the static background model is gone, as can be seen in the image in Fig. 7.7.

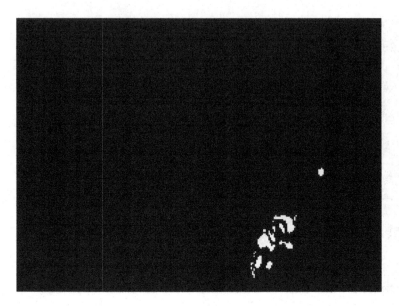

Figure 7.7 Top portion of Frame 229 foreground with a 10% alpha-blended background model.

Of course, some of the foreground (in this case the dog) is also suppressed, so there is a trade-off between alpha blending and sensitivity. However, in any real-world application, some maintenance of the background model is necessary. Some lighting noise started to creep into our sample video already, and it is only a few seconds long. A security video application needs to run for days on end, during which some lighting changes are inevitable. The level of alpha blending can be adjusted depending on the application and level of sensitivity required. A higher alpha, say 50%, updates the background quickly, nearly completely refreshing it in just a few frames. The result is that if a person comes into the scene and holds still, then he will quickly become merged into the background. Depending on the application, this may be acceptable. A lower value of alpha, say just 2%, will update the background more slowly, which can be desired if you need to keep objects from being merged into the background. However, once an object becomes merged, it is "burnt" into the background model, so when it does move, a shadow is left behind. A solution to this is to use a mask to *not* update portions of the background where objects are being actively tracked. This would require a more complicated graph and perhaps some user nodes, which are beyond the scope of this chapter. But hopefully this example provides an introduction to the OpenVX tools you can use to adjust the knobs of threshold and alpha blend to suit the background modeling needs of your application.

7.3 Applying morphology operators to the foreground

Once an initial foreground mask is created, some "clean-up" of the mask can help in localizing particular objects. You may have noticed that the dog in our example is usually broken up into a large number of disconnected "blobs." OpenVX provides some morphology operators that can merge nearby blobs into a single (or at least smaller number) of blobs to stream-line the downstream processing of detected objects. In particular, OpenVX provides "dilate" and "erode" functions that are commonly used to clean up foreground masks.

The dilate operator expands blobs to fill in gaps between nearby blobs. The erode operator contracts the blobs. Typically, the dilate operator is used to merge some blobs, and then the erode operator is applied to reduce the size of the resulting blob for better localization. The combination of a dilate followed by an erode is called a morphological "close" operation. Let us see how to apply a close operation to our sample video and observe the results.

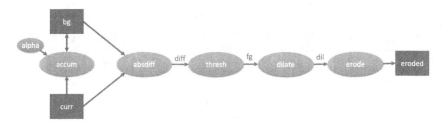

Figure 7.8 A background subtraction graph with morphology.

To do this, we will add a few lines to our graph construction code to postprocess the foreground mask and create the graph in Fig. 7.8. We will create additional images needed for the dilated and eroded versions of the mask. Only the final output needs to be "real," so the rest can be virtual. We will change our initial foreground mask to be virtual, and the dilated image is also virtual. The final eroded output is nonvirtual, so we can access it after the graph executes.

```
vx_image fg_image = vxCreateVirtualImage(graph, w, h, VX_DF_IMAGE_U8);
vx_image dilated_image = vxCreateVirtualImage(graph, w, h,
    VX_DF_IMAGE_U8);
vx_image eroded_image = vxCreateImage(context, w, h, VX_DF_IMAGE_U8);
```

Then we will create the node operators to execute the morphology:

```
vx_node dilate_node = vxDilate3x3Node(graph, fg_image, dilated_image);
vx_node erode_node = vxErode3x3Node(graph, dilated_image, eroded_image);
```

The images in Fig. 7.9 show the effect of the morphology operators on frame 212 of the video sequence. The first is the initial foreground mask, then the dilated version, and finally the eroded version. The dilated version connects several blobs together, but the result looks a little "puffy," with the blobs being larger than the underlying object. The eroded version cuts this down to a more accurate size. The erosion also expands some of the holes in the objects, but the blobs that were joined by the dilation remain joined. More aggressive morphology could join more of the blobs together, either by doing multiple dilates, using a larger dilation operator (via the vxNonLinearFilterNode), or by just working at a lower resolution.

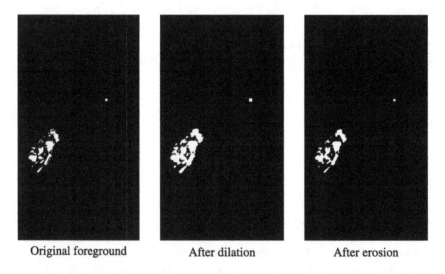

Original foreground   After dilation   After erosion

Figure 7.9 Morphological processing on Frame 212.

CHAPTER 8

Computational photography

Contents

Computer vision is taking an increasingly important place in processing images that we get from cameras attached to embedded compute platforms. Applications running in real time on mobile and automotive compute systems, such as digital image zoom, high dynamic range, and panoramic imaging, became important for several industries. In this chapter, we will consider one of the use cases, image stitching, implemented with OpenVX.

Let us consider two images taken with a camera from the same position but with different orientations. The goal is to generate a single seamless image from the input pair of images. OpenVX has no advanced tools for image registration required for this task, so we will use OpenCV to prepare stitching data. Obviously, this does not make sense if we want to stitch two images just once. However, in case we have videostreams from two cameras that we need to stitch, registration can be done once (e.g., on one pair of images), and stitching each couple of frames with OpenVX in real time can be very efficient. We will generally follow the multiband approach described in [37,38]. However, we will start with a simpler approach of naïve image blending.

8.1 Naïve image blending

Image stitching is based on the fact that the overlapping areas of two images taken with a rotating camera are related to each other with a homography

Copyright © 2020 Elsevier Inc.
All rights reserved.

transformation [26]. Image registration is done by finding salient keypoints in both images, matching them with their descriptors, and then searching for a homography transformation compatible with a subset of these matches (inliers). Once we have the registration, we remap both images to the output image and add them together with blending coefficients, which decrease for pixels further away from an image center, down to zero at the image border. Remap transformations and blending coefficients will be computed with OpenCV, and then we will implement stitching in OpenVX.

8.1.1 The algorithm

For two input images $I_1(x_1, y_1)$ and $I_2(x_2, y_2)$, we define mappings from the output blended image to the input images:

$$
\begin{aligned}
(x_1, y_1) &= p_1(x, y), \\
(x_2, y_2) &= p_2(x, y).
\end{aligned}
\tag{8.1}
$$

If we make $p_1 = H$ equal to homography and p_2 the identity transform (so that $x_2 = x$ and $y_2 = y$), then we may have the most of the first image appear outside the output image boundaries. So, we need to introduce an additional panning transformation T that will project the first image inside the bounds of the output image. So, our final transformations are:

$$
\begin{aligned}
p_1 &= T \otimes H, \\
p_2 &= T.
\end{aligned}
\tag{8.2}
$$

The size of the output image is chosen accordingly to fit both images after the transformations defined before.

Then the intensity of pixels in the blended image $I(x, y)$ is defined by

$$
I(x, y) = \frac{c_1(p_1(x, y))I_1(p_1(x, y)) + c_2(p_2(x, y))I_2(p_1(x, y))}{c_1(p_1(x, y)) + c_2(p_2(x, y))}.
\tag{8.3}
$$

The blending weights c_1 and c_2 change linearly from 1 at the image center to 0 at the image boundaries:

$$
\begin{aligned}
c_1(x_1, y_1) &= (1 - |2x_1/w_1 - 1|)(1 - |2y_1/h_1 - 1|), \\
c_2(x_2, y_2) &= (1 - |2x_2/w_2 - 1|)(1 - |2y_2/h_2 - 1|),
\end{aligned}
\tag{8.4}
$$

where w_j and h_j are the width and height of the image I_j.

8.1.2 Preparing stitching data

Image registration and the computation of remaps and blending weights is implemented in "stitch/homography-opencv.cpp." Although this code is not based on OpenVX, we briefly review it here as an example of how to prepare data for OpenVX using OpenCV. First, we register two input images. Since the registration is done on greyscale images, we convert color input images to greyscale:

```
Mat img1_color = imread( argv[1]);
Mat img2_color = imread( argv[2]);
Mat img1, img2;
cvtColor(img1_color, img1, COLOR_RGB2GRAY);
cvtColor(img2_color, img2, COLOR_RGB2GRAY);
```

Registration is implemented in the function computeStitchParams, which takes greyscale images img1 and img2 and returns a homography transformation mapping from the first to the second, as well as the rectangle bounds, which contains both images after img1 is projected onto img2 with the homography transformation:

```
Mat homography;
Rect bounds;
computeStitchParams(img1, img2, homography, bounds, verbose);
```

Then we create an output image (which will contain the results of stitching the two images) and the images for blending weights using bounds:

```
Mat img_stitched(bounds.height, bounds.width, CV_8UC1);
Mat coeffs1 = Mat::zeros(img_stitched.size(), CV_32FC1);
Mat coeffs2 = Mat::zeros(img_stitched.size(), CV_32FC1);
```

We also generate stitching weight maps for both input images:

```
Mat weights1, weights2;
generateWeightImage(img1.size(), weights1);
generateWeightImage(img2.size(), weights2);
```

Now let us create the remap transformations for mapping the input images img1_color and img2_color to the output image img_stitched. We take into account a panning transformation for both images according to Eq. (8.2):

```
Rect roi = Rect(-bounds.x, -bounds.y, img2.cols, img2.rows);
Mat remap_homography, remap_pan;
```

```
computeHomographyRemap(img1.size(), img_stitched.size(),
    homography, remap_homography);
computePanRemap(img2.size(), img_stitched.size(), roi,
    remap_pan);
```

Once we have the remaps, we map both image weights to the output image space to obtain the blending coefficients c_1 and c_2 from (8.4):

```
remap(weights1, coeffs1, remap_homography, Mat(),
  INTER_LINEAR, BORDER_TRANSPARENT);
remap(weights2, coeffs2, remap_pan, Mat(),
  INTER_LINEAR, BORDER_TRANSPARENT);
```

Here `remap` is the OpenCV implementation of the remap transformation that maps an input image (e.g., `weights1` in the first call above) to the output image (`coeffs1`) using the remap `remap_homography` with linear interpolation and not modifying the output pixels mapped outside the input image boundary (`BORDER_TRANSPARENT`). The final step is normalizing the blending coefficients: we divide them by their sum at each pixel. We also have to account for the case where both coefficients are zero, so we set the minimum value of `coeff_total` to a nonzero value:

```
Mat coeff_total = max(coeffs1 + coeffs2, FLT_MIN);
divide(coeffs1, coeff_total, coeffs1);
divide(coeffs2, coeff_total, coeffs2);
```

Now we have everything we need to run image stitching, so we just need to save the remaps and blending coefficients. The blending coefficients are converted to signed 16-bit images supported by image arithmetic functions in OpenVX and scaled by a factor of 2^{12} for higher precision. Also, we save both input and output image sizes with each remap.

```
FileStorage fs(stitch_filename, FileStorage::WRITE);
fs << "remap1" << remap_homography;
fs << "remap1_src_width" << weights1.cols;
fs << "remap1_src_height" << weights1.rows;
fs << "remap1_dst_width" << coeffs1.cols;
fs << "remap1_dst_height" << coeffs1.rows;

fs << "remap2" << remap_pan;
fs << "remap2_src_width" << weights2.cols;
fs << "remap2_src_height" << weights2.rows;
fs << "remap2_dst_width" << coeffs2.cols;
```

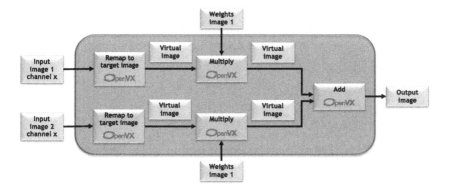

Figure 8.1 A naïve image stitching graph for a single channel.

```
fs << "remap2_dst_height" << coeffs2.rows;

Mat coeffs1_s16, coeffs2_s16;
coeffs1.convertTo(coeffs1_s16, CV_16SC1, (float)(1<<12));
fs << "coeffs1" << coeffs1_s16;

coeffs2.convertTo(coeffs2_s16, CV_16SC1, (float)(1<<12));
fs << "coeffs2" << coeffs2_s16;
```

8.1.3 The stitching algorithm implementation

Now we turn to the image stitching part, implemented in stitch.c with
OpenVX. The OpenVX graph for processing a single channel of an input
image is shown in Fig. 8.1.

We start by creating an OpenVX context and reading the stitching parameters, which we saved to the xml file:

```
const char* config_filename = argv[3];
vx_context context = vxCreateContext();
/* Read config images and remaps */
vx_image coeffs1, coeffs2;
if(vxa_import_opencv_image(config_filename, "coeffs1", context,
  &coeffs1, NULL, NULL) != 1)
{
  printf("Error reading coeffs1\n");
  return(-1);
}
```

```
if(vxa_import_opencv_image(config_filename, "coeffs2", context,
  &coeffs2, NULL, NULL) != 1)
{
  printf("Error reading coeffs2\n");
  return(-1);
}
int width, height;
vx_remap remap1, remap2;
if(vxa_import_opencv_remap(config_filename, "remap1", context, &remap1,
  &width, &height) != 1)
{
  printf("Error reading remap1\n");
  return(-1);
}
if(vxa_import_opencv_remap(config_filename, "remap2", context, &remap2,
  NULL, NULL) != 1)
{
  printf("Error reading remap2\n");
  return(-1);
}
```

Then we read input images from files and create the output image. The dimensions of the output image are taken from the remap transformation:

```
/* Read the input images*/
vx_image image1, image2;
if(vxa_read_image(image1_filename, context, &image1) != 1)
{
  printf("Error reading image 1\n");
  return(-1);
}
if(vxa_read_image(image2_filename, context, &image2) != 1)
{
  printf("Error reading image 2\n");
  return(-1);
}
/* Create an output image */
vx_image output = vxCreateImage(context, width, height, VX_DF_IMAGE_RGB);
```

Now it is time to create the OpenVX graph:

```
vx_status status;
vx_graph graph = makeStitchGraph(context, image1, image2,
```

```
remap1, coeffs1, remap2, coeffs2, output);
```

Let us look into the graph creation more closely. First, we create a graph:

```
vx_graph makeStitchGraph(vx_context context, vx_image image1, vx_image
    image2,
 vx_remap remap1, vx_image coeffs1, vx_remap remap2, vx_image coeffs2,
 vx_image output)
{
    /* Create virtual images */
    const int numu8 = 5;
    vx_image virtu8[numu8][3];
    const int nums16 = 3;
    vx_image virts16[nums16][3];

    vx_graph graph = vxCreateGraph(context);
```

Then we create the virtual images, both 8-bit and 16-bit, for storing intermediate results:

```
    for(i = 0; i < numu8; i++)
    {
        for (j = 0; j < 3; j++)
        virtu8[i][j] = vxCreateVirtualImage(graph, 0, 0, VX_DF_IMAGE_U8);
    }
    for(i = 0; i < nums16; i++)
    {
        for (j = 0; j < 3; j++)
        virts16[i][j] = vxCreateVirtualImage(graph, 0, 0, VX_DF_IMAGE_S16);
    }
```

Since we will use the Multiply node for blending and then the ConvertDepth node for getting an output as a VX_DF_IMAGE_U8 data type, we create scalars we will need for these nodes. Recall that we scaled the blending coefficients up to a factor of 2^{12} when converting the scaling weights from floating point to 16-bit, so now we will scale down the same factor when applying weights to images:

```
    float _scale = 1.0f/(1<<12);
    vx_scalar scale = vxCreateScalar(context, VX_TYPE_FLOAT32, &_scale);
    int _shift = 0;
    vx_scalar shift = vxCreateScalar(context, VX_TYPE_INT32, &_shift);
```

Now, as usual, we create nodes for each channel in a loop extracting each channel for both input images into 8-bit virtual images:

```
/* Create the same processing subgraph for each channel */
enum vx_channel_e channels[] = {VX_CHANNEL_R, VX_CHANNEL_G,
    VX_CHANNEL_B};
for(i = 0; i < 3; i++)
{
    /* First, extract input and logo R, G, and B channels to individual
    virtual images */
    vxChannelExtractNode(graph, image1, channels[i], virtu8[0][i]);
    vxChannelExtractNode(graph, image2, channels[i], virtu8[1][i]);
```

Then we map each channel of each input image to the output image space with remap transformations:

```
/* Add remap nodes */
vxRemapNode(graph, virtu8[0][i], remap1, VX_INTERPOLATION_BILINEAR,
    virtu8[3][i]);
vxRemapNode(graph, virtu8[1][i], remap2, VX_INTERPOLATION_BILINEAR,
    virtu8[4][i]);
```

We multiply each remapped image to the blending coefficients with the Multiply node:

```
/* add multiply nodes */
vxMultiplyNode(graph, virtu8[3][i], coeffs1, scale,
    VX_CONVERT_POLICY_SATURATE, VX_ROUND_POLICY_TO_NEAREST_EVEN,
    virts16[0][i]);
vxMultiplyNode(graph, virtu8[4][i], coeffs2, scale,
    VX_CONVERT_POLICY_SATURATE, VX_ROUND_POLICY_TO_NEAREST_EVEN,
    virts16[1][i]);
```

Now we add the weighted images to get the blended result, convert it to the 8-bit images, and then combine all the channels back together:

```
vxAddNode(graph, virts16[0][i], virts16[1][i],
    VX_CONVERT_POLICY_SATURATE, virts16[2][i]);

/* convert from S16 to U8 */
vxConvertDepthNode(graph, virts16[2][i], virtu8[2][i],
    VX_CONVERT_POLICY_SATURATE, shift);
}
```

```
vxChannelCombineNode(graph, virtu8[2][0], virtu8[2][1], virtu8[2][2],
    NULL, output);
```

We will skip the rest of the graph creation code that takes care of releasing data. Fig. 8.2 shows examples of two input images and the stitched output. Note that the blended image is blurred along the stitch line closer to the image borders. The effect is especially pronounced on the top of the mountain, where two copies of some trees are clearly visible. It is the result of imprecise registration, which is usually solved by multiband blending discussed in Section 8.3.

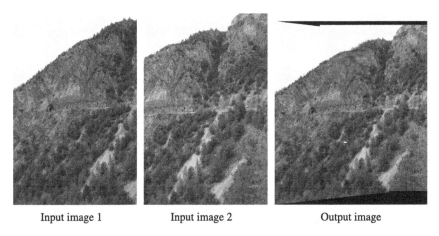

Input image 1   Input image 2   Output image

Figure 8.2 Input images and their stitching result.

8.2 Obtaining intermediate results

We may wonder what the results of a remap or applying blending weights look like. The implementation we just discussed does not allow us to look at these results, as we are using virtual images. If we want to obtain the results of intermediate calculations, then we need to replace these virtual images with real ones. This will require some changes in the graph, implemented in "stitch/stitch-debug.c." The graph now has more output color images, which is reflected in the definition of the makeStitchGraph function:

```
vx_graph makeStitchGraph(vx_context context, vx_image image1, vx_image
    image2,
  vx_remap remap1, vx_image coeffs1, vx_remap remap2, vx_image coeffs2,
  vx_image output, vx_image output_remapped1, vx_image output_remapped2,
```

```
vx_image output_weighted1, vx_image output_weighted2)
{
```

The implementation of the function is the same as that discussed in the previous section, with a few changes. First, we allocate real images to be used instead of virtual, so we have to specify image dimensions:

```
int output_width, output_height;
vxQueryImage(output, VX_IMAGE_WIDTH, &output_width, sizeof(int));
vxQueryImage(output, VX_IMAGE_HEIGHT, &output_height, sizeof(int));

/* Create temporary images */
vx_image image_remapped1[3], image_remapped2[3],
      image_weighted1[3], image_weighted2[3];

for(i = 0; i < 3; i++)
{
  image_remapped1[i] = vxCreateImage(context, output_width, output_height,
    VX_DF_IMAGE_U8);
  image_remapped2[i] = vxCreateImage(context, output_width, output_height,
    VX_DF_IMAGE_U8);
  image_weighted1[i] = vxCreateImage(context, output_width, output_height,
    VX_DF_IMAGE_S16);
  image_weighted2[i] = vxCreateImage(context, output_width, output_height,
    VX_DF_IMAGE_S16);
}
```

We are using image_remapped1 and image_remapped2 as outputs of the remap node:

```
vxRemapNode(graph, virtu8[0][i], remap1, VX_INTERPOLATION_BILINEAR,
  image_remapped1[i]);
vxRemapNode(graph, virtu8[1][i], remap2, VX_INTERPOLATION_BILINEAR,
  image_remapped2[i]);
```

Also, we use image_weighted1 and image_weighted2 as outputs of the multiplication node:

```
vxMultiplyNode(graph, image_remapped1[i], coeffs1, scale,
  VX_CONVERT_POLICY_SATURATE, VX_ROUND_POLICY_TO_NEAREST_EVEN,
  image_weighted1[i]);
vxMultiplyNode(graph, image_remapped2[i], coeffs2, scale,
  VX_CONVERT_POLICY_SATURATE, VX_ROUND_POLICY_TO_NEAREST_EVEN,
  image_weighted2[i]);
```

Since the images after the multiplication node are signed 16-bit, we convert them to unsigned 8-bit before combining single-channel images into color ones:

```
vxConvertDepthNode(graph, image_weighted1[i], virtu8[3][i],
    VX_CONVERT_POLICY_SATURATE, shift);
vxConvertDepthNode(graph, image_weighted2[i], virtu8[4][i],
    VX_CONVERT_POLICY_SATURATE, shift);
```

Finally, we generate color images:

```
vxChannelCombineNode(graph, image_remapped1[0], image_remapped1[1],
  image_remapped1[2], NULL, output_remapped1);
vxChannelCombineNode(graph, image_remapped2[0], image_remapped2[1],
    image_remapped2[2], NULL, output_remapped2);
vxChannelCombineNode(graph, virtu8[3][0], virtu8[3][1],
    virtu8[3][2], NULL, output_weighted1);
vxChannelCombineNode(graph, virtu8[4][0], virtu8[4][1],
    virtu8[4][2], NULL, output_weighted2);
```

The `main()` function takes care of creating the color images and then saving them to disk after executing the graph:

```
vxa_write_image(remapped1, "remapped1.png");
vxa_write_image(remapped2, "remapped2.png");
vxa_write_image(weighted1, "weighted1.png");
vxa_write_image(weighted2, "weighted2.png");
```

The images after the remap transformation and after applying the blending weights with the multiplication node are shown in Fig. 8.3.

8.3 Multiband image blending

This section focuses on a more advanced blending algorithm, which produces higher quality results than naïve blending. Also, it will give us a chance to work with a larger OpenVX graph. The problem with the naïve stitching described before is that both low and high frequencies are stitched with the same blending weights. If the weights boundaries are sharp, then we add more high frequencies, even in the areas where they were not present in the input images. As a result, we will observe a blending line in uniform areas of an output image. If, on the other hand, we blur the weights images, then we will blend high frequencies from two images with

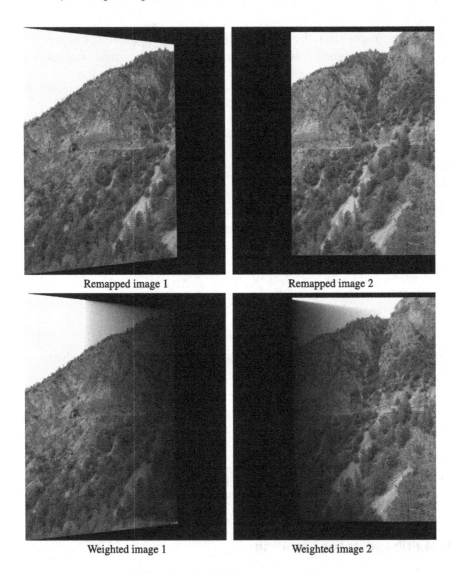

Figure 8.3 Naïve stitching intermediate results.

comparable weights. This, in the presence of even small misregistration, will result in an additional blur or two copies of the same scale object present in an output image. We are observing the latter effect in the output image of Fig. 8.2, where there are two instances of some trees on the top of the mountain. This problem can be solved by a method described in [37, 38]. The idea of the algorithm is that different frequency bands should be stitched with blending weights that are blurred depending on the frequency band, so that low frequencies are blended with strongly blurred weights, whereas high frequencies are blended with sharp weights. To achieve this, we will decompose the input images into Laplacian pyramids, blending weights into Gaussian pyramids, then blend images on each level to obtain the blended Laplacian pyramid, and then reconstruct the final image. First, let us define the input images and the blending weights mapped to the output image by the stitching transformation (8.2):

$$
\begin{aligned}
I_1^*(x, y) &= I_1(p_1(x, y)), \\
I_2^*(x, y) &= I_2(p_2(x, y)), \\
c_1^*(x, y) &= c_1(p_1(x, y)), \\
c_2^*(x, y) &= c_2(p_2(x, y)).
\end{aligned}
\tag{8.5}
$$

Initialize the blending weights by

$$
c_i^{\max}(x, y) = \begin{cases} 1 \text{if } i = \arg\max_i c_i^*(x, y), \\ 0 \text{ otherwise.} \end{cases}
\tag{8.6}
$$

Let us denote the kth level of the Laplacian pyramid of the image I_i^* by I_i^k and the kth level of the Gaussian pyramid of the blending weights image c_i^* by c_i^k. We use naïve blending (see Eq. (8.3)) on each pyramid level:

$$
I^k = \frac{c_1^k I_1^k + c_2^k I_2^k}{c_1^k + c_2^k}.
\tag{8.7}
$$

Finally, the output image is reconstructed from the Laplacian pyramid I^k. This way the low frequencies are blended with strongly blurred blending weights (the lower levels of a Gaussian pyramid), whereas the highest frequencies are blended with nonblurred blending weights.

Now let us look at the OpenVX graph implementation of this algorithm. The source code is available in "stitch/stitch-multiband.c." The remap and blending weights are stored in "stitch/stitch-multiband.xml."

Since the `main()` function is almost the same as for naïve stitching, let us focus on the graph creation function. The graph is quite large, so we have divided the implementation into several functions that we consider here one by one.

8.3.1 The main graph

The function makeGraph has almost the same list of arguments as for the naïve stitching. There is one more argument representing the number of pyramid levels pyr_levels. For this sample, we use pyr_levels = 4:

```
vx_graph makeGraph(vx_context context, vx_image image1, vx_image image2,
  vx_remap remap1, vx_image coeffs1, vx_remap remap2, vx_image coeffs2,
  int pyr_levels, vx_image output)
{
   /* Create virtual images */
   const int numu8 = 8;
   vx_image virtu8[numu8][3];

   const int nums16 = 5;
   vx_image virts16[nums16][max_pyr_levels][3];

   vx_image pyr_img_levels[3][max_pyr_levels][3];
   vx_image pyr_coeff_levels1[max_pyr_levels],
       pyr_coeff_levels2[max_pyr_levels];

   vx_pyramid pyr_image1[3], pyr_image2[3], pyr_output[3],
     pyr_coeffs1, pyr_coeffs2;
```

We start by creating a graph and temporary images. Also, we create some helper objects like shift scalar, which we will need for conversion between 8-bit and 16-bit images, and scale scalar, which will be used for multiplication:

```
   vx_graph graph = vxCreateGraph(context);

   int i, j, s;

   /* get width and height of the input images */
   vx_uint32 width, height;
   vxQueryRemap(remap1, VX_REMAP_DESTINATION_WIDTH, &width, sizeof(width));
   vxQueryRemap(remap1, VX_REMAP_DESTINATION_HEIGHT, &height,
       sizeof(height));

   // create virtual images
   for(i = 0; i < numu8; i++)
     for (j = 0; j < 3; j++)
     {
```

```
if(i == 2 || i == 3)
{
  virtu8[i][j] = vxCreateVirtualImage(graph, width, height,
      VX_DF_IMAGE_U8);
}
else if(i >= 4 && i <= 6)
{
  virtu8[i][j] = vxCreateVirtualImage(graph, width/(1 << (pyr_levels
      - 1)),
    height/(1 << (pyr_levels - 1)), VX_DF_IMAGE_U8);
}
else
{
  virtu8[i][j] = vxCreateVirtualImage(graph, 0, 0, VX_DF_IMAGE_U8);
}
}

for(s = 0; s < nums16; s++)
  for (j = 0; j < pyr_levels; j++)
    for(i = 0; i < 3; i++)
      virts16[s][j][i] = vxCreateVirtualImage(graph, 0, 0,
        VX_DF_IMAGE_S16);

/* Create the same processing subgraph for each channel */
enum vx_channel_e channels[] = {VX_CHANNEL_R, VX_CHANNEL_G,
    VX_CHANNEL_B};

float _scale = 1.0f/(1<<8);//1.0f/(1<<12);
vx_scalar scale = vxCreateScalar(context, VX_TYPE_FLOAT32, &_scale);

int _shift = 0;
vx_scalar shift = vxCreateScalar(context, VX_TYPE_INT32, &_shift);
```

We will need pyramid objects to store the Laplacian pyramids for the two input and one output images. A pyramid in OpenVX cannot store color images, so we create a pyramid for each of the three channels:

```
// create pyramids for images and coefficients
for(i = 0; i < 3; i++)
{
  pyr_image1[i] = vxCreatePyramid(context, pyr_levels - 1,
    VX_SCALE_PYRAMID_HALF, width, height, VX_DF_IMAGE_S16);
```

```
  pyr_image2[i] = vxCreatePyramid(context, pyr_levels - 1,
    VX_SCALE_PYRAMID_HALF, width, height, VX_DF_IMAGE_S16);
  pyr_output[i] = vxCreatePyramid(context, pyr_levels - 1,
    VX_SCALE_PYRAMID_HALF, width, height, VX_DF_IMAGE_S16);
}
```

Note that `pyr_level` in our code has the meaning of the total number of resolutions used for blending. `vxLaplacianPyramidNode` generates an image of the lowest resolution that is not a part of the pyramid, so the Laplacian pyramids here are created with `pyr_levels - 1` levels each. Blending weights need to be normalized on each level, so storing them in pyramid objects will actually result in more code. So we will store the Gaussian pyramids of the blending weights as arrays of images:

```
// build a gaussian pyramid images for each level
for(j = 0; j < pyr_levels; j++)
{
  pyr_coeff_levels1[j] = vxCreateVirtualImage(graph, 0, 0,
    VX_DF_IMAGE_U8);
  pyr_coeff_levels2[j] = vxCreateVirtualImage(graph, 0, 0,
    VX_DF_IMAGE_U8);
}

createBlendingWeightImages(graph, coeffs1, coeffs2, pyr_levels,
  pyr_coeff_levels1, pyr_coeff_levels2);
```

The function `createBlendingWeightImages` creates a Gaussian pyramid for each of the two blending weights; the implementation of this function will be considered in the next section. Once we set up the blending pyramids computation, we are ready to implement the main part of the graph. We start by extracting each channel from the input images, remapping them to the output image space, and computing their Laplacian pyramids:

```
for(i = 0; i < 3; i++)
{
  /* First, extract input and logo R, G, and B channels to individual
  virtual images */
  vxChannelExtractNode(graph, image1, channels[i], virtu8[0][i]);
  vxChannelExtractNode(graph, image2, channels[i], virtu8[1][i]);

  /* Add remap nodes */
  vxRemapNode(graph, virtu8[0][i], remap1, VX_INTERPOLATION_BILINEAR,
```

```
virtu8[2][i]);
vxRemapNode(graph, virtu8[1][i], remap2, VX_INTERPOLATION_BILINEAR,
    virtu8[3][i]);

// compute laplacian pyramid for each image channel
vxLaplacianPyramidNode(graph, virtu8[2][i], pyr_image1[i],
    virtu8[4][i]);
vxLaplacianPyramidNode(graph, virtu8[3][i], pyr_image2[i],
    virtu8[5][i]);
```

vxRemapNode requires us to explicitly set the output image size, so virtu8[2] and virtu8[3] are created with the dimensions taken from the remap object. Also, note that the number of levels in the pyramids pyr_image1 and pyr_image2 is pyr_levels - 1. The last level is returned separately to virtu8[4] and virtu8[5], respectively. Now, for each pyramid level, we implement the blending. First, we cycle through the levels of the vx_pyramid objects, and the last level of the Laplacian pyramid has to be addressed separately:

```
for(int j = 0; j < pyr_levels - 1; j++)
{
  pyr_img_levels[0][j][i] = vxGetPyramidLevel(pyr_image1[i], j);
  pyr_img_levels[1][j][i] = vxGetPyramidLevel(pyr_image2[i], j);
  pyr_img_levels[2][j][i] = vxGetPyramidLevel(pyr_output[i], j);

  // add multiply nodes
  vxMultiplyNode(graph, pyr_img_levels[0][j][i], pyr_coeff_levels1[j],
    scale, VX_CONVERT_POLICY_SATURATE, VX_ROUND_POLICY_TO_NEAREST_EVEN,
    virts16[0][j][i]);
  vxMultiplyNode(graph, pyr_img_levels[1][j][i], pyr_coeff_levels2[j],
    scale, VX_CONVERT_POLICY_SATURATE, VX_ROUND_POLICY_TO_NEAREST_EVEN,
    virts16[1][j][i]);
  vxAddNode(graph, virts16[0][j][i], virts16[1][j][i],
    VX_CONVERT_POLICY_SATURATE, pyr_img_levels[2][j][i]);
}

// add multiply nodes for the last pyramid levels
vxMultiplyNode(graph, virtu8[4][i], pyr_coeff_levels1[pyr_levels - 1],
    scale, VX_CONVERT_POLICY_SATURATE, VX_ROUND_POLICY_TO_NEAREST_EVEN,
    virts16[2][pyr_levels - 1][i]);
vxMultiplyNode(graph, virtu8[5][i], pyr_coeff_levels2[pyr_levels - 1],
    scale, VX_CONVERT_POLICY_SATURATE, VX_ROUND_POLICY_TO_NEAREST_EVEN,
    virts16[3][pyr_levels - 1][i]);
```

```
vxAddNode(graph, virts16[2][pyr_levels - 1][i],
    virts16[3][pyr_levels - 1][i], VX_CONVERT_POLICY_SATURATE,
    virts16[4][pyr_levels - 1][i]);
```

We cannot directly apply the denominator in formula (8.7) since there is no division function in OpenVX. So, we take care of normalization during the computation of Gaussian pyramids, and the function createBlendingWeightImages generates the weights such that their sum is a constant value for all pixels. We will discuss how to do this in the next section.

Although the blending coefficients are stored in 8-bit images, the outputs of the multiplication and addition are 16-bit. We need to convert the last level of the blended pyramid into 8-bit before running the Laplacian reconstruction. Once we have the output images for all channels, we just need to combine all the channels in a color image:

```
// convert from S16 to U8
vxConvertDepthNode(graph, virts16[4][pyr_levels - 1][i], virtu8[6][i],
    VX_CONVERT_POLICY_SATURATE, shift);

vxLaplacianReconstructNode(graph, pyr_output[i], virtu8[6][i],
    virtu8[7][i]);
}
vxChannelCombineNode(graph, virtu8[7][0], virtu8[7][1], virtu8[7][2],
    NULL, output);
```

Finally, we need to release all the temporary images that we created in this function. Also, we need to release the images created via calls to vxGetPyramidLevel as this function also increases a reference counter for the corresponding object:

```
for (s = 0; s < 3; s++)
  for(j = 0; j < pyr_levels - 1; j++)
    for(i = 0; i < 3; i++)
    vxReleaseImage(&pyr_img_levels[s][j][i]);
```

We ran this graph on the same images as in the results of Section 8.1 in the image shown in Fig. 8.4. Note that the trees on the top of the mountain near the blending line are now sharp.

Naïve blending output   Multiband blending output

Figure 8.4 Naïve and multiband stitching results.

8.4 Building a Gaussian pyramid for the blending weights

The main challenge with building a Gaussian pyramid for the blending weights is that OpenVX has no division function, so applying a denominator in the blending formula (8.7) is challenging. We will solve it using a lookup table, which can be handy for any per-pixel transformation that OpenVX does not support directly. Let us take a look at the implementation of the function `createBlendingWeightImages`. It takes the blending coefficients `coeffs1` and `coeffs2` as inputs and returns the arrays of images `pyr_coeff_levels1` and `pyr_coeff_levels2` as an output. First, we need to allocate temporary images:

```
void createBlendingWeightImages(vx_graph graph, vx_image coeffs1,
    vx_image coeffs2,
  int pyr_levels, vx_image* pyr_coeff_levels1, vx_image*
    pyr_coeff_levels2)
{
  vx_context context = vxGetContext((vx_reference)graph);

  int _shift4 = 4;
  vx_scalar shift4 = vxCreateScalar(context, VX_TYPE_INT32, &_shift4);

  int _shift0 = 0;
```

```
vx_scalar shift0 = vxCreateScalar(context, VX_TYPE_INT32, &_shift0);

float _scale = 1.0f/2;
vx_scalar scale = vxCreateScalar(context, VX_TYPE_FLOAT32, &_scale);

const int numu8 = 4;
vx_image coeff_levels[numu8][max_pyr_levels];

const int nums16 = 4;
vx_image coeff_levels_s16[nums16][max_pyr_levels];

for(int i = 0; i < numu8; i++)
{
  for(int j = 0; j < pyr_levels; j++)
  {
    coeff_levels[i][j] = vxCreateVirtualImage(graph, 0, 0,
        VX_DF_IMAGE_U8);
  }
}

for(int i = 0; i < nums16; i++)
{
  for(int j = 0; j < pyr_levels; j++)
  {
    coeff_levels_s16[i][j] = vxCreateVirtualImage(graph, 0, 0,
        VX_DF_IMAGE_S16);
  }
}
```

Another challenge that we meet here is that OpenVX does not widely support 16-bit image operations. Specifically, there is no function for resizing 16-bit images. Since coeffs1 and coeffs2 are 16-bit, we will need to convert them to 8-bit. The intensity values in these images vary from 0 to $2^{12} - 1$, and so during the conversion, we shift 4 bits to the right to leave the leftmost 8 bits. Also, we blur each blending image by applying the 3×3 Gaussian filter:

```
vxConvertDepthNode(graph, coeffs1, coeff_levels[0][0],
  VX_CONVERT_POLICY_SATURATE, shift4);
vxGaussian3x3Node(graph, coeff_levels[0][0], coeff_levels[2][0]);

vxConvertDepthNode(graph, coeffs2, coeff_levels[1][0],
```

```
VX_CONVERT_POLICY_SATURATE, shift4);
vxGaussian3x3Node(graph, coeff_levels[1][0], coeff_levels[3][0]);
```

Now we build a pyramid by scaling down and blurring:

```
// building a pyramid and applying smoothing to each level
for(int j = 1; j < pyr_levels; j++)
{
  vxHalfScaleGaussianNode(graph, coeff_levels[0][j - 1],
    coeff_levels[0][j], 3);
  vxGaussian3x3Node(graph, coeff_levels[0][j], coeff_levels[2][j]);

  vxHalfScaleGaussianNode(graph, coeff_levels[1][j - 1],
    coeff_levels[1][j], 3);
  vxGaussian3x3Node(graph, coeff_levels[1][j], coeff_levels[3][j]);
}
```

Now let us see how we can normalize each image so that their sum is a constant. We need to add the two images together and divide each image by the sum. Since OpenVX has no division operation, instead of dividing by the sum, we will create an image with inverse values and multiply by it. If two values from 8-bit images $c_1^k(x, y)$ and $c_2^k(x, y)$ (where k is the pyramid level index) are summed together, then the result $s^k(x, y)$ varies from 0 to 510. We will create a 16-bit image s_{inv}^k with the values

$$s_{inv}^k(x, y) = 510/\max(s^k(x, y), 1), \qquad (8.8)$$

where the max function is used to make sure the denominator does not take zero values. Then the normalized images b_i^k can be computed as follows:

$$b_i^k(x, y) = c_i(x, y) * s_{inv}^k(x, y) * 0.5. \qquad (8.9)$$

The 0.5 factor ensures that the result varies from 0 to 255. The only remaining problem is how to efficiently compute the image s_{inv}^k. Fortunately, OpenVX has a tool called a lookup table, which implements arbitrary mappings of pixel values. We will use it to map a value $s^k(x, y)$ to $s_{inv}^k(x, y)$ according to formula (8.8). Since $s^k(x, y)$ is a sum of two 8-bit images, it takes only 511 distinct values, and the size of the lookup table is limited to 1024.

Now let us see how this computation can be implemented within an OpenVX graph. We start by creating a lookup table object and retrieving the order number of the zero index. (Since the lookup table is created for VX_DF_IMAGE_S16 image type, it maps both positive and negative indices.)

```
// prepare a lookup table
vx_lut lut = vxCreateLUT(context, VX_TYPE_INT16, 1024);

// obtain the index of the 0 element
vx_uint32 lut_offset;
vxQueryLUT(lut, VX_LUT_OFFSET, &lut_offset, sizeof(vx_uint32));
```

Then we create an array of integer values for the lookup table and copy it into the lut object:

```
vx_int16 lut_data[1024];
for(int i = 0; i < lut_offset; i++)
{
  lut_data[i] = 0;
}

for(int i = 0; i < 512; i++)
{
  lut_data[i + lut_offset] = 510/(i == 0 ? 1 : i);
}

vxCopyLUT(lut, lut_data, VX_WRITE_ONLY, VX_MEMORY_TYPE_HOST);
```

Now the lookup table is ready, and we can implement the computation of normalized blending weights. Images on each pyramid level are summed up, resulting in 16-bit images, which are fed into the TableLookup node. The output is multiplied by each image (with the factor 0.5):

```
// summing up weights and building a normalization image
for(int j = 0; j < pyr_levels; j++)
{
  vxAddNode(graph, coeff_levels[2][j], coeff_levels[3][j],
    VX_CONVERT_POLICY_SATURATE, coeff_levels_s16[0][j]);

  vxTableLookupNode(graph, coeff_levels_s16[0][j], lut,
    coeff_levels_s16[1][j]);

  vxMultiplyNode(graph, coeff_levels[2][j], coeff_levels_s16[1][j],
    scale,
```

```
  VX_CONVERT_POLICY_SATURATE, VX_ROUND_POLICY_TO_ZERO,
      coeff_levels_s16[2][j]);
vxConvertDepthNode(graph, coeff_levels_s16[2][j],
    pyr_coeff_levels1[j],
  VX_CONVERT_POLICY_SATURATE, shift0);


vxMultiplyNode(graph, coeff_levels[3][j], coeff_levels_s16[1][j],
    scale,
  VX_CONVERT_POLICY_SATURATE, VX_ROUND_POLICY_TO_ZERO,
      coeff_levels_s16[3][j]);
vxConvertDepthNode(graph, coeff_levels_s16[3][j],
    pyr_coeff_levels2[j],
  VX_CONVERT_POLICY_SATURATE, shift0);
}
```

8.5 Implementing Laplacian pyramid functions with OpenVX graph

At the time of writing this book, the OpenVX sample implementation [30] of vxLaplacianPyramidNode and vxLaplacianReconstructNode had issues, so, in order to create the multiband stitching sample discussed in this chapter work, we have reimplemented both functions with other OpenVX functions. The implementation described here is not conformant with the OpenVX spec, since we are using Gaussian 3×3 convolutions instead of 5×5, a different algorithm for upscaling and a few other differences. However, it is an important demonstration that even with quite limited functionality, an OpenVX graph is a very powerful and flexible tool. The implementations of both functions are available in the same file "stitch/stitch-multiband.c." We start with building a Laplacian pyramid.

8.5.1 Implementing a Laplacian pyramid

The building of a Laplacian pyramid is implemented in the function _vxLaplacianPyramidNode. This function takes a single 8-bit image as an input and returns a Laplacian pyramid with 16-bit images on each level, with width and height two times smaller for each next level. It also returns an output 8-bit image with dimensions two times smaller than the lowest level of the Laplacian pyramid. The corresponding OpenVX functions can also take 16-bit input and output images. However, due to lack of 16-bit image support in OpenVX 1.2, we limit this implementation to 8-bit input and output images only.

The _vxLaplacianPyramidNode function has the same interface as the corresponding OpenVX function. The implementation starts by getting the context and the input image dimensions. We also create a Gaussian pyramid from an input image and put it in a virtual vx_pyramid object:

```
vx_status _vxLaplacianPyramidNode(vx_graph graph, vx_image image,
    vx_pyramid pyr_image, vx_image output)
{
  vx_context context = vxGetContext((vx_reference)graph);

  /* get the number of pyramid levels */
  vx_size level_num;
  vxQueryPyramid(pyr_image, VX_PYRAMID_LEVELS, &level_num,
    sizeof(vx_size));



  /* get width and height of the input image */
  vx_uint32 width, height;
  vxQueryImage(image, VX_IMAGE_WIDTH, &width, sizeof(width));
  vxQueryImage(image, VX_IMAGE_HEIGHT, &height, sizeof(height));

  vx_pyramid pyr_gauss = vxCreateVirtualPyramid(graph, level_num + 1,
    VX_SCALE_PYRAMID_HALF,
   width, height, VX_DF_IMAGE_U8);

  vxGaussianPyramidNode(graph, image, pyr_gauss);
```

Now we calculate a Laplacian pyramid level from a couple of Gaussian pyramid levels using the following algorithm:
*   take a lower resolution Gaussian level,
*   upscale it 2× each dimension, so that the size matches the next level of the Gaussian pyramid,
*   smooth it using a Gaussian 3 × 3 filter,
*   and, finally, subtract the result from the higher resolution Gaussian level and put it in the corresponding Laplacian pyramid level.

Here is the OpenVX graph implementation of this algorithm:

```
for(int i = 0; i < level_num; i++)
{
  vx_image level1 = vxGetPyramidLevel(pyr_gauss, i);
```

```
vx_image level2 = vxGetPyramidLevel(pyr_gauss, i + 1);

// get width and height of the level1
vx_uint32 width_level1, height_level1;
vxQueryImage(level1, VX_IMAGE_WIDTH, &width_level1,
    sizeof(width_level1));
vxQueryImage(level1, VX_IMAGE_HEIGHT, &height_level1,
    sizeof(height_level1));

// create temporary images for upscaling
vx_image upscale = vxCreateVirtualImage(graph, width_level1,
    height_level1, VX_DF_IMAGE_U8);
vx_image smoothed = vxCreateVirtualImage(graph, width_level1,
    height_level1, VX_DF_IMAGE_U8);

// upscale the lower level and run a Gaussian filter on it
vxScaleImageNode(graph, level2, upscale,
    VX_INTERPOLATION_NEAREST_NEIGHBOR);
vxGaussian3x3Node(graph, upscale, smoothed);

// subtract from the higher level to obtain a Laplacian pyramid level
vx_image laplacian_level = vxGetPyramidLevel(pyr_image, i);
vxSubtractNode(graph, level1, smoothed, VX_CONVERT_POLICY_SATURATE,
    laplacian_level);

vxReleaseImage(&level1);
vxReleaseImage(&level2);
vxReleaseImage(&upscale);
vxReleaseImage(&smoothed);
vxReleaseImage(&laplacian_level);
}
```

vxSubtractNode will generate a VX_DF_IMAGE_S16 image unless the output image type is explicitly set to VX_DF_IMAGE_U8. The Laplacian pyramid is 16-bit, so the laplacian_level image is of type VX_DF_IMAGE_S16. Like in Section 8.3, we have to release not just the temporary images upscale and smoothed, but also the pyramid level images level1, level2, and laplacian_level, initialized with calls to vxGetPyramidLevel.

Finally, we downscale 2× each dimension the last level of the Gaussian pyramid to create the output image and release the pyramid object:

```
vxHalfScaleGaussianNode(graph, vxGetPyramidLevel(pyr_gauss, level_num -
    1), output, 5);

vxReleasePyramid(&pyr_gauss);

return VX_SUCCESS;
}
```

8.5.2 Implementing Laplacian pyramid reconstruction

The `vxLaplacianReconstructNode` function implements an operation inverse to the `vxLaplacianPyramidNode`: given a Laplacian pyramid and an image generated by `vxLaplacianPyramidNode`, reconstruct an input image to the `vxLaplacianPyramidNode`. The algorithm is pretty simple: we upscale the image exactly the same way as when building the pyramid (upscale 2× each dimension with nearest neighbors and then smooth with a Gaussian 3 × 3 filter), add it with the lowest level of the pyramid, and then repeat with this image for the next level of the pyramid. The pyramid contains 16-bit images, so after adding images, we should also get a 16-bit image. However, if this pyramid was created by a `vxLaplacianPyramidNode` or `_vxLaplacianPyramidNode`, then we know that this result will have pixel values varying only from 0 to 255, so we will convert it to an 8-bit image on each step. We need to do it not just because of performance issues, but also because OpenVX 1.2 does not provide a function to upscale a 16-bit image.

We start the implementation of this function by getting the context, finding the number of input pyramid levels and creating a scalar needed for a conversion of a 16-bit image to an 8-bit image.

```
vx_status _vxLaplacianReconstructNode(vx_graph graph, vx_pyramid
    pyr_image, vx_image input, vx_image output)
{
    vx_context context = vxGetContext((vx_reference)graph);

    /* get the number of pyramid levels */
    vx_size level_num;
    vxQueryPyramid(pyr_image, VX_PYRAMID_LEVELS, &level_num,
        sizeof(vx_size));

    vx_image sum[level_num];
```

```
int _shift = 0;
vx_scalar shift = vxCreateScalar(context, VX_TYPE_INT32, &_shift);
```

Then, for each pyramid level, we upscale either the input image
or the temporary image created in the previous loop iteration. The
vxScaleImageNode requires explicit dimensions for the output image, so we
have to query the image dimensions of the current pyramid level and then
create a virtual image upscale with exactly these dimensions:

```
for(int i = level_num - 1; i >= 0; i--)
{
  vx_image level1 = vxGetPyramidLevel(pyr_image, i);
  vx_image level2 = i == level_num - 1 ? input : sum[i + 1];

  // get width and height of the level2
  vx_uint32 width_level2, height_level2;
  vxQueryImage(level2, VX_IMAGE_WIDTH, &width_level2,
      sizeof(width_level2));
  vxQueryImage(level2, VX_IMAGE_HEIGHT, &height_level2,
      sizeof(height_level2));

  // upsample the current level
  vx_image upscale = vxCreateVirtualImage(graph, 2*width_level2,
      2*height_level2, VX_DF_IMAGE_U8);
  vx_image smoothed = vxCreateVirtualImage(graph, 0, 0, VX_DF_IMAGE_U8);
  vxScaleImageNode(graph, level2, upscale,
      VX_INTERPOLATION_NEAREST_NEIGHBOR);
  vxGaussian3x3Node(graph, upscale, smoothed);
```

Now we have to add the upscaled image to the pyramid level and convert the result to an 8-bit image:

```
  // add it with the next level
  vx_image _sum = vxCreateVirtualImage(graph, 0, 0, VX_DF_IMAGE_S16);
  vxAddNode(graph, smoothed, level1, VX_CONVERT_POLICY_SATURATE, _sum);

  sum[i] = vxCreateVirtualImage(graph, 2*width_level2, 2*height_level2,
      VX_DF_IMAGE_U8);
  vxConvertDepthNode(graph, _sum, i > 0 ? sum[i] : output,
      VX_CONVERT_POLICY_SATURATE, shift);
```

The image _sum will have values varying from 0 to 255, so when converting it to an 8-bit image, no shift is required. We finalize the function by releasing the data allocated inside and outside of the loop:

```
  vxReleaseImage(&upscale);
  vxReleaseImage(&smoothed);
  vxReleaseImage(&level1);
  vxReleaseImage(&_sum);
}

vxReleaseScalar(&shift);

for(int i = 0; i < level_num - 1; i++)
{
  vxReleaseImage(&sum[i]);
}

  return(VX_SUCCESS);
}
```

Finally, we note that the implementation of Laplacian pyramids with other OpenVX functions results in quite a large graph for multiband stitching with a total of 194 nodes.

CHAPTER 9

Tracking

Contents

9.1 Introduction

By "tracking" we mean following the perceived movement, or apparent movement, of an object or set of features between successive frames of a video sequence. This has a number of applications:

- Estimation of speed and trajectory
- Prediction of position at some point in the future
- Estimation of structure from motion
- Video compression
- Video stabilization
- Automatic panning or zooming

The first two items refer to the position in two dimensions of the features we are tracking; we have knowledge neither of distance from the viewer nor of absolute scale. We will see that movement in the Z direction, resulting in a change of size of an object, can be confusing, especially if there is no

Copyright © 2020 Elsevier Inc.
All rights reserved.

concept of "object." A change of scale will manifest in movement of a set of distinct features, for example, corners, toward or away from a common point. Prediction of future position is useful not only in collision avoidance but also when what we are tracking, for example, a face in a crowd, which becomes obscured, and we have to find the features again. It saves time if we know roughly whereabouts to look. Conversely, the third item, the structure from motion, exploits characteristics such as relative motion of features and movement toward or away from a common point to estimate distance from the viewer and solidity, that is, which features together form a distinct object. Movement over time is important in video compression, since it enables a third degree of freedom giving far greater opportunity to reduce bandwidth. Video stabilization is achieved by reducing the size of the image and framing it in such a way that the majority of features remain in a constant position, whereas panning and zooming generally do the opposite, placing a smaller set of features of interest in the middle of the image.

9.2 Tracking methods

Perhaps the most obvious way of tracking a feature is to repeatedly detect it in subsequent frames. However, if the feature is trivial, like a corner, then how do we distinguish it from all the other corners? Logically, this method of tracking is only going to work for relatively complex, composite sets of features and so will be inefficient. There have been a number of algorithms proposed based upon taking the content of a bounding box as an example of an object that will be tracked frame by frame. Three such algorithms, "BOOSTING" (based on AdaBoost), "MIL" (for Multiple Instance Learning), and "KCF" (for Kernelized Correlation Filters) are available in implementations of OpenCV. Also available are "TLD" (for Tracking, Learning, and Detection) and "MEDIANFLOW," which are also based upon the idea of learning what the object was and looking for it again in subsequent frames. "MOSSE" (Minimum Output Sum of Squared Error) uses adaptive correlation. All these methods do essentially the same thing; given an initially example or set of examples, they create a detector that gives as an output the position of an object within a window and then reposition the window centrally around this position in preparation for the next frame.

9.3 Optical flow

Algorithms based upon optical flow work in a different way to the tracking methods briefly described before. Optical flow, or optic flow, is defined as the apparent motion of objects, surfaces, and edges in a scene caused by the relative movement of an observer and the scene, that is, the object and camera. The concept was originally introduced by the American psychologist James J. Gibson in the 1940s to describe the visual stimulus provided to organisms moving through their environment. It is a two-dimensional vector field where each vector is a displacement vector showing the movement of points from moment to moment and frame to frame. Rather than being based around object detection, methods based upon optical flow consider the properties of a set of pixels belonging to an object in contrast to pixels elsewhere and is based upon the simple assumptions:

- The pixel intensities of an object do not change between frames
- Neighboring pixels have similar motion

Thus algorithms based upon optical flow know nothing of "objects" and are inherently simpler and faster than the methods that seek to detect and redetect objects frame by frame.

Consider a pixel at location (x, y) and time t that has the intensity $I(x, y, t)$ in one frame. In the next frame, time Δt later, it has moved by $(\Delta x, \Delta y)$ and has the intensity $I(x+\Delta x, y+\Delta y, t+\Delta t)$. By our first assumption, otherwise known as the *brightness constancy constraint*, we can write

$$I(x, y, t) = I(x + \Delta x, y + \Delta y, t + \Delta t).$$

Assuming that the displacement $\Delta x, \Delta y, \Delta t$ is small, we can expand this using the Taylor series:

$$I(x + \Delta x, y + \Delta y, t + \Delta t) = I(x, y, t) + \frac{\partial I}{\partial x}\Delta x + \frac{\partial I}{\partial y}\Delta y + \frac{\partial I}{\partial t}\Delta t$$
$$+ \text{higher-order terms.}$$

From this it follows that to a first approximation:

$$\frac{\partial I}{\partial x}\Delta x + \frac{\partial I}{\partial y}\Delta y + \frac{\partial I}{\partial t}\Delta t = 0.$$

Dividing throughout by Δt, we obtain:

$$\frac{\partial I}{\partial x}\frac{\Delta x}{\Delta t} + \frac{\partial I}{\partial y}\frac{\Delta y}{\Delta t} + \frac{\partial I}{\partial t}\frac{\Delta t}{\Delta t} = 0 = \frac{\partial I}{\partial x}V_x + \frac{\partial I}{\partial y}V_y + \frac{\partial I}{\partial t}.$$

In this equation, V_x and V_y are the x and y components of the velocity, or optical flow of $I(x, y, t)$, and $\frac{\partial I}{\partial x}$, $\frac{\partial I}{\partial y}$, and $\frac{\partial I}{\partial t}$ are the derivatives of the intensity with respect to the space and time coordinates. Writing these derivatives as I_x, I_y, and I_t, we obtain:

$$I_x V_x + I_x V_y = -I_t,$$

or, in vector notation,

$$\nabla VI^T \cdot \vec{V} = -I_t.$$

In other words, what we say that after a time t, the intensity will change depending upon the direction of movement and the intensity gradient in that direction, which makes intuitive sense. As it stands, this equation cannot be solved, since there is one equation and two unknowns. However, we made two assumptions, and we have only used one of them. The other assumption is that neighboring pixels move together, or in other words, we need to have more than one pixel to constitute an object to track. But which pixels to choose? This dilemma is similar to the *aperture problem* in optical flow, described in the next section, but in practice, our pixel selection has little bearing on this.

9.4 The aperture problem

In the picture in Fig. 9.1, we have taken two close-ups of the railings through a hole, one displaced slightly to the other. However, the displacement can be at a wide variety of angles and achieve the same result. The motion direction of pixels is ambiguous, because the motion component parallel to the line cannot be inferred based on the visual input.

The aperture problem is a higher-level problem than the issue of finding movement of individual pixels, and it serves to illustrate that whatever we calculate based upon our close-up, the pixelated view must be "taken with a pinch of salt," and it can be impossible to determine real movements based upon the information we are given.

9.5 The Lucas–Kanade algorithm for sparse feature sets

Optical flow may be calculated for all pixels positions of an image, but in most cases, we are interested in just a few points of interest, or *sparse feature sets*. Clearly, the fewer points we have to calculate, then there is potentially

Figure 9.1 *The aperture problem.* In the second small image the bars have clearly moved horizontally, but it's impossible to say if there has also been vertical movement, nor indeed if the horizontal movement was to the left or the right. (Redrawn from an image at https://www.ultrarailing.com/uar-270-3r-railing.html.)

less resource required, or we can use the resource to obtain more accurate results. Note that this general rule may not hold for implementations that have access to massively parallel computation where there may be almost no gain in being able to reduce the number of points beyond some lower limit. The Lucas–Kanade algorithm is designed for sparse feature sets and uses the second assumption that neighboring pixels have the same motion in the following way. Taking the pixels that are immediate neighbors to the chosen point, it is fairly safe to assume that the majority of those pixels will belong to the same object, unless the object is very small or we have not picked the center of the object. So for the smallest window of neighbors, we end up with nine equations, two unknowns, and some errors. A suitable method of estimating the unknowns in the presence of errors is the least-squares linear regression, resulting in the following equation:

$$\vec{V} = \begin{bmatrix} \sum_i I_{x_i}{}^2 & \sum_i I_{x_i} I_{y_i} \\ \sum_i I_{x_i} I_{y_i} & \sum_i I_{y_i}{}^2 \end{bmatrix}^{-1} \begin{bmatrix} -\sum_i I_{x_i} I_{t_i} \\ -\sum_i I_{x_i} I_{t_i} \end{bmatrix}.$$

In fact, this equation may be extended to any size of window; however, a 3 × 3 window is usually adequate and involves significantly less computation than the next size up, which would involve 25 pixels. This least-squares solution gives the same importance to all the pixels in the window, and it would be better to give more weight to the center of the patch, and Gaussian weighting is often used. The equation above is deceptive; it gives the impression that the problem may be solved in simple one-step way by calculating the sums, inverting the matrix, and performing the multiplication. In practice, it is never done this way; methods such as simple Gaussian elimination, Givens transformations, pivoting, and so on, are all employed to solve linear regression without specifically inverting the matrix, which is never guaranteed to be invertible. When we have the possibility of uniform areas of images where variation is most probably noise, these linear approaches may fail to give sensible results altogether. For this reason, iterative methods are usually used and in practice achieve consistently reliable results in fast times—if only the iteration may be designed to include any number of guards against unlikely solutions and inherent robustness in the presence of nonlinearity. Because the Lucas–Kanade method [39,40] only considers a very small area of pixels at a time, it just does not work if all those pixels happen to be uniform or if there is a large movement to a different area of the image, so it really is of interest because it is the basis for other methods.

9.6 Bouguet's implementation using image pyramids

The implementation of the Lucas–Kanade method used in OpenVX is based upon a paper by Bouguet [41], who uses image pyramids; in other words, it works on several different scale replicas of the image at once. In this implementation the partial derivatives of intensities I_x and I_y are obtained by using the Scharr gradients on the input image, rather than a Sobel filter, which would have simple Gaussian weighting. The change with respect to time, I_t, is found simply by subtracting the corresponding pixels in adjacent frames.

A window dimension of just nine pixels (OpenVX specifies that implementations must be able to support this size of window) may not be enough to accommodate large changes in position, which is where the pyramids come in. At the smallest scale the nine-pixel window is sufficient to find larger displacements, but small movements will be hidden. Similarly, at the largest scale, small movements can be found, but large displacements cannot be measured. This approach with pyramids goes some way to help solve the aperture problem, especially if movement can be detected at all scales.

The general approach of the algorithm is finding a solution to the optical flow of points of interest at the lowest resolution using an iterative Lucas–Kanade method based upon Newton–Raphson techniques, with a first guess for the displacement vector as zero. The result of that calculation is then used as a first guess for the iterations at the next higher-resolution pyramid, and so on in turn until level 0 of the pyramid, the raw image, is reached. In this way, large movements can be accommodated at the highest resolution, overcoming the aperture problem if proper design considerations are made. There is a trade off between the depth of the pyramid and the maximum displacement that may be reliably detected and must be taken into account in a system design. We must be careful with very deep pyramids, because if there are finely repeating features in your image (such as the railings in our aperture problem example), then the lower resolution images in the pyramid could suffer from aliasing, resulting in estimates of movement that are too large.

For the intimate details of the algorithm, the reader is referred to the original paper at http://robots.stanford.edu/cs223b04/algo_tracking.pdf.

9.6.1 The OpenVX API for optical flow

Let us take a look at the OpenVX API and examine what we can do with it. The declaration of the node function is:

```
vx_node vxOpticalFlowPyrLKNode(
      vx_graph graph,
      vx_pyramid old_images,
      vx_pyramid new_images,
      vx_array old_points,
      vx_array new_points_estimates,
      vx_array new_points,
      vx_enum  termination,
      vx_scalar epsilon,
      vx_scalar num_iterations,
      vx_scalar use_initial_estimate,
      vx_size   window_dimension);
```

There are quite a lot of parameters, perhaps more than we would expect from the description of the algorithm so far. The input parameters named old_images and new_images refer to greyscale pyramids (VX_DF_IMAGE_U8) and are otherwise self-explanatory, as perhaps are the input old_points and output new_points, but what about new_points_estimates? In fact, this parameter is included so that if we wish, then we can point the algorithm in the right direction if we know that, for example, a camera is panning, or we can predict movement based upon the momentum of an object such as a vehicle. We do not have to provide these estimates; whether they are to be used or not depends upon the value of the use_initial_estimate parameter, which is a Boolean value provided in a vx_scalar, so it may change at run-time.

The points parameters are arrays of VX_TYPE_KEYPOINT, referring to elements of this type:

```
typedef struct _vx_keypoint_t {
      vx_int32   x;
      vx_int32   y;
      vx_float32 strength;
      vx_float32 scale;
      vx_float32 orientation;
      vx_int32   tracking_status;
      vx_float32 error;
} vx_keypoint_t;
```

The specification requires that this node will change only the x, y and tracking_status fields, setting tracking_status to zero if a point is lost; however, we know that some implementations, including the Khronos sample implementation, also set other fields to zero. A point is lost if its new position is off the image or if no solution to the optical flow equation was found. Removing lost points from the array before processing of the next frame may improve efficiency, depending upon the implementation, but it is not necessary.

The final parameter window_dimension specifies the window size over which the algorithm is going to operate, that is, how far away from the original pixel position it is going to search for a new solution. This window size interacts with the initial estimates, if they are given, because the first part of Bouget's algorithm is applying the initial estimates by moving the pixel patch defined by the window size to be centered on the estimates. This first occurs at the lowest resolution of the pyramid, so quite large movements may be accommodated even if initial estimates are not given. The maximum window size that the algorithm can handle is implementation-dependent, but it is guaranteed to be at least 9 × 9, and may be found by querying the context for `VX_CONTEXT_OPTICAL_FLOW_MAX_WINDOW_DIMENSION`. Larger values of the integration window may be used to look for larger displacements; there is a trade-off here with the pyramid depth. In general, using a deeper pyramid is more efficient than a larger integration window, but be careful of aliasing in the lower-resolution images; if you find that your tracking is over-estimating movement or jumping around, then it can be that your pyramid is too deep. Notice that the window size must be set when the graph is created and cannot be changed at run-time.

The other parameters, `termination`, `epsilon`, and `num_iterations`, determine how the Lucas–Kanade iteration operation will stop. At graph creation time, you can choose `termination` as either `VX_TERM_CRITERIA_ITERATIONS`, `VX_TERM_CRITERIA_EPSILON`, or `VX_TERM_CRITERIA_BOTH`. The actual values may be determined at run-time as they are provided in scalars, and Bouget suggests maximum values of 20 iterations or a difference of 0.03 pixels as suitable values, although convergence is typically within 5 iterations. We suggest not to use the termination criteria `VX_TERM_CRITERIA_EPSILON` simply because this does not actually guarantee termination and recommend `VX_TERM_CRITERIA_BOTH`.

9.7 Selection of features to track

Bouget's implementation, like all methods based upon the Lucas–Kanade least-squares formulation of the problem, gives performance of a quality dependent upon the quality of its input. We made the point during the discussion of the Lucas–Kanade method that the matrix is not guaranteed to be invertible. This is most likely the case if the input pixels are uniform, or correlated, not conveying much information. If the matrix is not invertible, then the Newton–Raphson method does not converge either, so Bouget's implementation will give up after its maximum number of iterations is done. Therefore it is important to pick pixels that are part of some obvious feature with a distinct intensity gradient, for example, a corner. But if we want to track a face or another object, then how do we do that?

One scheme would be as follows:
- Run object recognition on the first frame to find your object
- Establish a region of interest including just the object found
- Run corner detection in the region of interest to find pixels to track
- Establish the relationship between the pixels and the border, or the centroid, of the region of interest

- Run OpenVX Optical Flow on the next frame
- Calculate the new region of interest using the new pixel positions

OpenVX provides two corner detection methods, Harris Corners and FAST Corners. Although FAST is an acronym (Features from Accelerated Segment Test), the algorithm is indeed significantly faster than the Harris method and hence probably more suitable for use in video applications. Note that we use the term "corner" very loosely to describe some trackable feature.

9.7.1 The OpenVX API for FAST corners

The OpenVX specification document contains quite a good description of both the Harris and FAST corners methods; the former is more configurable, and hence the API requires more parameters, whereas as noted earlier, the latter method is probably more suited to processing video frames. The function signature for creation of a FAST corners node is as follows:

```
vx_node vxFastCornersNode(
        vx_graph    graph,
        vx_image input,
        vx_scalar strength_thresh,
        vx_bool  nonmax_suppression,
        vx_array corners,
        vx_scalar   num_corners);
```

In the function signature, corners is a vx_array of vx_keypoint_t structures as described before. If more features are found than the array has capacity for, then they will not be recorded. The last parameter is optional, and if given, the total number of features found will be returned.

The strength_thresh is the parameter that controls the selection of features and must have a value between zero and 256; it can be set at run-time. The nonmax_suppression parameter is set at graph-building time, and if true means that nonmax suppression will be applied to the output features and also that the strength field in each vx_keypoint_t entry will be calculated; otherwise, it will be undefined.

9.8 Centroid tracking

If we wish to track an entire object, referred to by its bounding box, then we need a method to establish the relationship between this and the set of features we are tracking. One method of doing this is using the centroid.

When tracking features, we may find that the features move closer together or further apart in the x and y directions. This could be because the object is actually moving in the z direction, so the scale is changing, or the object is rotating, so that perspective comes into play. Each of the features may not maintain its distinct position, because our object may be flexible, like a face or a flag waving in the wind. So how can we relate our set of features to the bounding box of our object?

Let us make some assumptions. Let us assume that on average, the centroid of our feature set is in the same proportionate position within the bounding box of our object. By "proportionate position" we mean that the ratio of the size of the bounding box to the distance between the centroid of the feature set and centroid of the bounding box is constant. We also assume that the spread of our feature set is proportional to the size of our bounding box. For the initial frame, we can calculate the following items:

• The bounding box centroid

$$C_B = \left(\frac{x_{max} + x_{min}}{2}, \frac{y_{max} + y_{min}}{2} \right)$$

• The bounding box spread, equal to the root mean square distance from the centroid

$$S_B = \left(\frac{x_{max} - x_{min}}{2}, \frac{y_{max} - y_{min}}{2} \right)$$

• The centroid of the feature set

$$C_f = (\overline{x_f}, \overline{y_f})$$

• The spread of the feature set as the RMS distance from the centroid, that is, the standard deviation

$$S_f = (\sigma(x_f), \sigma(y_f))$$

• The size of the bounding box relative to the feature set, $\oslash$ denoting elementwise division:

$$R = S_B \oslash S_f$$

• The normalized displacement of the bounding box relative to the feature set

$$D = (C_B - C_f) \oslash S_f$$

Note that it is important that S_f is nonzero in both dimensions, or we can calculate neither the relative size nor the normalized displacement.

For subsequent frames, we can calculate a new feature spread S_f' and centroid C_f' and from these calculate a new bounding box.

- A new bounding box size, ∘ denoting elementwise multiplication:

$$S_B' = R \circ S_f'$$

- A new bounding box centroid:

$$C_B' = C_f' + D \circ S_f'$$

Using the standard deviation σ or the RMS distance from the centroid as a measure of spread is preferable to using the difference between maximum and minimum values because it is less reliant on individual points that may have been chosen initially in error or be subject to variation due to object orientation or flexibility.

We use the spread in separate x and y directions to allow for distortion of the object or apparent distortion due to partial occlusion or rotation; if the object could be guaranteed to be of fixed shape, then we could use the absolute distance from the centroid, but this is not the case.

9.8.1 Difficulties

We have already mentioned one difficulty, namely we need nonzero feature spread in both dimensions. It is advisable to have as many features as possible within the object bounding box, since this gives a better estimation of the centroid as features move relative to each other because of noise or flexibility.

Initial choice of features to track is a source of error; for example, there may be a bright corner within the bounding box of an object that is not part of the object. This feature may move relatively to the object, causing perceived distortion of the net of points making up the object. Using the standard deviation to measure the spread of the features means that such erroneous points can be identified by noting that a change in distance from the centroid is surprisingly large or simply that the point is no longer within the calculated bounding box of the object. An example of such a rogue feature can be a fly sitting on the object when it was first identified, which subsequently flies off.

How then should we remove a point from the constellation of features we are tracking, without adversely affecting the estimation of the bounding box position and size? If we keep a record of the original position of the corners and the original centroid and spread of the bounding box, then we can recalculate the relative size and normalized displacement.

Expect features to disappear because of occlusion, rotation, noise, or simply because the object moves out of the field of view. The case of rotation is further discussed in the section entitled "The mirror ball." As the number of tracked features diminishes, we can expect the newly calculated values for position and size of the bounding box to become less reliable. Thus we should set some minimum absolute or relative value for the number of features we are tracking, and if the numbers fall below that value or if the spread becomes zero in either dimension, then take an appropriate action. Possible actions are:

- Run corner detection again, with the same parameters as were initially used. This should correct for points that were lost through noise or temporary partial occlusion.
- Run the original object detection algorithm again, that is, restart the process.

If the corner detection is run, then again the results should be compared with those previously estimated from the tracker, and if there is a large difference in spread or position, then it may be wise to also rerun object detection.

We should stress that the features or "corners" that we find to track be well-defined, because we are relying upon them. There must be a sufficient number of them. For example, if we select just four features, and one of them disappears perhaps because it was a transient specular reflection, then that could dramatically affect our measure of spread and centroid.

9.8.2 User nodes to handle centroid tracking

OpenVX does not have built-in support for centroid tracking; we need either to handle this outside the graphs or to define one or more user nodes to do the calculations. In the latter case, we could use APIs like the following:

```
typedef struct {
    vx_rectangle_t    bounding_box; // The last calculated object
        bounding box
    vx_coordinates2df_t bb_centroid; // The original bounding box
        centroid
```

```
    vx_coordinates2df_t bb_std_dev; // The original bounding box
        standard deviation
    vx_coordinates2df_t spread_ratio; // The ratio of bounding box to
        features std.dev.
    vx_coordinates2df_t displacement; // The displacement of bounding
        box from features
    vx_coordinates2df_t bb_vector; // The rate of change in
        displacement of the bounding box
    vx_coordinates2df_t bb_zoom;  // The rate of change in scale of
        the bounding box
    vx_uint32              num_corners; // The last valid number of
        features
} userTrackingData;


vx_node intialCentroidCalculationNode(
    /*
            Create a node to perform the initial centroid tracking
                calculations.
            The initial data consists of detected features and an object
                bounding box.
            The output scalar "valid" is a boolean that determines if
                tracking can continue.
    */
    vx_graph    graph,
    vx_scalar   bounding_box, // Object coordinates (input)
    vx_array    corners,          // Detected features (input)
    vx_scalar   output_data, // Holds a userTrackingData (output)
    vx_array    output_corners, // Output parameter of filtered
        features, same capacity as input array
    vx_scalar   valid              // Holds a vx_bool
    );


vx_node trackCentroidsNode(
    /*
            Create a node to perform the centroid tracking update
                calculation
            We calculate a new position and size for the bounding box,
                and also the
            rate of change of displacement and size.
            We reject any features that are not behaving correctly, and
                recalculate the ratio and displacement.
```

```
        We signal with an output boolean if tracking can continue,
            or if new features need to be found
*/
vx_graph    graph,
vx_array    originals,        // Original input features (in case
        we need to recalculate)
vx_array    corners,         // Input features
vx_scalar   input_data,      // Holds a userTrackingData (input)
vx_scalar   output_data, // Holds a userTrackingData (output)
vx_array    output_corners, // Filtered features (output), same
        capacity as input array
vx_scalar   valid            // Holds a vx_bool
);
```

Let us take these in turn, starting with the initial centroid calculation.

9.9 Example of tracking using OpenVX

In our code example, we will take a short sequence of film and demonstrate the following:
- Detect and obtain a bounding box for a specific object
- Find suitable features to track within that box
- Track features using Pyramidal Optical Flow, drawing an estimated bounding box on each frame
- Deal with disappearing features and features that are unreliable

Our initial code will just choose to track the first candidate object we find. Because our object detection gives us a bounding box for the object, we will use a region of interest in our input image to find the features to track. For the purposes of this example, the region of interest is predefined on a particular frame, and we will bother about the object detection. We will start by having two graphs, one for the initial feature detection and one for the feature and centroid tracking.

Our feature and centroid tracker uses the vxOpticalFlowPyrLKNode to track features using optical flow and then a user node to calculate the new centroid and draw the bounding box on the image.

To calculate our initial features of interest using FAST corners, we will have to either find all the corners in our image and then reject those that fall outside our bounding box or restrict our search for features to just the area of the image defined by the bounding box. Clearly, the latter method is more efficient, but it does require that the bounding box is known before the graph is created. This is because the OpenVX FAST corners API does not include a provision for searching only within certain bounds, plus there is no graph node that will create an image from a region of interest. However, if we use the former method, then there is also another potential problem: if there are very many corners found outside our bounding box, then the array of output features can fill before any corners we actually want are found. This can be solved by supplying a very large array, further compounding inefficiency.

Another alternative is generating a user node that first creates a new image from a region of interest in the input image, then performs FAST on this using the immediate mode function, and finally offsets the output points using the start_x and start_y values of the bounding box. Although at first glance this method seems attractive, we are not going to use it for two reasons:

1. It requires the creation and destruction of an extra object, the region of interest
2. It requires the use of the immediate mode library

It is quite possible that an implementation of OpenVX in our deployment environment will not contain or allow one or both of these items, for example, in a safety critical application.

We have a compromise solution:

1. Create an image without any features outside the bounding box by zeroing pixels
2. Run FAST corners on this image
3. Eliminate corners found at the periphery of the bounding box

The last stage is necessary since we will create contrast at the box border where in fact there may be none in the original image, and as a result, we could see erroneous disappearing features in subsequent frames. The last stage can be tacked on to the front of our initial centroid calculation node, but to implement it, the first stage will need a new user node defined as follows:

```
vx_node clearOutsideBoundsNode(
  /*
    Create a node to clear all pixels outside a bounding box
  */
  vx_graph    graph,
  vx_image    input_image,
  vx_scalar   bounds, // Holds a vx_rect (input)
```

```
  vx_image    output_image
);
```

The code to implement this user node is quite simple; after setting all the pixels in the output image to zero, we map the area defined by the bounds in the input image and then use `vxCopyImagePatch` to copy this region to the same location in the output image:

```
vx_status VX_CALLBACK clearOutsideBounds_function(vx_node node, const
    vx_reference * refs, vx_uint32 num)
{
    /*
    Output image equals input image but only for the bounding box
        region. Everything else is zeroed out...
    */
    vx_image input_image=(vx_image)refs[0];
    vx_image output_image=(vx_image)refs[2];
    vx_rectangle_t bounds;
    vx_map_id map_id;
    vx_imagepatch_addressing_t addr;
    vx_pixel_value_t pixel;
    void *ptr;
    /* Zero out the output image, assume setting u32 to zero will be
        good for any format we would use*/
    pixel.U32 = 0;
    ERROR_CHECK_STATUS(vxSetImagePixelValues(output_image, &pixel));
    /* Get the bounding box */
    ERROR_CHECK_STATUS(vxCopyScalarWithSize((vx_scalar)refs[1],
        sizeof(bounds), &bounds, VX_READ_ONLY, VX_MEMORY_TYPE_HOST));
    /* Map the input image for reading the area of the bounding box */
    ERROR_CHECK_STATUS(vxMapImagePatch(input_image, &bounds, 0,
        &map_id, &addr, &ptr, VX_READ_ONLY, VX_MEMORY_TYPE_NONE, 0));
    /* Now copy just what is inside the bounding box, from the input
        image to the output */
    ERROR_CHECK_STATUS(vxCopyImagePatch(output_image, &bounds, 0,
        &addr, ptr, VX_WRITE_ONLY, VX_MEMORY_TYPE_HOST));
    /* unmap the input image */
    ERROR_CHECK_STATUS(vxUnmapImagePatch(input_image, map_id));
    return VX_SUCCESS;
}
```

At the time of writing the Khronos sample implementation does not support the functions `vxCreateScalarWithSize` and `vxCopyScalarWithSize`, so in fact the example code for this chapter uses an array of size one rather than a scalar, so that it will work with libopenvx from Khronos, or indeed implementations conforming to version 1.1.

9.9.1 Calculating the initial tracking data

We have already presented the prototype of a user node creation function that implements the initial tracking data calculation. You can find a code that implements this in the examples in the file "centroid_tracking.c." We further present the code that implements the algorithm. Recall that we are using an array of one element to hold single structures, rather than scalars, since this is then compatible with implementations that do not support vxCreateScalarWithSize. It may also be convenient if you wish to extend the code to support tracking multiple objects. We use vxTruncateArray to make sure that the output arrays contain only the data we put in them. Input arrays of key points are mapped, but the output array of key points is filled one item at a time using vxCopyArrayRange. Note that only points found inside the bounding box are put in the output array. This means that any artificial features found at the edge of the bounding box are rejected initially.

```
vx_status VX_CALLBACK initialCentroidCalculation_function(vx_node node,
    const vx_reference * refs, vx_uint32 num)
{
        vx_array bounding_box = (vx_array)refs[0];
        vx_array corners = (vx_array)refs[1];
        vx_array output_data = (vx_array)refs[2];
        vx_array output_corners = (vx_array)refs[3];
        vx_scalar valid = (vx_array)refs[4];
        userTrackingData tracking_data;
        vx_bool valid = vx_true_e;
        vx_size num_corners = 0, orig_num_corners = 0;
        double sumx = 0.0, sumy = 0.0, sumsqx = 0.0, sumsqy = 0.0, meanx,
            meany, sigmax, sigmay;
        vx_map_id input_map_id;
        vx_size stride;
        char *array_data = NULL;
        ERROR_CHECK_STATUS(vxTruncateArray(output_data, 0));
        ERROR_CHECK_STATUS(vxTruncateArray(output_corners, 0));
        // Initial value of the bounding box in the tracking data is the
            input bounding box
```

```
ERROR_CHECK_STATUS( vxCopyArrayRange(bounding_box, 0, 1,
    sizeof(tracking_data.bounding_box),
    &tracking_data.bounding_box, VX_READ_ONLY,
    VX_MEMORY_TYPE_HOST));
// Initial value of the bounding box centroid:
tracking_data.bb_centroid.x = (tracking_data.bounding_box.end_x +
    tracking_data.bounding_box.start_x) / 2.0;
tracking_data.bb_centroid.y = (tracking_data.bounding_box.end_y +
    tracking_data.bounding_box.start_y) / 2.0;
// Initial value of the bounding box standard deviations
tracking_data.bb_std_dev.x = (tracking_data.bounding_box.end_x -
    tracking_data.bounding_box.start_x) / 2.0;
tracking_data.bb_std_dev.y = (tracking_data.bounding_box.end_y -
    tracking_data.bounding_box.start_y) / 2.0;
// Check for validity - we must have a bounding box with some area:
if (tracking_data.bb_std_dev.x < 1.0 || tracking_data.bb_std_dev.y
    < 1.0 )
{
    valid = vx_false_e;
}
// Initial velocities are all set to zero
tracking_data.bb_vector.x = 0.0;
tracking_data.bb_vector.y = 0.0;
tracking_data.bb_zoom.x = 0.0;
tracking_data.bb_zoom.y = 0.0;
// Find the sums and sums of squares of the corners, rejecting any
    that do not lie within the bounding box
// Copy good data to the output corner array
ERROR_CHECK_STATUS(vxQueryArray(corners, VX_ARRAY_NUMITEMS,
    &orig_num_corners, sizeof(num_corners)));
ERROR_CHECK_STATUS(vxMapArrayRange(corners, 0, orig_num_corners,
    &input_map_id, &stride, (void **)&array_data, VX_READ_ONLY,
    VX_MEMORY_TYPE_NONE, 0));
for (vx_uint32 i = 0; i < orig_num_corners; ++i, array_data +=
    stride)
{
    vx_keypoint_t *feature = (vx_keypoint_t *)array_data;
    // a tracking_status of zero indicates a lost point
    // we will mark a point as lost if it is already outside the
        bounding box
    // or on the bounding margin, as may be the case initially
    if (feature->tracking_status != 0 &&
```

```
                    feature->x > tracking_data.bounding_box.start_x &&
                    feature->x < tracking_data.bounding_box.end_x &&
                    feature->y > tracking_data.bounding_box.start_y &&
                    feature->y < tracking_data.bounding_box.end_y)
        {

            sumx += feature->x;
            sumy += feature->y;
            sumsqx += feature->x * feature->x;
            sumsqy += feature->y * feature->y;
            vxAddArrayItems(output_corners, 1, array_data, stride);
            ++num_corners;
        }
        else
        {
            feature->tracking_status = 0;
        }
    }
ERROR_CHECK_STATUS(vxUnmapArrayRange(corners, input_map_id));
// Now calculate centroid (mean) and standard deviation of the
    corners using the sums and sums of squares.
// We can also assess validity during this operation
// From the means and standard deviations we calculate the spread
    ratio and normalized displacement
if (num_corners < 2)
{
    // need at least two features to be able to establish a
        centroid and spread
    valid = vx_false_e;
    tracking_data.spread_ratio.x = 1.0;
    tracking_data.spread_ratio.y = 1.0;
    tracking_data.displacement.x = 0.0;
    tracking_data.displacement.y = 0.0;
}
else
{
    meanx = sumx / num_corners;
    meany = sumy / num_corners;
    sigmax = sqrt( sumsqx / num_corners - meanx * meanx);
    sigmay = sqrt( sumsqy / num_corners - meany * meany);
    if (sigmax < 1.0 || sigmay < 1.0)
    {
```

```
            // Need some area in the features to be able to
               calculate a new bounding box
            valid = vx_false_e;
            sigmax = 1.0; // just to stop divide-by-zero errors
            sigmay = 1.0;
        }
        tracking_data.spread_ratio.x = tracking_data.bb_std_dev.x /
            sigmax;
        tracking_data.spread_ratio.y = tracking_data.bb_std_dev.y /
            sigmay;
        tracking_data.displacement.x = (tracking_data.bb_centroid.x
            - meanx) / sigmax;
        tracking_data.displacement.y = (tracking_data.bb_centroid.y
            - meany) / sigmay;
    }

    tracking_data.num_corners = num_corners;
    // set output "output_data" parameter
    ERROR_CHECK_STATUS(vxAddArrayItems(output_data, 1, &tracking_data,
        sizeof(tracking_data)))
    // Set output "valid" parameter
    ERROR_CHECK_STATUS(vxCopyScalar(valid, &valid, VX_WRITE_ONLY,
        VX_MEMORY_TYPE_HOST));
    return VX_SUCCESS;
}
```

In the file "tracking_example.cpp," we create a graph using this user node, which outputs two copies of the filtered features array, by using vxCopyNode. We would like two copies because the centroid tracking graph may have to recalculate initial data when features are lost. We use two user nodes here: the node that will clear the image area outside the bounding box prior to finding features with FAST corners and our initial centroid calculation node. The graph is represented pictorially in Fig. 9.2.

The function is as follows:

```
vx_graph initial_feature_detection_graph(
                vx_context context,
                vx_rectangle_t *bounding_box,
                vx_image initial_image,
                vx_pyramid initial_pyramid,
                vx_array output_data,
                vx_array output_corners,
```

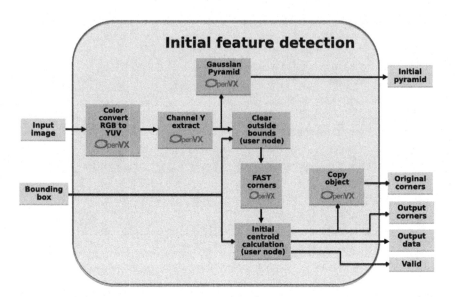

Figure 9.2 *Initial feature detection graph.* Two user nodes are required, one to clear data outside the bounding box and one to create the initial tracking data.

```
                vx_array original_corners,
                vx_scalar valid)
{
    /*
    Create the graph that performs the initial feature detection,
        given the bounding box.
    This graph will search for features using FAST corners, in a
        region of interest of the
    input image bounded by the given rectangle
    */
    vx_graph graph = vxCreateGraph(context);
    vx_image yuv_image = vxCreateVirtualImage(graph, 0, 0,
        VX_DF_IMAGE_IYUV);
    ERROR_CHECK_OBJECT(yuv_image)
    vx_image y_image = vxCreateVirtualImage(graph, 0, 0,
        VX_DF_IMAGE_U8);
    ERROR_CHECK_OBJECT(y_image)
    vx_image roi = vxCreateVirtualImage(graph, 0, 0, VX_DF_IMAGE_VIRT);
    ERROR_CHECK_OBJECT(roi)
    vx_array bounds = vxCreateArray(context, VX_TYPE_RECTANGLE, 1);
    ERROR_CHECK_OBJECT(bounds)
```

```
ERROR_CHECK_STATUS(vxAddArrayItems(bounds, 1, bounding_box,
    sizeof(*bounding_box)))
vx_float32 fast_corners_strength = 3.0;
vx_scalar strength_thresh = vxCreateScalar(context,
    VX_TYPE_FLOAT32, &fast_corners_strength);
ERROR_CHECK_OBJECT(strength_thresh)
vx_array first_corners = vxCreateVirtualArray(graph,
    VX_TYPE_KEYPOINT, NUM_KEYPOINTS);
ERROR_CHECK_OBJECT(first_corners)
ERROR_CHECK_OBJECT(vxColorConvertNode(graph, initial_image,
    yuv_image))
ERROR_CHECK_OBJECT(vxChannelExtractNode(graph, yuv_image,
    VX_CHANNEL_Y, y_image))
ERROR_CHECK_OBJECT(clearOutsideBoundsNode(graph, y_image, bounds,
    roi))
ERROR_CHECK_OBJECT(vxGaussianPyramidNode(graph, y_image,
    initial_pyramid))
ERROR_CHECK_OBJECT(vxFastCornersNode(graph, roi, strength_thresh,
    vx_true_e, first_corners, NULL))
ERROR_CHECK_OBJECT(intialCentroidCalculationNode(graph, bounds,
    first_corners, output_data, output_corners, valid))
ERROR_CHECK_OBJECT(vxCopyNode(graph, (vx_reference)output_corners,
    (vx_reference)original_corners))
ERROR_CHECK_STATUS(vxReleaseImage(&yuv_image))
ERROR_CHECK_STATUS(vxReleaseImage(&y_image))
ERROR_CHECK_STATUS(vxReleaseImage(&roi))
ERROR_CHECK_STATUS(vxReleaseArray(&bounds))
ERROR_CHECK_STATUS(vxReleaseScalar(&strength_thresh))
ERROR_CHECK_STATUS(vxReleaseArray(&first_corners))
return graph;
}
```

9.9.2 Calculating the bounding box position in the next frame

To find the bounding box position in the next frame, we use the optical flow algorithm to track where our chosen points have moved to. We hope that most of them will be on our object in the bounding box, but inevitably some of them will be on the background or in the foreground, so they do not move with our object. Also, the optical flow algorithm may not be able to find a new position for some of the key points, so it will invalidate them. We discussed earlier various strategies for recognizing these scenarios and dealing with them. In our implementation of centroid tracking, we will first calculate a new bounding box using the equations as discussed before and then mark as rejected any of the key points that do not fall inside the new bounding box. If any key points have been rejected either by the optical flow algorithm or our primitive rejection of points outside the new box, then we recalculate the initial tracking data using the original key points for the array positions that are still valid, and then recalculate the bounding box for the frame. Since we have gotten a new bounding box, we can again consider if any of the remaining key points are outside and should be rejected, and we iterate until either we reject no more key points or there are less than two left. We cannot calculate a new bounding box if we do not have a minimum of two key points.

We have two utility functions, one which calculates a new bounding box, returning the number of corners used, and one that rejects corners if they are out of limits. The second function also returns the number of new corners rejected.

Thus the main code for the `track_centroids` function is as follows:

```
do
{
    corners_used = calculate_new_bounding_box(orig_num_corners,
        &tracking_data, old_array_data, array_data, stride);
} while (validate_corners(orig_num_corners, &tracking_data, array_data,
    stride));
```

The first function, `calculate_new_bounding_box`, is responsible not just for calculating a new bounding box based upon the new points, but also for recognizing when the number of new points is different from the original and recalculating new initial tracking data if necessary. The code for the tracking nodes may be found in the examples in the file "centroid_tracking.c," and we reproduce some of it here.

Some salient points about this code:
- We always use the stride returned from `vxMapArrayRange` to step through the array, because we cannot make assumptions about how the implementation stores arrays.
- We always calculate the sums and sums of squares of the original data, before we know if we need it, to save having another loop. This could be made more efficient by using, for example, OpenMP to leverage multiple cores.
- Remove the calls to `printf` to get more performance!

- It would probably be possible to save having the `orig_num_corners` parameter by storing the original x and y positions of the key point in some of the unused parts of the key point structure if they can be guaranteed to be unused. (The specification says they should be, but in practice the conformance tests do not check this.)
- We also make an attempt to calculate velocities of the object in the x and y directions and rate of increase or decrease in size using a simple IIR filter. These are of course all relative to the frame rate. The results are stored in the `vector` and `zoom` fields of the `userTrackingData` structure.

```
static vx_size calculate_new_bounding_box(vx_size orig_num_corners,
    userTrackingData *tracking_data, vx_keypoint_t *old_features,
    vx_keypoint_t *features, vx_size stride)
{
    /* This function calculates a new bounding box in tracking_data,
        and returns the number of corners used */
    // Find the the sums and sums of squares of the corners
    double sumx = 0.0, sumy = 0.0, sumsqx = 0.0, sumsqy = 0.0, meanx,
        meany, sigmax, sigmay;
    double osumx = 0.0, osumy = 0.0, osumsqx = 0.0, osumsqy = 0.0;
    vx_size num_corners = 0;
    vx_char * ptr = (char *)features, * old_ptr = (char *)old_features;
    for (vx_uint32 i = 0; i < orig_num_corners; ++i, ptr+=stride, old_ptr
        += stride)
    {
        vx_keypoint_t * feature = (vx_keypoint_t*)ptr;
        vx_keypoint_t * old_feature = (vx_keypoint_t*) old_ptr;
        // a tracking_status of zero indicates a lost point
        // and we don't process old points
        if (feature->tracking_status != 0)
        {
            sumx += feature->x;
            sumy += feature->y;
            sumsqx += feature->x * feature->x;
            sumsqy += feature->y * feature->y;
            osumx += old_feature->x;
            osumy += old_feature->y;
            osumsqx += old_feature->x * old_feature->x;
            osumsqy += old_feature->y * old_feature->y;
            ++num_corners;
        }
    }
}
```

```
// Now calculate centroid (mean) and standard deviation of the
    corners using the sums and sums of squares.
// We can also assess validity during this operation. Notice that
    during tracking we consider tracking of
// the object lost if any feature is lost - it may be possible to
    recover
// From the means and standard deviations we calculate the new
    bounding box estimate
if (num_corners >= 2)
{
    // need at least two features to be able to establish a
        centroid and spread
    if ( tracking_data->num_corners != num_corners)
    {
        printf("Number of corners was %d, is now %ld\n",
            tracking_data->num_corners, num_corners);
        meanx = osumx / num_corners;
        meany = osumy / num_corners;
        sigmax = sqrt( osumsqx / num_corners - meanx * meanx);
        sigmay = sqrt( osumsqy / num_corners - meany * meany);
        printf("mean (stddev) = [ %f (%f), %f (%f) ]\n",
            meanx, sigmax, meany, sigmay);
        if (sigmax < 1.0 || sigmay < 1.0)
        {
            // Need some area in the features to be able to
                calculate a new bounding box
            sigmax = 1.0; // just to stop divide-by-zero
                errors
            sigmay = 1.0;
        }
        tracking_data->spread_ratio.x =
            tracking_data->bb_std_dev.x / sigmax;
        tracking_data->spread_ratio.y =
            tracking_data->bb_std_dev.y / sigmay;
        tracking_data->displacement.x =
            (tracking_data->bb_centroid.x - meanx) / sigmax;
        tracking_data->displacement.y =
            (tracking_data->bb_centroid.y - meany) / sigmay;
    }

    meanx = sumx / num_corners;
    meany = sumy / num_corners;
```

```
sigmax = sqrt( sumsqx / num_corners - meanx * meanx);
sigmay = sqrt( sumsqy / num_corners - meany * meany);
if (sigmax < 1.0 || sigmay < 1.0)
{
    // Need some area in the features to be able to
        calculate a new bounding box
    sigmax = 1.0; // just to stop divide-by-zero errors
    sigmay = 1.0;
}
// Calculate new bounding box
vx_rectangle_t bb;

bb.start_x = meanx + (tracking_data->displacement.x -
    tracking_data->spread_ratio.x) * sigmax;
bb.end_x = meanx + (tracking_data->displacement.x +
    tracking_data->spread_ratio.x) * sigmax + 0.5;
bb.start_y = meany + (tracking_data->displacement.y -
    tracking_data->spread_ratio.y) * sigmay;
bb.end_y = meany + (tracking_data->displacement.y +
    tracking_data->spread_ratio.y) * sigmay + 0.5;
// Calculate bounding box velocities using simple
    differences, apply some smoothing using a simple IIR
    filter
double bbmeanxdelta = (bb.start_x + bb.end_x -
    tracking_data->bounding_box.start_x -
    tracking_data->bounding_box.end_x) / 2.0;
double bbmeanydelta = (bb.start_y + bb.end_y -
    tracking_data->bounding_box.start_y -
    tracking_data->bounding_box.end_y) / 2.0;
double bbsizexdelta = (bb.end_x - bb.start_x -
    tracking_data->bounding_box.end_x +
    tracking_data->bounding_box.start_x) / 2.0;
double bbsizeydelta = (bb.end_y - bb.start_y -
    tracking_data->bounding_box.end_y +
    tracking_data->bounding_box.start_y) / 2.0;
tracking_data->bb_vector.x = tracking_data->bb_vector.x *
    0.25 + bbmeanxdelta * 0.75;
tracking_data->bb_vector.y = tracking_data->bb_vector.y *
    0.25 + bbmeanydelta * 0.75;
tracking_data->bb_zoom.x = tracking_data->bb_zoom.x * 0.25 +
    bbsizexdelta * 0.75;
```

```
                 tracking_data->bb_zoom.y = tracking_data->bb_zoom.y * 0.25 +
                     bbsizeydelta * 0.75;
                 // set new bounding box
                 tracking_data->bounding_box.start_x = bb.start_x;
                 tracking_data->bounding_box.end_x = bb.end_x;
                 tracking_data->bounding_box.start_y = bb.start_y;
                 tracking_data->bounding_box.end_y = bb.end_y;
        }
        else
        {
                 printf("Less than 2 corners!\n");
        }

        tracking_data->num_corners = num_corners;
        return num_corners;
}
```

The code of rejecting points outside the new bounding box is relatively trivial. Once again, we use the stride to step through the array rather than incrementing an array pointer in the usual way, since we cannot be sure how an implementation will store the data. Note that the key points have floating point coordinates, but that the bounding box has integral coordinates, and therefore we take extra care with the comparisons, or we will unnecessarily reject points due to rounding errors. The scheme for rejecting points we use is by no means the only or the best one. As an example of another scheme, the original RGB image can be referenced to decide if the points were the correct color:

```
static int validate_corners(vx_size orig_num_corners, userTrackingData
    *tracking_data, vx_keypoint_t *features, vx_size stride)
{
        /* This function validates the corners, setting them to nonvalid
             if they are outside the bounding box
        it returns the number of corners that were newly invalidated
        */
        int rejected_corners = 0;
        char *ptr = (char *)features;
        for (vx_uint32 i = 0; i < orig_num_corners; ++i, ptr+=stride)
        {
                 vx_keypoint_t *feature = (vx_keypoint_t*)ptr;
                 // a tracking_status of zero indicates a lost point
```

```
// we will mark a point as lost if it is outside the
    bounding box
if (feature->tracking_status != 0 && (
feature->x < tracking_data->bounding_box.start_x - 1||
feature->x > tracking_data->bounding_box.end_x +1||
feature->y < tracking_data->bounding_box.start_y -1||
feature->y > tracking_data->bounding_box.end_y +1))
    {
        ++rejected_corners;
        feature->tracking_status = 0;
    }
    }
    return rejected_corners;
}
```

We create a graph using this user node operating on the output of optical flow, as depicted in Fig. 9.3. Delays are used that are aged each frame so that the output of one frame becomes the input of the next. The code

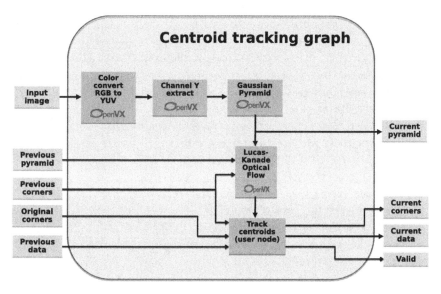

Figure 9.3 *Centroid tracking graph.* The current and previous pyramids, corners, and data are all stored in delays that are aged at every frame.

for this may be found in the file "tracking_example.cpp" and is listed here:

```
vx_graph centroid_tracking_graph(
```

```
vx_context context, vx_image input_image, vx_array
    original_corners,
vx_delay images, vx_delay tracking_data, vx_delay corners,
vx_scalar valid)
{

/*
Extract intensity from the RGB input
Create pyramid
Do optical flow
Do centroid tracking calculation
*/
vx_enum lk_termination    = VX_TERM_CRITERIA_BOTH; // iteration
    termination criteria (eps & iterations)
vx_float32 lk_epsilon     = 0.01f;              // convergence
    criterion
vx_uint32 lk_num_iterations = 5;                 // maximum number of
    iterations
vx_bool lk_use_initial_estimate = vx_false_e; // don't use initial
    estimate
vx_uint32 lk_window_dimension = 6;               // window size for
    evaluation
vx_scalar epsilon        = vxCreateScalar( context, VX_TYPE_FLOAT32,
    &lk_epsilon );
vx_scalar num_iterations = vxCreateScalar( context,
    VX_TYPE_UINT32, &lk_num_iterations );
vx_scalar use_initial_estimate = vxCreateScalar( context,
    VX_TYPE_BOOL, &lk_use_initial_estimate );
vx_graph graph = vxCreateGraph(context);
ERROR_CHECK_OBJECT(graph)
vx_array unfiltered_keypoints = vxCreateVirtualArray(graph,
    VX_TYPE_KEYPOINT, NUM_KEYPOINTS);
ERROR_CHECK_OBJECT(unfiltered_keypoints)
vx_image yuv_image = vxCreateVirtualImage(graph, 0, 0,
    VX_DF_IMAGE_IYUV);
ERROR_CHECK_OBJECT(yuv_image)
vx_image y_image = vxCreateVirtualImage(graph, 0, 0,
    VX_DF_IMAGE_U8);
ERROR_CHECK_OBJECT(y_image)
vx_pyramid current_pyramid =
    (vx_pyramid)vxGetReferenceFromDelay(images, 0);
ERROR_CHECK_OBJECT(current_pyramid)
```

```
vx_pyramid previous_pyramid =
    (vx_pyramid)vxGetReferenceFromDelay(images, -1);
ERROR_CHECK_OBJECT(previous_pyramid)
vx_array current_corners =
    (vx_array)vxGetReferenceFromDelay(corners, 0);
ERROR_CHECK_OBJECT(current_corners)
vx_array previous_corners =
    (vx_array)vxGetReferenceFromDelay(corners, -1);
ERROR_CHECK_OBJECT(previous_corners)
vx_array current_data =
    (vx_array)vxGetReferenceFromDelay(tracking_data, 0);
ERROR_CHECK_OBJECT(current_data)
vx_array previous_data =
    (vx_array)vxGetReferenceFromDelay(tracking_data, -1);
ERROR_CHECK_OBJECT(previous_data)
ERROR_CHECK_OBJECT(vxColorConvertNode(graph, input_image,
    yuv_image))
ERROR_CHECK_OBJECT(vxChannelExtractNode(graph, yuv_image,
    VX_CHANNEL_Y, y_image))
ERROR_CHECK_OBJECT(vxGaussianPyramidNode(graph, y_image,
    current_pyramid))
ERROR_CHECK_OBJECT(vxOpticalFlowPyrLKNode(graph, previous_pyramid,
    current_pyramid,
                            previous_corners, previous_corners,
                                unfiltered_keypoints,
                            lk_termination, epsilon,
                                num_iterations,
                            use_initial_estimate,
                                lk_window_dimension ))
ERROR_CHECK_OBJECT(trackCentroidsNode(graph, original_corners,
    previous_data, unfiltered_keypoints, current_data,
    current_corners, valid))
ERROR_CHECK_STATUS(vxReleaseScalar(&epsilon))
ERROR_CHECK_STATUS(vxReleaseScalar(&num_iterations))
ERROR_CHECK_STATUS(vxReleaseArray(&unfiltered_keypoints))
ERROR_CHECK_STATUS(vxReleaseImage(&yuv_image))
ERROR_CHECK_STATUS(vxReleaseImage(&y_image))
return graph;
}
```

Figure 9.4 *Output from the tracking example.* The head of the individual in white was selected with a bounding box and tracked. The path of the center of the yellow (white in print version) box is shown with the line of red (mid gray in print version) points. (Original video sequence copyright University of Reading.)

9.9.3 Running the tracking example application

As well as building the examples using CMake, you will also have to download the example video sequence and place it in the same folder as the tracking_example application. The video sequence "PETS09-S1-L1-View001.avi" should be downloaded from http://ewh.ieee.org/r6/scv/sps/openvx-material/PETS09-S1-L1-View001.avi. This video sequence and the starting bounding box that frames the head of one of the pedestrians is hard-coded into the example program "tracking_example.cpp" in the macros VIDEO_FILE, START_X, START_Y, END_X and END_Y defined at the top of the code. Typical output from the example program when using this data is shown in Fig. 9.4. If you want to use a different video file or a different bounding box, or both, then this is where you change it. Alternatively, you can use command-line parameters to provide the values and more easily explore the performance of the code under different circumstances. The original video sequence is copyright University of Reading, please see http://www.cvg.reading.ac.uk/PETS2009/a.html.

9.10 Multiple objects

Typically, an object detector can find multiple objects in a scene; we must decide how to handle this. If we expect only one object, then we assume that there are false positives, and we choose the best scoring candidate. If there can be several objects, then we should track which object is which. The simplest solution to this is using the optical flow method to track separate sets of features; in other words, for each frame, calling the Pyramidal Optical Flow function as many times as there are objects.

A better method perhaps is including all the key points for all the objects in one array, processing this with `vxOpticalFlowPyrLKNode` and then extending our user nodes `intialCentroidCalculationNode` and `trackCentroidsNode` to process the array of key points using multiple tracking data elements in a `vx_array`. We can identify which points belong to which object by marking them in the `tracking_status` field of the `vx_keypoint_t` entries in the `originals vx_array` parameter. We also have to return a `vx_array` of type `VX_TYPE_BOOL` as the `valid` parameter, one for each object.

The implementation of multiple object tracking is left as an exercise for the reader.

9.11 Occlusion and trajectories

If our object of interest goes behind another object, all the tracking points should be lost. In practice, what happens with the optical flow algorithm is that some of the key points are incorrectly tracked to features on the object that is doing the occluding and remain there. This is in fact a major failing of the algorithm and in our example can be seen with the recommended video sequence if the initial bounding box is placed on one of the pedestrians that goes behind the sign in the center of the image. One thing worse than this happening is the inability to detect it. So how to detect it?

Our centroid-tracking algorithm conveniently gives us three pieces of information that will help with detection of the number of key points being tracked, the direction of motion, and the "zoom" or scale. We may expect that all these will change, but we can put limits on what we consider as a normal rate of change. For example, there is a limit to how quickly a person can stop and start or run toward or away from the camera, and although we expect to lose a few tracking points, a sudden change in the number should arouse suspicion. In fact, it may be possible to study film sequences and arrive at typical ranges for various sorts of object. If the results fall outside our limits, then we suspect there is something amiss and can run object classification on the image within our bounding box. If what should be there is still there, then we can rerun FAST corners to refresh our key points.

This suggests a change in our centroid tracking node, perhaps to give it some limits to check so that the vx_scalar valid can be set to vx_false_e. We further suggest a possible new structure definition for userTrackingData. Note that by changing the structure, rather than providing new parameters for the node, multiple objects may easily be supported, and detection schemes that call for dynamically changing limits are also possible. Exactly how the limits are used may depend upon a given application:

```
typedef struct {
    vx_rectangle_t      bounding_box; // The last calculated object
        bounding box
    vx_coordinates2df_t bb_centroid; // The original bounding box centroid
    vx_coordinates2df_t bb_std_dev;  // The original bounding box
        standard deviation
    vx_coordinates2df_t spread_ratio; // The ratio of bounding box to
        features std.dev.
    vx_coordinates2df_t displacement; // The displacement of bounding box
        from features
    vx_coordinates2df_t bb_vector;    // The rate of change in
        displacement of the bounding box
    vx_coordinates2df_t bb_zoom;      // The rate of change in scale of
        the bounding box
    vx_uint32           num_corners; // The last valid number of features
    vx_coordinates2df_t bb_vector_high; // High limit for the value of
        the vector
    vx_coordinates2df_t bb_vector_low; // Low limit for the value of the
        vector
    vx_coordinates2df_t bb_zoom_high; // High limit for the value of zoom
    vx_coordinates2df_t bb_zoom_low; // Low limit for the value of zoom
    vx_float32          corners_delta; // Limit for the proportion of
        corners that may be lost in one frame
} userTrackingData;
```

Since the procedure for recovering from lost tracking is in this case fairly complex, we suggest that it is not done in one user node, but as part of a graph. Either the classifier graph is run if required after the centroid tracking, or it is part of the same graph, and its output is selected using a vxSelectNode controlled by the vx_scalar valid.

If the result of the classifier is that the bounding box no longer contains the object of interest, then we can assume that it has been occluded. Based upon historical values of the vector and zoom fields of the tracking data, that is, the values from the frame before we noticed occlusion, we can predict a new value of bounding box at each frame assuming that it follows the same trajectory (we can record historic values and make this as complex as we wish) and look for the object with our classifier in this new position until perhaps we can find it again.

Discussion of classifiers is well beyond the scope of this chapter.

9.12 The mirror ball and other failings of our algorithm

As an interesting case of object tracking with optical flow, let us consider a disco ball, a rotating multifaceted mirror ball. Let us assume that we are looking at this sideways-on, so neither of the polar regions is visible. Because the ball is covered with many identically sized rectangular mirrors, it will yield many corners or features to track. Also, suppose that all these corners are located on the ball, perhaps one per mirror. If the frame rate is sufficiently high, so that aliasing is not a problem even for the fastest moving features at the center of the ball, then we are able to track all our features accurately, and in one half-rotation of the ball, all our features are lost as they disappear from view around the back of the ball. If we do not rerun corner or object detection, then the ball has effectively become invisible to the tracking algorithm, even though it has not moved out of the frame or been covered by another object. The same is true for any rotating object where aliasing is not an issue.

What is more interesting, however, is what happens at lower frame rates. You can imagine a mirror ball lit by strobe lighting. At a certain frequency of strobe, equivalent to our frame rate, the ball appears to be stationary, because if the strobe matches exactly the time it takes for the next mirror to end up in the place occupied by the previous mirror, then the image remains almost identical. At other frequencies the ball may seem to rotate slowly in either direction, as the placing of the mirrors is not quite accurate. This is the effect you may have seen in films where car wheels or chariot wheels with obvious spokes appear to rotate in the wrong direction.

For our mirror ball, the frame rate to avoid aliasing need not be very high at all. A typical mirror ball could be 60 cm in diameter with 1-cm square mirrors; a quick calculation shows there can be no more than 188 such mirrors around the equator. With rotational speeds in the region of 1 to 2 rpm, each mirror will be replaced by the next at a rate of at most $\frac{188}{60}$. To avoid aliasing, we only need to double that, so we are definitely going to lose our constellation of features representing the mirror ball in the first half-second or so, unless our frame rate is below 5 or 6 Hz.

Using our centroid tracking algorithm, we will see the newly estimated bounding box of the object, both moving to one side and at the same time diminishing in size, but the constellation of features would not retain its shape; in fact, it will appear like an occlusion from the opposite side to where the features disappear. We retain tracking of part of the mirror ball only if one of the polar regions remains visible.

This is by far not the only issue with the mirror ball; after all, the main purpose of a mirror ball is reflecting dots of light onto the surroundings, and in any case, our camera is not likely to be pointing at the mirror ball itself, far more likely that it is there to monitor the crowd below. Now when we use our corner detector to find features to track in our rectangle of interest, perhaps framing a particular face, we are quite likely to find among the corners at least one of these dots, because it will be one of the brightest features. Just like a fly, it is not part of the object we are tracking and moves off at some point. We have to correctly recognize this as a lost feature and not allow it to distort the estimation of the new bounding box position.

The mirror ball is a device designed to confuse human perception of optical flow, which is why we enjoy it. Equally, it confuses our machine implementation of optical flow, and the problems it raises do have relevance to other situations that are encountered in places other than night clubs, for example, rotating objects and reflections, especially from moving lights at night.

9.13 Image stabilization, panning, and zooming

Image stabilization may be achieved using optical flow in much the same way that tracking may be done. There are a number of choices here. Firstly, what sort of stabilization would you like, and what is possible?

• Some identified static background remains in the same position relative to the image border

• Some identified moving background (e.g., trees blowing in the wind) remain in the same average position relative to the image border
• An identified rigid background may move smoothly relative to the image border, but sharp or higher frequency changes are removed
• The images are being processed a frame at a time as the data arrives
• We have an entire recorded video sequence to work with

To achieve stabilization, the basic method is tracking the carefully chosen key points within a large bounding box slightly smaller than the frame and then cropping the frame to the bounding box as each new box position is found. The way in which the points are chosen, the new box position is calculated, and how the points are rejected will vary according to what type of stabilization is required.

Image stabilization in the presence of panning and zooming becomes a little trickier. Here instead of keeping an image still, we would like to make the movement smooth. If we have a recorded video sequence, then we can think of a plot of the movement of our chosen key points across a canvas—we want a constant or smoothly changing velocity, with no little shakes and wiggles. We could, for example, collect x and y for all our points in all the frames and perform a linear regression to fit a smooth curve, then predict using the resulting equation where we should have our crop in each frame. For example, consider the following x coordinates for the centroid of our key points in a sequence of frames:

20, 26, 31, 34, 39, 46, 50, 56.

For a smooth pan, it would be better if the change in position were the same each frame in this case, that is,

20, 25, 30, 35, 40, 45, 50, 55.

Consequently, to make the pan nice and smooth with respect to this point, we can use a rectangle just two pixels smaller than the frame at both ends and crop at pixels numbered:

1, 2, 2, 0, 0, 2, 1, 2.

If we have no recorded sequence but are doing this in real-time, then we have our calculated vector and zoom fields in the tracking data, which may be used to find the next ideal location for each point, although the current simplistic calculation could do with some improvement.

For changes in scale (zoom), we would like this also to happen smoothly, but in this case, we cannot just crop, and we need to actually change the scale of the image. In any case, we may like our input and output video sequences to be of the same size, so we need to be able to change the scale anyway. In fact, we want to take our series of input points and decide where we really want them to be in the output image or, in other words, create a mapping. So what we need for this job is a `vx_remap` object, which we then apply to the input image using `vxRemapNode`. This also allows us to have completely different input and output image sizes.

The Remap object can be thought of as a table of entries, one for each pixel in the output image, that define where to retrieve data in the input image. The coordinates pointing to the input image are floating point, implying that the implementation may use some interpolation method to arrive at the output values. In fact, the type of interpolation to be used may be chosen by the `policy` parameter of `vxRemapNode`:

```
vx_node vxRemapNode(
        vx_graph graph,
        vx_image input,
        vx_remap table,
        vx_enum policy,
        vx_image output);
```

The `policy` may be either `VX_INTERPOLATION_NEAREST_NEIGHBOR` to just take the nearest pixel or `VX_INTERPOLATION_BILINEAR` to make a linear approximation. The input and output images for `vxRemapNode` must be of type `VX_DF_IMAGE_U8`, so to perform the correction on RGB or YUV frames, it is necessary to create a graph that extracts each plane using `vxChannelExtract`, corrects it individually, and then recombines them using `vxChannelCombine`. What is missing in the puzzle now is just a method of creating a Remap object from the `userTrackingData` created by our `trackCcentroidsNode`. A suggested signature would be:

```
vx_node createRemapFromTrackingDataNode(
        vx_graph graph,
        vx_array tracking_data, // Input, this is an array of one element
            of type userTrackingData created by trackCentroidsNode
        vx_remap remap          // Output, a remap object that will
            correct for stabilization
        );
```

Finally, building upon the code we defined before for the centroid tracking graph, a graph to implement stabilization based upon some input points chosen carefully as rigid background or an object of interest can be as shown in Fig. 9.5 and in the following code:

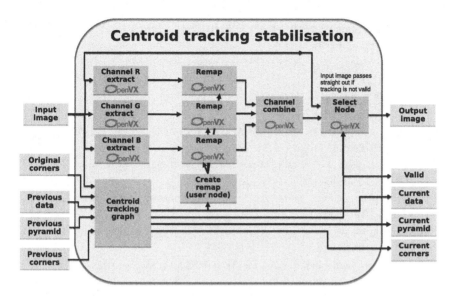

Figure 9.5 *Stabilization using centroid tracking.* We build upon the centroid tracking graph, outputting a remapped input image if the tracking is valid.

```
vx_graph centroid_tracking_stabilisation_graph(
    vx_context context, vx_image input_image, vx_array
        original_corners,
    vx_delay images, vx_delay tracking_data, vx_delay corners,
    vx_scalar valid, vx_image output_image)
{
    /*
        Extract intensity from the RGB input
        Create pyramid
        Do optical flow
        Do centroid tracking calculation
        Calculate a remap and apply it to the input image, if
            tracking is still valid
        We've omitted error checking and releasing of objects for
            the sake of brevity and clarity
    */
    vx_graph graph = centroid_tracking_graph(context, input_image,
        original_corners, images, tracking_data, corners, valid);
    vx_array current_data =
        (vx_array)vxGetReferenceFromDelay(tracking_data, 0);
    vx_uint32 width, height;
    vxQueryImage(input_image, VX_IMAGE_WIDTH, &width, sizeof(width));
```

```
vxQueryImage(input_image, VX_IMAGE_HEIGHT, &height,
    sizeof(height));
vx_image r_image_in = vxCreateVirtualImage(graph, width, height,
    VX_DF_IMAGE_U8);
vx_image g_image_in = vxCreateVirtualImage(graph, width, height,
    VX_DF_IMAGE_U8);
vx_image b_image_in = vxCreateVirtualImage(graph, width, height,
    VX_DF_IMAGE_U8);
vx_image r_image_out = vxCreateVirtualImage(graph, width, height,
    VX_DF_IMAGE_U8);
vx_image g_image_out = vxCreateVirtualImage(graph, width, height,
    VX_DF_IMAGE_U8);
vx_image b_image_out = vxCreateVirtualImage(graph, width, height,
    VX_DF_IMAGE_U8);
vx_image rgb_image_out = vxCreateVirtualImage(graph, width,
    height, VX_DF_IMAGE_RGB);
vx_remap remap = vxCreateVirtualRemap(graph, width, height, width,
    height);
vxChannelExtractNode(graph, input_image, VX_CHANNEL_R, r_image_in);
vxChannelExtractNode(graph, input_image, VX_CHANNEL_G, g_image_in);
vxChannelExtractNode(graph, input_image, VX_CHANNEL_B, b_image_in);
createRemapFromTrackingDataNode(graph, current_data, remap);
vxRemapNode(graph, r_image_in, remap, VX_INTERPOLATION_BILINEAR,
    r_image_out);
vxRemapNode(graph, g_image_in, remap, VX_INTERPOLATION_BILINEAR,
    g_image_out);
vxRemapNode(graph, b_image_in, remap, VX_INTERPOLATION_BILINEAR,
    b_image_out);
vxChannelCombineNode(graph, r_image_out, g_image_out, b_image_out,
    NULL, rgb_image_out);
vxSelectNode(graph, valid, (vx_reference) rgb_image_out,
    input_image, output_image);
// Releasing of objects created in this function omitted
return graph;
}
```

As well as illustrating the use of channel extract, remap, and channel combine, this code demonstrates how to use vxSelectNode to make decisions. Note that the implementation is free to schedule the operations as it wishes. The vxRemapNodes cannot be executed until the remap has been written, but at that time the value of the vx_scalar valid is known, so it may not be necessary to execute `vxRemapNode`. At that point the `vxChannelExtractNodes` may or may not have been executed.

We leave it as an exercise for the reader to implement a stabilization algorithm using the ideas in this chapter.

CHAPTER 10

Neural networks

Contents

In recent times the Convolution Neural Networks (CNNs) are used ubiquitously in computer vision tasks, such as classification, detection, and segmentation. A CNN is composed of stacking several tensor level operations, such as convolution layers, activation layers (e.g., *ReLU*), pooling layers (e.g., max pooling), fully connected layers, and so on, as shown in Fig. 10.1. The weights used in these operations, such as convolution weight tensors, are calculated from an application-specific training dataset using deep learning frameworks.

In these applications the CNNs perform the critical classification, detection, or segmentation part of computer vision processing. A *classification* CNN takes an image as input and produces a label identifying the object in the image, such as "duck," "plane," or "tree." A *detection* CNN takes an image and possibly finds several things in the image. The output is a set of bounding-box coordinates and a separate label for the object in each bounding box. A *segmentation* CNN provides even more fine-grained information in which the output is another image, where each pixel value in the output image is a label for the type of object at that location in the input image. There are many (infinite) other things that can be done with neural networks, but these are the most common in vision processing.

Other parts of computer vision processing may come before or after the CNN in these applications and can include:

- *image-processing*: color conversion, image filtering, image resize, cropping, normalization, etc.

OpenVX Programming Guide
https://doi.org/10.1016/B978-0-12-816425-9.00016-4

Copyright © 2020 Elsevier Inc.
All rights reserved.

205

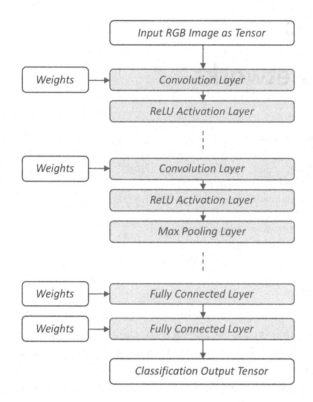

Figure 10.1 CNN Architecture.

- *postprocessing*: non-maximum suppression, overlay segmentation results on input images, etc.

In this chapter, you will learn about how to use OpenVX to deploy CNNs in computer vision applications. In addition, you will also learn about OpenVX extensions that enable inserting CNNs inside an OpenVX graph.

- `vx_khr_nn`: neural network extension to insert CNN model layer-by-layer
- `vx_khr_import_kernel`: kernel import extension to insert CNN model as a single node

10.1 OpenVX neural network extension

The OpenVX Neural Network Extension (`vx_khr_nn`) provides a means to integrate CNN layers into an OpenVX graph. In this specification the

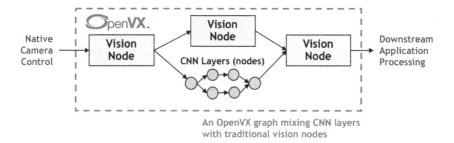

An OpenVX graph mixing CNN layers
with traditional vision nodes

Figure 10.2 OpenVX graph with CNN layers and traditional vision nodes.

CNN layers are represented as OpenVX nodes connected by vx_tensor data objects. You can mix both the CNN layers and traditional vision nodes inside an OpenVX graph as shown in Fig. 10.2.

You can find the Neural Network extension specification at https://www.khronos.org/registry/OpenVX. The direct link to the vx_khr_nn version 1.3 is https://www.khronos.org/registry/OpenVX/extensions/vx_khr_nn/1.3/html/vx_khr_nn_1_3.html. We list neural network layer APIs supported by this extension:

- vxActivationLayer: activation layer for *relu, brelu, tanh, sqrt*, etc.
- vxConvolutionLayer: convolution layer
- vxDeconvolutionLayer: deconvolution layer
- vxFullyConnectedLayer: fully connected layer
- vxLocalResponseNormalizationLayer: normalization layer
- vxPoolingLayer: max pooling and average pooling layers
- vxROIPoolingLayer: ROI pooling layer
- vxSoftmaxLayer: softmax layer

The vx_khr_nn extension requires constructing the neural network layer by layer using the nodes listed. Most neural networks are constructed using one of the popular frameworks such as Caffe, TensorFlow, PyTorch, and others. Some vendors offer a translation tool, which reads the output description from popular neural framework formats and outputs a sequence of vx_khr_nn calls to construct that network.

10.2 Inserting an entire neural network into an OpenVX graph as a single node

An alternative method of incorporating a neural network into an OpenVX graph is provided by the Import Kernel extension (vx_khr_import_kernel), described at https://www.khronos.org/registry/OpenVX/extensions/vx_khr_import_kernel/1.3/html/vx_khr_import_kernel_1_3.html. Rather than constructing the neural network layer by layer, the entire pretrained neural network is treated as a single kernel, which can be instantiated as a node in a graph. This can simplify the task of the OpenVX application developer, who can treat the neural network as a black box that you feed images, and some descriptive data come out. Behind the scenes, the neural network implementation can take advantages of any optimizations or special-purpose hardware the vendor can provide.

To meet the compute demands of the Convolutional Neural Networks (CNNs), several hardware vendors are building hardware accelerators. The programmability of these accelerators varies a lot depending on whether the underlying architecture is a fully programmable processor or a fixed-function block. To meet the rapidly changing AI market demands with best-in-class compute/power efficiency, the hardware vendors are providing SDKs with inference engines instead of just the programming toolkits. It can be difficult to manage working with several vendor SDKs when the APIs are very different.

Another roadblock to portability and deployment comes from the use of proprietary formats to represent pretrained CNN models. This drove requirements for several proprietary importers to support all these formats. To address the portability of pretrained CNN models, Khronos released the NNEF standard file format and a sample toolkit to import and export pretrained models from and to other proprietary formats.

With these tools, you just need to follow the three steps:
- export pretrained models into the NNEF data format
- import NNEF data into an OpenVX context as an OpenVX kernel
- build an OpenVX graph with pretrained model instantiated as an OpenVX node

10.3 NNEF: the Khronos neural network exchange format

NNEF is a Khronos standard data format for exchanging descriptions of neural networks. The NNEF data format enables the export of pretrained models from deep learning frameworks such as Torch, Caffe, Tensorflow, Theano, Chainer, Caffe2, PyTorch, and MXNet to a common format, so that you do not have to worry about portability and compatibility across vendors and upgrades as shown in Fig. 10.3. It reduces machine learning deployment fragmentation by enabling a rich mix of neural network train-

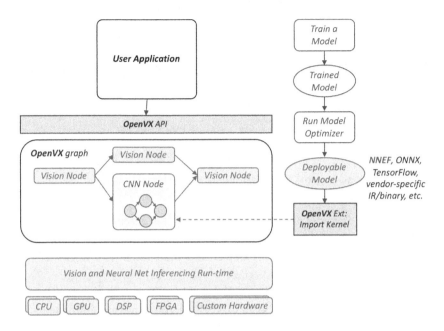

Figure 10.3 Computer vision application with Convolution Neural Networks.

ing tools and inference engines to be used by applications across a diverse range of devices and platforms. You can find the NNEF specification and further details at https://www.khronos.org/registry/NNEF.

The Khronos is also developing open-source tools for exchanging neural network models between deep learning frameworks and NNEF. These tools can be used to convert a pretrained neural network model into NNEF format from other formats, such as Tensorflow, ONNX, and so on. This enables inference engines to implement just one NNEF importer instead of creating and maintaining separate model importers for every deep learning framework. Here is the link to Khronos open-source GitHub repo for NNEF tools: https://github.com/KhronosGroup/NNEF-Tools.

For your experimentation with NNEF, you can find pretrained neural network models at https://github.com/KhronosGroup/NNEF-Tools/tree/master/models.

10.4 Import NNEF models into OpenVX

The Khronos OpenVX Import Kernel Extension (vx_khr_import_kernel) provides a way of importing an OpenVX kernel at a location specified by

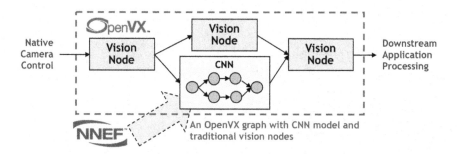

Figure 10.4 OpenVX graph with CNN model and traditional vision nodes.

a URL. Unlike the export and import extension, this extension can only import kernel objects. You can use this extension to import a pretrained CNN model as an OpenVX kernel object and then instantiate nodes in OpenVX graphs that execute this kernel.

Most embedded platform vendors will provide offline tools to compile pretrained CNN models from NNEF/ONNX/Tensorflow/etc. into their own binary formats, which can be directly imported and executed on their hardware using the vx_khr_import_kernel extension. Compiling a pretrained CNN model into a device binary may not be a trivial process. A user may iterate several times to tune a binary to meet their accuracy and/or performance goals.

The vx_khr_import_kernel extension can also be used to import directly from standard data formats. For example, you may be able to import a CNN model in NNEF data format with pretuned weights in fixed-point representation. This will require just-in-time graph compiler to optimize the CNN when used inside the OpenVX graph as shown in Fig. 10.4.

You can find more information about the OpenVX Import Kernel Extension at https://www.khronos.org/registry/OpenVX.

10.4.1 Inserting a neural network into an OpenVX graph

This section outlines a step-by-step procedure to build the OpenVX graph that contains a pretrained CNN model.

Step 1: import a pretrained CNN model

As discussed earlier, there are two ways to import a pretrained CNN model into the OpenVX context.

- Use an offline compiler to generate precompiled binary tuned for specific hardware platform

- Import directly from standard CNN model data formats
  A precompiled binary can be imported into the OpenVX context as an
  OpenVX kernel using the vxImportKernelFromURL API.

```
// this example needs the OpenVX Import Kernel Extension
#include <VX/vx_khr_import_kernel.h>

vx_status import_cnn_from_myvendor(vx_context context, vx_kernel&
    cnn_kernel)
{
  // The myvendor's offline compiler generated a precompiled binary from
  // a pretrained CNN model. The import requires specifying:
  // - vendor-specific identifier for the precompiled binary
  // - folder containing the precompiled binary
  const char * type = "vx_myvendor_folder";
  const char * url = "/assets/mobilenet_bin/";

  // import the precompiled binary as an OpenVX kernel
  cnn_kernel = vxImportKernelFromURL(context, type, url);

  return vxGetStatus((vx_reference) cnn_kernel);
}
```

If the vendor supports importing directly from standard neural network
model data formats, such as NNEF, then a corresponding type identifier
of the data format must be used. The vx_khr_import_kernel specification
did not explicitly specify these identifiers for any of the standard data formats. But the identifiers that start with "vx_khr_" are reserved for future
specifications. Possible examples of such identifiers are "vx_khr_nnef" and
"vx_xxx_onnx".

```
// A just-in-time compiler can import an OpenVX kernel directly from
// standard neural network data formats
const char * type = "vx_xxx_onnx";
const char * url = "/assets/mobilenet.onnx";

// import the pretrained CNN model directly
cnn_kernel = vxImportKernelFromURL(context, type, url);
```

Step 2: add CNN model into OpenVX graph

Now that you have imported the OpenVX kernel object that corresponds to the CNN model, you can instantiate the CNN model into the OpenVX graph just like a user node:

```
// add CNN model as a node in the OpenVX graph
vx_node node = vxCreateGenericNode(graph, cnn_kernel);

// set input and output tensors
vxSetParameterByIndex(node, 0, cnn_input);
vxSetParameterByIndex(node, 1, cnn_output);
```

Note that the basic classification CNN models are trained using fixed input image dimensions and a fixed number of output classes. For example, the MobileNet pretrained CNN model takes an *RGB* image with *width=224*, *height=224*, and the number of output classes is *1001*. So the cnn_input and the cnn_output tensors objects must be created to match these dimensions:

```
// create CNN input tensor that corresponds to 224x224 RGB image
vx_size cnn_input_dims[4] = { 224, 224, 3, 1 };
vx_tensor cnn_input = vxCreateVirtualTensor(graph, 4, cnn_input_dims,
    VX_TYPE_UINT8, 0);

// create CNN output tensor that corresponds to the output of the
    last fully connected layer
vx_size cnn_output_dims[2] = { 1001, 1 };
vx_tensor cnn_output = vxCreateVirtualTensor(graph, 2,
    cnn_output_dims, VX_TYPE_INT16, 8);
```

Step 3: preprocess input image to produce the input tensor

The input from JPEG images or cameras usually come in RGB format and in different dimensions. To make use of this MobileNet model, we need to scale the input image and convert it into a tensor for input to the CNN.

To efficiently convert and scale the input RGB image to tensor object, you need to access 2D planes in the tensor as separate vx_image objects. Then the data buffers of these images will point to the corresponding offsets in the tensor object data buffer, so that the data copies between the tensor and its image planes can be eliminated. When these image planes are used as outputs from the RGB color conversion and the image scaling nodes, the

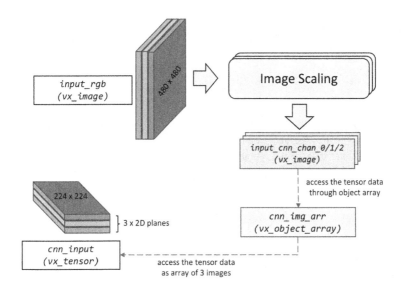

Figure 10.5 Preprocessing input image into CNN input tensor.

image data will be written directly into the tensor object without having to make explicit copies as shown in Fig. 10.5.

The OpenVX API provides a mechanism to access 2D planes of a tensor as images. A vx_tensor can be exported into an object array of images:

```
// get access to individual 2D planes of input tensor as an array of
    images
vx_rectangle_t cnn_input_rect = { 0, 0, 224, 224 };
vx_object_array cnn_img_arr =
    vxCreateImageObjectArrayFromTensor(cnn_input,
        &cnn_input_rect, 3, 1, VX_DF_IMAGE_U8);
```

Now the individual images can be extracted from the vx_object_array objects. Note that these extracted images still refer to the data in the cnn_input tensor with *width=224* and *height=224*:

```
// get images that correspond all 3 channels of input tensor
vx_image input_cnn_chan_0 =
    (vx_image)vxGetObjectArrayItem(cnn_img_arr, 0);
vx_image input_cnn_chan_1 =
    (vx_image)vxGetObjectArrayItem(cnn_img_arr, 1);
vx_image input_cnn_chan_2 =
    (vx_image)vxGetObjectArrayItem(cnn_img_arr, 2);
```

Now that the input tensor is accessible as vx_image objects, the input image can be scaled into the cnn_input tensor using these channels:

```
// extract R,G,B channels from input image
vx_image input_r = vxCreateVirtualImage(graph, 0, 0, VX_DF_IMAGE_U8);
vx_image input_g = vxCreateVirtualImage(graph, 0, 0, VX_DF_IMAGE_U8);
vx_image input_b = vxCreateVirtualImage(graph, 0, 0, VX_DF_IMAGE_U8);
vxChannelExtractNode(graph, input_rgb, input_r, VX_CHANNEL_R);
vxChannelExtractNode(graph, input_rgb, input_g, VX_CHANNEL_G);
vxChannelExtractNode(graph, input_rgb, input_b, VX_CHANNEL_B);

// scale input R,G,B planes into 224x224 input channels for CNN
vxScaleImageNode(graph, input_r, input_cnn_chan_0,
    VX_INTERPOLATION_BILINEAR);
vxScaleImageNode(graph, input_g, input_cnn_chan_1,
    VX_INTERPOLATION_BILINEAR);
vxScaleImageNode(graph, input_b, input_cnn_chan_2,
    VX_INTERPOLATION_BILINEAR);
```

Step 4: postprocess the output tensor from CNN model

The output from MobileNet is a tensor coming from a fully connected layer. These values of the tensor are not normalized because there is no softmax operation at the end of the model. The class of the input image can be extracted by finding the index of the maximum value in the output tensor. This operation is referred to as **ArgMax**.

If the application needs to make a decision to trigger further processing in the same graph using control flow, then the *ArgMax* function needs to be inserted into the graph to output class number into a vx_scalar object of VX_TYPE_INT32.

Unfortunately, there is no standard OpenVX function for *ArgMax*. So you need to create a user kernel or ask the vendor to provide similar functionality.

10.4.2 Summary

The Khronos OpenVX Import Kernel Extension (vx_khr_import_kernel) can be used to deploy deep learning models. It requires just two steps:
- import a pretrained CNN model as an OpenVX kernel
- insert a node of imported kernel into OpenVX graph

CHAPTER 11

Openvx safety-critical applications

Contents

Copyright © 2020 Elsevier Inc.
All rights reserved.
215

11.1 Safety-critical applications and standards

There are an increasingly varied number of areas in which computer vision and neural networks are being employed. Many of these have obvious safety implications, such as the use of both in autonomous vehicles. For other applications, the need is less obvious. In some cases an application may currently be considered trivial, a novelty where safety need not be paramount, but this may change, and safety may become increasingly important in the future as this technology becomes commonplace and we come to rely upon it more heavily.

11.1.1 What sort of applications have safety implications?
Sensing

These applications are those where data from a sensor is processed and presented to a user and can be as simple as measuring a temperature and displaying it. In the OpenVX realm, this could be a rear-facing camera used as a parking aid on a car or truck. The safety implications in this case arise because the driver is relying upon the camera and display to maneuver the vehicle. If the picture is incorrect, for example, if it freezes, then the driver may be unaware of hazards. Notice that in this example, we regard the whole pipeline from the camera lens to the driver's eye as the sensor. Importantly, sensor data are being relied on and if incorrect could be interpreted in a way that results in a dangerous situation.

Activation, control, and calibration

Again, there are obvious examples in automotive. Brakes must work when the brake pedal is pressed, and nowadays there are both software and hardware between the driver's foot and the brake shoe. However, it is not obvious how OpenVX would be used in a brake activator or in any other simple activation. However, in more complex situations where feedback loops are involved, applications of OpenVX can be very useful.

An engine controller consumes many inputs and produces many outputs in a deterministic way; mathematically, this can be expressed in terms of vector or matrix operations and coded up with a variety of methods including OpenVX, although this is not the current state-of-the-art. Calibration coefficients for such control loops may be calculated using diverse techniques. The mathematical tools or code libraries employed are relied upon to produce results such that the control loop will work in the expected predictable fashion. An error in the code or a rogue coefficient can result in loss of control, for example, an unintended acceleration.

Decision

By this we mean an application that takes in data, processes it in some way, and gives a possibly summarized output to be relied and potentially acted upon. The result may be used by a human or by another machine; the key thing is that the original data have been replaced with data manufactured by an algorithm and its integrity must be guaranteed or resulting actions could be inappropriate.

Examples could be a medical diagnosis made by a neural network based upon patient data, both anecdotal and measured, or a collision avoidance system in a vehicle. In the former case a misdiagnosis can result in a wrong treatment being prescribed with potentially damaging results, and in the latter a vehicle could swerve to avoid a shadow or fail to warn that a real collision is imminent.

Autonomous

We use the term "autonomous" most frequently nowadays to describe vehicles where the elements of sensing, decision, activation, and control have been joined together, perhaps even without the possibility of any human intervention. This could be just for parallel parking or for the whole journey, but it is only one example of autonomous systems in current use. Others include shop-floor robots in factories, airplane autopilots, and even a simple automatically opening door, which could become more capable in the near future, for example, making decisions about whom to let in and out, which must be modified in the event of fire.

11.1.2 Applicable standards

Applicable safety standards vary in the details relating to software; however, the principles should be the same whether directly stated or implied. The newest standards give the best overview both because the art of safety regulations is evolving, and also over the last few years the importance of expert software systems has risen so dramatically: witness emerging technologies such as OpenVX and NNEF. There is in fact a bewildering array of standards, as the following subsections demonstrate. If you are not interested in this rather dry list, then skip to the section that describes the general contents of the standards.

Automotive

The most recent and perhaps most relevant standard to this discussion is ISO 26262 "Road Vehicles – Functional Safety," which was first published in 2011, updated in 2018, and has chapters dedicated solely to software development and its associated processes. ISO 26262 defines four "Automotive Safety Integrity Levels" (ASIL), A through D, with D being the most stringent. For applications of computer vision and neural networks in the automotive industry, the ability to meet these different levels is largely determined by hardware, there being no technical reasons that software cannot be written to comply with the highest level. Indeed, once a suitable process has been put in place and engineers have been taught the appropriate methodologies, there exists no barrier, neither technical nor financial, to producing new software at ASIL D. Much of the process can be thought of just as "good software engineering," although the standard does make some specific demands. Barriers do exist, however, to adopting already existing software packages into a design, simply because of availability; presently, libraries implementing commonly used algorithms that can be shown to comply with ISO 26262 are limited in number.

The ISO26262 standard is available from the International Organization for Standardization [42] [43] [44].

ISO 26262 makes mention of the MISRA (Motor Industry Software Reliability Association) standards for C [45] and C++ [46], which put some restrictions upon how much of the language should be used and in what way [47]. There are other such rules and regulations, such as the

AUTOSAR (Automotive Open System Architecture) "Guidelines for the use of the C++14 language in critical and safety-related systems" published in March 2017 [48].

More recently, the standard ISO/PAS 21448:2019 [49] addresses issues raised by advanced driver assistance systems (ADAS), particularly lack of determinism encountered due to the interaction between the uncontrolled external environment and complex algorithms including vision processing and neural networks. It is effectively an extension to ISO26262, discussing "Safety of the intended functionality" (SOTIF). There are appendices specifically addressing verification of automotive perception systems, and implications for offline training, which may be pertinent to applications using OpenVX. This standard also categorizes scenarios, for the purpose of the risk assessment of SOTIF, into four areas:

- Area 1: Known safe
- Area 2: Known unsafe
- Area 3: Unknown unsafe
- Area 4: Unknown safe

Following ISO/PAS 21448, we use a process to increase the SOTIF by increasing area (1) at the expense of areas (2) and (3). Section 8 of ISO/PAS 21448 is entitled "Functional modifications to reduce SOTIF related risks" and discusses a number of pertinent methods.

Avionics

Also published in 2011 was DO-178C, "Software Considerations in Airborne Systems and Equipment Certification" [50–52], the primary document by which authorities such as FAA, EASA, and Transport Canada approve all commercial software-based aerospace systems. When comparing safety descriptions referring to this specification and those relating to ISO26262, take great care with the safety level. In DO-178C the "Software Level," also known as the "Design Assurance Level," ranges from A to E, where A in this case means that a failure would have a catastrophic effect in the system and exceeds ASIL D in the ISO26262 standard.

Rail

CENELEC (The European Committee for Electro-technical Standardization [53] has developed technical railway standards concerning Function Safety applicable to both heavy rail systems, light rail and urban mass transportation. The standards have IEC equivalents and cover the following subjects:

- EN 50126 (IEC 62278) – Reliability, Availability, Maintainability, and Safety (RAMS) [54] [55]
- EN 50128 (IEC 62279) – Software [56]
- EN 50129 (IEC 62425) – System safety [57]

In the UK the Rail Safety and Standards Board (RSSB) has in 2017 published Rail Industry Guidance Note GEGN8650 "Guidance on High-Integrity Software Based Systems for Railway Applications" [58], which asserts the following about relevant standards:

- "EN 50128:2011 is currently the only European standard that includes detailed requirements for software for the rail industry and it addresses communication, signaling and control, and protection systems. Software for use on rolling stock will be covered by EN 50657, which is currently being developed."
- "EN 50155:2007 includes some generic requirements for software, which are particularly applicable to COTS products."
- "EN ISO 9001:2015 provides requirements on quality management of software."
- "EN 50159:2010 includes some generic requirements for software relating to transmission systems."
- "EN 50126:1999 sets out the requirements for system Safety Integrity Levels (SILs) and safety management requirements."
- "ISO 13849-2:2012 includes some requirements for software for machinery."
- "On Track Machines and On Track Plant have to comply with the Machinery Directive and may use ISO 13849-2:2012 as a presumption of conformance."

Maritime

The "Industry Standard on Software Maintenance of Shipboard Equipment Version 1.0" [59] was published in December 2017 by a Joint Working Group comprising members of Comité International Radio-Maritime (CIRM, http://www.cirm.org/), the international association of marine electronics companies, and BIMCO (https://www.bimco.org/), the world's largest shipping association. This standard is remarkably short at just 25 pages; however, it references several other standards that cannot be considered lightweight:

- IEC 61162-460 Ed. 1.0, Maritime navigation and radio communication equipment and systems - Digital interfaces [60]
- Part 460: Multiple talker and multiple listeners – Ethernet interconnection – Safety and security
- IMO International Ship and Port Facility Security (ISPS) Code [61]
- International Safety Management (ISM) Code, Resolution A.741(18) as amended by MSC.104(73), MSC.179(79) [62,63]
- MSC.195(80) and MSC.273(85)
- IMO MSC.1/Circ.1389, Guidance on Procedures for Updating Shipborne Navigation and Communication Equipment [61]
- IMO SN.1/Circ.266/Rev.1, Maintenance of Electronic Chart Display and Information System (ECDIS) Software [61]
- ISM Code, Chapter 5, Section 10, Maintenance of the Ship and Equipment [61]
- ISO 9001, Quality management systems – Requirements [42]
- ISO 17894, Ships and marine technology – Computer applications – General principles for the development and use of programmable electronic systems in marine applications
- ISO/IEC 90003, Guidelines for the application of ISO 9001 to computer software
- ISO/IEC 12207, Systems and software engineering – Software lifecycle processes
- ISO/IEC 15288, Systems and software engineering – System life cycle processes
- ISO/IEC 25010, Systems and software engineering – Systems and software Quality Requirements and Evaluation
- (SQuaRE) – System and software quality models [64]

Medical

IEC 62304 [65] requires risk management is carried out and defines three simple classes as follows:

- Class A: No injury or damage to health is possible
- Class B: Nonserious injury is possible
- Class C: Death or serious injury is possible

Once this is done, various demands are made upon the software development process that become more stringent as the level of risk increases.

However, the software safety experts advise not to take IEC 62304 in isolation, but rather in the context of other applicable standards not entirely related to software, for example, IEC 6061. First published in 1977, this is a series of technical standards for the safety and effectiveness of medical electrical equipment, and by 2011 it consisted of a general standard, about 10 collateral standards, and about 60 particular standards [66].

Factory automation

Among relevant standards appear to be: IEC 61511 [67], IEC 62061 [68], ISA84 [69], ANSI B11.0: 2010 [70], ISO 13849, and ISO 12100: 2010 [71].

General safety

The general standard for software safety, referenced extensively by the other standards, is IEC–65108 [72].

Comparison of safety levels

Table 11.1   Rough cross-domain mapping of safety levels.

Domain	Domain-specific safety levels				
Automotive (ISO 26262/PAS 21448)	QM	ASIL A	ASIL B/C	ASIL D	–
Aviation (DO-187C)	DAL-E	DAL-D	DAL-C	DAL-B	DAL-A
Rail (CENELEC 50126/128/129)	–	SIL-1	SIL-2	SIL-3	SIL-4
Medical (IEC-62304)		Class A	Class B	Class C	–
General (IEC-65108)	–	SIL-1	SIL-2	SIL-3	SIL-4

Table 11.1 shows the approximate equivalence of safety levels described in different standards.

11.2 What is in these standards?

As perhaps could be expected since all these standards deal with safety-critical systems, they have a lot in common. They all make demands of process, testing, and risk analysis. They all require traceability, the ability to prove that the process has been followed, and that requirements have been met and tested. To a large extent, this could all be described as good software engineering and project management. There are particular processes to be followed and work products to be produced; these may vary a little between the standards employed and the engineers working in different industries.

11.3 What could possibly go wrong?

11.3.1 A spelling mistake with potentially disastrous consequences

The following is an example of a typical error in a Python program that goes undetected by the Python parser. Since variables do not need to be declared, the example is perfectly legal Python code, which is supposed to set a global variable to a value and return that value. Instead, it silently forgets the new value and returns the old value due to the misspelling of `somevaraible` in the assignment line.

```python
def set_somevariable(self, parameter):
    global somevariable
    somevaraible = parameter
    return somevariable
```

Errors exactly like this are not possible with languages like C where all variables must be declared before use.

11.3.2 Misuse of enumerated types

It is very easy to use enumerations to declare constants and then forget which constant is in which enumeration; C does not help you to remember, either. Consider the following:

```c
enum race_enum {ready, steady, go};
enum light_enum {off, blinking, on};
....
enum light_enum light;
...
if (steady == light)
{
    /* This will be executed when light is blinking */
}
```

11.4 Errors and avoiding them

11.4.1 Requirement, design, programming and transient errors

Requirement errors generally originate at the outset of a project and can be down to unrealistic expectations, miscommunication, or a lack of requirements engineering. If a design is not correct, because it either cannot or does not implement the requirements or is too inflexible or indeed too flexible, then it can be a real problem. Most of the standards such as ISO26262 are based upon the assumption that a waterfall "V" process is being used, demanding that the design is finished before coding begins. This is not and never has been either practical or really used in practice. Alternatives are discussed in the next section.

Programming errors are mistakes made due to lack of understanding or care, which results in improper operation of the application. With good test design and extensive testing, these errors should be all detectable and capable of correction.

Transient errors, or soft errors as they are sometimes known, are issues that arise for a short period of time and then correct themselves. They may be caused by factors such as radiation, electrical noise, or mechanical vibration, or they may be as the result of a connectivity loss to another component that has suffered some other type of error. For example:

- A transient memory fault caused by interaction with an alpha-particle
- A communication error caused by a lightning strike
- Intermittent connection due to mechanical vibration
- Server component resets because of some type of error (design, programming, or transient), and the client consequently suffers a transient error
- High temperature causes the processor clock to throttle back, and some calculation is not completed within a design deadline

Of course, this is a book about OpenVX, and general discussions about the prevention, avoidance, and mitigation of these risks is outside of its scope. However, it is worth noting that undetected transient errors can easily result in the corruption of data. If your system is intended for operation at a high safety level, then data integrity may be helped by hardware such as ECC memory (Error Correcting Code Memory) or parity checking. The OpenVX specification also implies that much of the onus for checking values of parameters supplied to APIs is on the user of the API rather than on the implementation; it is worth checking documentation for your implementation to ascertain exactly what will happen if "illegal" parameters are given. If that is not available, then assume the worst. Much of the data in vision applications is fairly large (images!), and it may be that if you have no ECC memory and risk evaluation suggests it, then you should consider calculating CRCs if images are to stay unchanged in RAM for some time. Transmission of images between components should always be carried out using a protocol that includes error detection. Transient errors by their nature are difficult to test, and this is usually done by "fault injection." There are two types of test:

• Tests injecting errors that the software has been specifically designed to detect and mitigate, or to protect against.

• Tests that inject errors at random or systematically throughout areas, without knowledge of any measure designed into the code. Preferably, the tests are driven with some knowledge of the likelihood of a particular failure.

In some respects the first type of test can be regarded as "business as usual" for testing, since it is necessary to achieve 100% code coverage. The second type of test is very useful as it can uncover areas where the design may be improved, but it is not possible to be completely thorough with this type of testing; there has to be some limit at which you say "this is so improbable, so we will take the risk." Therefore there will always be the possibility of some unexpected transient errors.

11.4.2 Defensive programming

A quick google search will reveal many papers about defensive programming and indeed offensive programming, which is a form of defensive programming that trusts the local code. There is a good compromise to be drawn between these two, as suggested in standards such as ISO26262, where it is recommended that every parameter of an API is range-checked unless it may be guaranteed by design that whenever an API is called, its parameters will meet requirements. Internal documentation should clearly state whether arguments are checked by the called function or should be guaranteed by the caller, and this in turn will affect test design.

An example of an API that supports offensive programming is the Vulkan^{TM} graphics library, designed to be fast and light and used with care. Implementations are encouraged to not waste cycles on parameter checking but require proper use. OpenVX makes no particular stipulation about what implementations should do, but the specification does list requirements for parameter values.

Overly defensive programming can lead to unreachable code and be a testing nightmare, requiring extensive fault injection, especially at higher safety levels where evidence of 100% mc/dc coverage may be required by auditors.

11.4.3 Feature subsets

Some of the standards suggest using language or API subsets. The purpose of this is to limit the number of ways in which the programmer may express a design, meaning that the code becomes easier to read for maintainers as the style automatically becomes more uniform and less dependent upon the specific author. In a way, this is like the use of language subsets to write operation manuals: because a smaller dictionary is used, the result is more accessible to a greater number of people. You can have team members with reduced expertise, or your highly talented team will make fewer mistakes. Use of language subsets also allows features of the language that can cause confusion to be entirely removed; for example, in C++, it really is not a good idea to redefine the "+" operator for integers, or to dereference a null pointer.

OpenVX-SC also allows API subsets, one for developing your product and one for shipping inside it. The subset to ship is smaller and contains no features that are not needed except in development, so you cannot use them by mistake.

11.5 How to do agile development and still meet the ISO26262 requirements

ISO26262, in common with many standards, imposes a waterfall process based upon the "V" model. However, you should remember that this process is observable (by auditors) through the work products and that the process not only allows for but also demands a change management process. It does not specify the change management process; it just requires the process to be documented and followed. So to meet ISO26262 requirements and still use an agile development process, the following are required:

- Live requirements throughout the project
- Live designs throughout the project
- Well-documented change management process (your scrum story or ticketing system works well for this)
- Strong source code management (e.g., git is suitable)
- Effective platform for documented code reviews, integrated with source code management
- Continuous test and integration (e.g., Jenkins)
- Is this beginning to look familiar?

Of course, you must produce the required work products and be able to specify a sprint that will result in everything (requirements, design, implementation, test) being in sync for a release, but in between you can work piecewise toward your goal, with each sprint being like a separate mini-V model. Always make sure that your specification, tests, design, and implementation are in sync. This last point is very important; if after a scrum or a design meeting, different people go off and independently in parallel update the specification, tests, design, and the implementation, then things could go very wrong if they have all left the meeting with slightly different ideas about what was decided. Even if you have a good secondary review process that is 100% accurate, you could end up wasting a lot of effort. It is better to agree the requirements first, then write the functional tests (or at least test designs) and audit them against those requirements, before proceeding with design and implementation. To achieve the best quality and guarantee that you meet your safety goals, you should have a process of continuous improvement, with metrics such as code coverage and static analysis results that must not degrade. For example, you can use the following criteria as a gate to acceptance of a merge request:

- Code coverage by test as a percentage of code must not go down
- No regressions in existing tests unless they can be justified as a temporary situation (requires discussion)
- No new violations from static analysis (waivers are accepted but require discussion)
- Request must be justifiable as contributing to an existing story
- Code passes peer review
- Code satisfies complexity requirements
- Code meets style guidelines (this should be automated)

11.6 Determinism

ISO26262 and other standards require a code to be deterministic. At first sight, this perhaps would seem to be a nonrequirement: why would your code not do the same each time for the same inputs? How else would you test it?

In that last question, perhaps is the answer to the riddle. In practice, large systems implemented on complex pieces of hardware are **not** deterministic. This can be for many reasons; to illustrate this, let us invent a scenario.

Suppose you wish to find objects in a scene, say, the edge of the road. You find candidate lines and then sort through them to decide which is the actual edge of the road. Because you know that sometimes there could be a lot of candidate lines and you only have a limited amount of time to do the processing, you limit the maximum number of lines, stopping processing after you have found 100 lines.

For a given image input, will you always find the same lines, and will they be in the same order in your list? In fact, if they are not in the same order, then there is a very high probability that the lines in your list will not be the same ones. But why might they not be in the same order? Well, the answer could be down to the hardware. Suppose the task is divided over a number of separate, independently clocked cores that are polled for their data in turn. Small variations in clock speed (or even clock jitter if the cores are supposedly clocked together) can result in changes in the order in which the data arrives. Effectively, you are letting things that are out of your control affect the results. Careful design of both the hardware and the software could eliminate this problem, but it could be at the expense of other things, and in fact it might be counterproductive.

In this particular case, you probably do not want to find the same lines every time: if there are a large number and you consistently choose the first "n", then you could miss finding the edge of the road altogether. It could be that a good design actually inserts some randomness into the algorithm, to ensure that over a sequence of frames a sufficient number of lines, under varying light conditions and from different angles, are found so that the real edge of the road may be recognized. Since there is so much randomness in the real data that will be analyzed, testing an artificial situation with repeatable input data (a recorded video sequence) and hardware and software engineered to be as deterministic and repeatable as possible (the software could use a pseudorandom number generator, so for testing purposes, the "randomness" is repeatable) would not seem to be very useful. It would be better to accept the nondeterminism and average results from data taken in a large variety of different situations.

In fact, ISO/PAS21448, the most recent supplement to ISO26262, contains some guidance in Annex D "Automotive perception systems verification and validation" for testing systems containing algorithms like this.

11.7 OpenVX-SC

The OpenVX-SC specification was an attempt by the Khronos OpenVX working group to define a specification that could be more easily used to create and use Khronos-conformant implementations in environments that respect safety-critical standards such as ISO 26262. The OpenVX-SC specification was originally a separate document from the regular OpenVX specification. The SC specification was based on version 1.1 of the regular OpenVX specification document, with updates supporting SC applications. The most recent version of this separate version of the SC specification is OpenVX1.1-SC, released on March 8, 2017. In parallel with the development of the SC spec based on OpenVX 1.1, the OpenVX 1.2 specification was developed, and it did not yet include the SC features. The most recent version of the OpenVX 1.2 main specification is version 1.2.1 (August 15, 2018), and it is only a formatting difference from version 1.2 (October 20, 2017).

Version 1.3 of the OpenVX specification (July 24, 2019) merges the SC features into the main specification, so there is no longer a separate stand-alone SC specification; the OpenVX 1.3 main specification includes the SC features needed. OpenVX 1.3 includes the concept of "feature sets," which define subsets of all the features available in the main specification, and this concept is leveraged to define subsets of OpenVX for "development" and "deployment" supporting SC applications as described further. These feature sets are described in a companion document to the main specification called The OpenVX Feature Set Definitions (version 1.0, July 24, 2019).

11.7.1 Differences between OpenVX and OpenVX-SC

The main differences in the SC version are separation of the specification into "development" and "deployment" feature sets and inclusion of the Export and Import Extension as a necessary part. The reasoning behind this was that most safety-critical specifications do not expect or allow modifications of the system, so those parts of the OpenVX specification related to creation, optimization, and compilation (if this is what an implementation does) of an OpenVX graph are not needed in a deployed safety-critical system. The Export and Import Extension provides a means of taking a finished, ready-to-run graph out from the environment in which it was created (the development feature set) into a different deployment subset that contains only the parts of the implementation required to actually execute the graph. This division allows the larger development feature set (the full OpenVX API) of the implementation to be free of some of the more stringent requirements of safety-critical standards, since it becomes essentially a tool that produces code in the form of the exported graph, whereas the smaller deployment subset will has to conform to all the rules of a safety-critical system. In the case of ISO 26262 the development feature set will have to be qualified as a tool, and if designed and used correctly, the effort here may be minimal. Because the deployment subset is much smaller, the implementers have fewer APIs to implement and test, and the application developers have fewer APIs to use in their safety-critical system. Hence there is less work to do all-round, the size of the documents comprising the work products is considerably smaller, and there is less chance of mistakes being made.

The deployment feature subset

The "development feature set" in OpenVX SC is the full API and so needs no further explanation. The "deployment subset" is very restricted. The philosophy is that graphs are created and verified using the development feature set and then exported using the Export and Import extension in some format ready to be used by the "deployment feature set." The deployment feature set therefore requires no APIs concerned with the construction or verification of graphs. There are APIs neither for the construction of nodes (although of course the code for execution of vision functions must be in the deployment feature set) nor for creating or accessing kernels. All nonvirtual data objects may be created using the deployment feature set. Import objects may be created (using the import API), but no objects may be exported.

11.7.2 Drawbacks of OpenVX-SC
Enumerations vs. constants

Apart from the separation into development and deployment subsets, the only other real difference with OpenVX-SC is that the many enumerations in the header files have been replaced with preprocessor symbols, although this is not ideal. The reason for the replacement is that the way enumerations were defined and used in OpenVX1.1 is contrary to the rules in the specification MISRA C (2012) [45], which requires strict typing and no arithmetic. OpenVX uses arithmetic to calculate values of enumeration constants in the header files, then expects the application programmer to pass them like integer constants (of type vx_enum) and the implementer to interpret the vx_enum as various different enumerated types, in contravention of the strict typing rules. Therefore the header files of OpenVX version 1.2 and earlier do not comply to MISRA, and it is almost impossible to use or implement the APIs in a way conformant with MISRA. OpenVX-SC and OpenVX 1.3 seek to amend the enumerated type issue by using the preprocessor to define constants. This results in conformance with MISRA C

(2012); however, not only is it clumsy, but there arise a whole new set of problems if either the implementation or application developer wishes to use C++, since use of the preprocessor is banned in MISRA C++ (2008) [46], except for #include and #include guards.

Design of containers

There are other inherent drawbacks of OpenVX that make it not ideally suitable for safety-critical systems; in other words, there is room for improvement. These are mostly to do with object lifecycles. For example, there are inconsistencies in the way the reference counts of objects are handled, for example, when retrieving references to objects held in delays (vxGetReferenceFromDelay) versus those held in object arrays (vxGetObjectArrayItem). To help with this and to support those occasions when it may be necessary to create a copy of a reference, the ability to manipulate the reference count is provided by the functions vxRetainReference and vxReleaseReference. In a safety-critical context, the use of these functions and copying references is a dangerous practice.

Some objects, for example, the pyramid and object array, are collections of other objects, and references to these objects may be obtained. The OpenVX specification (including the SC version) is not clear about what happens to objects within the collection when the container is destroyed. If a Pyramid is created, a reference is obtained to the image at the base of the Pyramid, and the Pyramid destroyed, then what happens to the image for which we have a reference? The specification says that we must release this reference, but if the Pyramid no longer exists, then this may present problems, and different implementations may interpret the specification in different ways. One thing that the specification is clear about is that when the context is destroyed, everything is destroyed, and references are no longer valid. This suggests two approaches to dealing with references to objects in containers (and references generally):

1. Never bother to release references. Everything will be sorted out when the context is destroyed. This solution is particularly attractive to systems where all resources are claimed at the start and there are no changes required in the numbers of different objects.
2. Take extreme care to release all references obtained from containers before releasing references to those containers.

Usually in safety-critical systems, it is possible to use the first method, since this is an ideal model for such systems.

Lack of overloaded functions

The C language has no concept of overloaded functions, so the OpenVX API finds a way around this using the usual C idiom of passing a pointer to void and a size. In addition, a constant is passed in many functions (e.g., the SetAttribute and Query functions for various object types) that also describes the usage of the data, further defining its type. This is an accepted use, and C programmers are well aware of the pitfalls. However, it is not safe, and the use of C++ (next section) to wrap the C API is a better solution.

Reliance on pointers

There is much use of pointers and structures containing pointers in the OpenVX API, especially for extracting data from and inserting data in images. Here we refer to the APIs that use the vx_imagepatch_addressing_t structure or manipulate arrays of pointers. Although this is almost inevitable, it is certainly not ideal from a safety-critical point of view, and the OpenVX Specification does not hold enough explanatory text to fully satisfy auditors. The application developers will find themselves required to produce a lot of documentation, justifications, and possibly MISRA or other waivers, none of which is going to be a popular task. To reduce the amount of this type of work, it should be concentrated in one place by creating wrappers that implement the more restricted functionality required by a particular application in a nice way, mapping to the general features of the OpenVX API. For example, in some applications, images are held in a proprietary format, and a simple API may be designed to create an OpenVX image from an image in this format without reference to any arrays of pointers. This is created and passed to the vxCreateImageFromHandle() function in one place, as illustrated below, rather than calling it from everywhere:

```
vx_image createImageFromMyFormat(vx_context my_context, my_image_format
    *myImage)
{
    /* Lots of documentation */
    vx_image new_image = NULL;
    vx_df_image color = getColorFromMyImage(myImage);
    vx_uint16 num_ptrs = getNumPtrsFromMyImage(myImage);
    vx_imagepatch_addressing_t *addrs = (vx_imagepatch_addressing_t
        *)my_safe_calloc(num_ptrs,
        sizeof(vx_imagepatch_addressing_t));
    void **ptrs = (void **)my_safe_calloc(num_ptrs, sizeof(void *));
```

```
if ((NULL != addrs )&& (NULL != ptrs))
{
        new_image = vxCreateImageFromHandle(mv_context, color,
            addrs, ptrs, VX_MEMORY_TYPE_HOST);
}
my_safe_free(addrs);
my_safe_free(ptrs);
return new_image;
}
```

11.7.3 A targeted shim layer

One way of reducing the complexity and avoiding remaining compliance issues on the OpenVX API is producing a shim layer targeted for your particular application and environment. The last example, createImageFromMyFormat, does just that for one API. It is easy to see how this may be extended for other APIs, and then this collection makes up a shim layer with all the safety-dubious items together in one place, where they may be documented with clarity. There are many APIs in OpenVX, written with general purpose applicability in mind, that may be simplified for specific environments. In an extreme case, you may wish to create your own API subset and have all references to the OpenVX API in one module; this is also what you will want to do if you are programming in a language other than C.

11.8 Programming with C++

Most high-level automotive applications will probably be written using C++14. The AUTOSAR Adaptive Platform specification is aimed at this language, defining guidelines for the use of C++14 in safety-critical systems in its later releases (the most current at the time of writing being AP-19-03, i.e., dated March 2019). These guidelines uphold the rules of MISRA C++ (2008) [46], which states the preprocessor should be used only for include directives; bad news for all the #defines in the OpenVX1.1-SC headers!

Of course, at first glance, because of the way that the OpenVX objects are opaque and defined in terms of a common vx_reference type, it looks as though it should be an easy business to use them just like C++ derived types, with, for example, a vx_image inheriting from vx_reference, or at least to wrap the types in convenient classes. But there are difficulties: just as with the enumerated types, the OpenVX specification is far from perfect.

(Being some of those doing the thinking, we feel we are both in a place to criticize and also perhaps more critical than would be someone on the outside looking in.)

We will outline a general structure for how the OpenVX-SC deployment feature set could be wrapped in C++ classes in a way that not only can be AUTOSAR AP-19-03 compliant, but also avoids use of the heap and limits the use of pointers as far as possible. It should be possible to use the shim layer without invoking **new** or **delete**. The development feature set is bigger and messier, but does not have to comply, so let us not bother. An example of how this C++ API could be used to import previously created graphs has already been given in Chapter 5.

11.9 Data objects

In the C API the objects are hidden from the application, and pointers to objects are returned by factories, which naturally can be thought of member functions of the context object, for example,

- `vxCreateImage( context, ...)` becomes `context.createImage(...)`,
- `vxCreateScalar( context, ...)` becomes `context.createScalar(...)` etc.

Similarly, all the following C functions would translate into member functions of a class `VxReference`:

```
vxQueryReference
vxSetReferenceName
vxGetStatus
vxHint
```

11.9.1 Constructors and destructors

In a C++ definition of the API, we can replace the references to objects by objects in a class hierarchy, using the pointer-to-implementation idiom within the class. Pointers can be completely managed by factory functions, constructors, copy constructors, and destructors.

11.9.2 Query attribute and SetAttribute

For C++, we consider this OpenVX attribute API to be inherently dangerous. Although the idiom (pointer to void, size) is well known to C programmers, that is not the case for many C++ programmers. It is possible to have many different types of the same size, one especially erroneous situation being created if pointers and integers are muddled up. This is easy to do when the type is implied by the attribute constant (e.g., do we supply a number or a pointer to the number?). To overcome this, we can create templates that map the vx_enum, which defines the attribute to the type required, and hide the mechanics of requiring specific data type and the size of that type in a template function. This is all checked at compile time and requires that the attribute is passed as a constant; it can no longer be determined at run-time. We are not sure that there really is a use case for a nonconstant attribute tag, so no real loss of functionality. There are other places in OpenVX where a constant is usually passed, and defining template functions in these cases will allow more checking to be done at compile time without significant loss of functionality.

11.9.3 Arrays of references

Arrays of generic references are used when exporting and importing objects, and unfortunately, they are a potential source of problems if used incorrectly. To help prevent incorrect use, it is a good idea to limit their use to specific places in the code. In the example further, we wrap the array of references in a class VxRefArray and make it much safer; it is not possible, for example, to put a reference of one type in a specific place in the array and then use it as if it was a different type later on. As the arrays of references are only ever used for importing and exporting and there must be an associated array of "uses" of the same length to describe how each of the references is to be used, that data is also stored, avoiding any issues of the arrays being different lengths.

11.10 A practical example

The code that follows seeks to create C++ classes that hide the OpenVX C implementation and take care of reference counting through the use of the vxRetainReference and vxReleaseReference functions, eliminating the danger that there will be unmatched calls to those functions. The Query and SetAttribute functions are wrapped to ensure that the correct types are also introduced. Templates are used to provide overloaded methods, although there will be run-time checking of the actual types passed; for example, with VxReference.query, methods will be created for all types passed although vxQueryReference may not be able to support that type. A more complete design should explicitly create overloaded functions for those types actually supported and reintroduce the attribute enumerations for each data type to enforce some compile-time checking.

The listing is by no means complete; an implementation of C++ wrappers for the deployment feature set is available in the public domain [32]; at the time of writing the development feature set was not available.

11.10.1 vx_reference

We wrap vx_reference, which is a pointer, in a class VxReference and take care of the reference counting by defining a copy constructor, an assignment operator, and a destructor. Notice that we check for **nullptr** in several places; in fact, if **nullptr** is found there, then this is probably a programming error, and perhaps it would be a good idea to raise an exception or otherwise log an error for debugging purposes. We make it impossible to create objects of type VxReference by making the destructor protected; we find that in practice there is no need to have any base references. Although there is a type hierarchy in that other objects inherit the basic functionality of a VxReference, we do not use virtual functions to achieve polymorphism, but rather use templates to create overloaded functions where necessary. This means that there are no virtual pointers in the classes, and a VxReference object takes up exactly the same amount of data memory as the underlying vx_reference object. We are in fact trying to define classes that will not generate any extra run-time code but force the programmer to write safer code. Note the protected constructor that checks the type of the underlying OpenVX object. The idea of this is that if an attempt is made to create an object, such as a VxImage, derived from a VxReference using an OpenVX object of the wrong type, then the underlying object will be inaccessible. It would also be possible to put some debugging code in the constructor to log the error or to raise an exception. Unfortunately, we are not able to catch all these errors at compile time. There are more notes in the comments.

```
class VxReference
{
public:
        // Get the context from this reference
        VxContext getContext();

        // There are no virtual functions in this class.
        // Objects of type VxReference may not be instantiated.
protected:
```

```
    // remember that the OpenVX C definition of vx_reference is a
    // pointer to an opaque type. Derived classes will need to be able
        to
    // access the implementation pointer, but the application using
        this
    // shim should not.
    vx_reference pimpl;

    // Any of the derived classes and friends may cast VxReference or
    // a derived class to vx_reference.
    operator const vx_reference() const { return
        reinterpret_cast<const vx_reference>( pimpl ); }

public:
    template <vx_enum A>
    typename tagmap<A>::vx_type queryReference(typename
        tagmap<A>::vx_type init={0}) const
    {
        static_assert( (tag & VX_TYPE_MASK) == (VX_TYPE_REFERENCE <<
            8), "You must use a Reference type attribute!");
        auto data(init);
        if ( nullptr != pimpl )
        {
                vxQueryReference( pimpl, A, &data, sizeof( data ) );
        }
        return data;
    }

protected:
    // Protected constructor. VxReference can't be made without a
        pimpl.
    // pimpl must match given type enum or it's set to nullptr
    VxReference( vx_reference ref, vx_enum vxtype )
    : pimpl( ref )
    {
        // In this constructor we make sure that the reference count
            of
        // the OpenVX object is decremented if the pointer is the
            wrong
        // type
        if ( nullptr != pimpl )
        {
```

```cpp
            vx_enum the_type = queryReference<VX_REFERENCE_TYPE>( );
            if ( the_type != vxtype )
            {
                  vxReleaseReference( &ref );
                  pimpl = nullptr;
            }
      }
}


~VxReference( void )
{
      // Protected destructor. VxReference objects are not allowed!
      // In this destructor we make sure that the underlying OpenVX
      // object has its reference count decremented, so that the
      // implementation will destroy it when we've removed all our
      // references to it. Notice we take care never to pass a
         nullptr
      // pointer to any OpenVX APIs. We rely upon the OpenVX API to
      // call the correct ReleaseXXX function when
         VxReleaseReference
      // is called.
      if ( nullptr != pimpl )
      {
            vxReleaseReference( &pimpl );
      }
}


VxReference( const VxReference& obj )
{
      // In the copy constructor we make sure that the reference
         count
      // of the OpenVX object is incremented when we take a copy of
      // the pointer
      pimpl = obj.pimpl;
      if ( nullptr != pimpl )
      {
            vxRetainReference( pimpl );
      }
}


friend class VxGraph;
friend class VxRefArray;
```

```
    friend class VxContext;

public:
    void operator=( const VxReference& obj )
    {
        // We define the assignment operator so as to be able to keep
        // track of the reference counts. An alternative would be to
        // raise an error if assigning to a reference that already
            has
        // a value in pimpl since this is most likely an error.
        // Notice that the operator does not return a value and hence
        // constructs of the type a = b = c cannot be made.
        if ( nullptr != pimpl )
        {
            vxReleaseReference( &pimpl );
        }
        pimpl = obj.pimpl;
        if ( nullptr != pimpl )
        {
            vxRetainReference( pimpl );
        }
    }


    // getName() is included for utility
    const std::string getName() const
    {
        return queryReference<VX_REFERENCE_NAME>("");
    }


    vx_status setName( const std::string& name ) { return
        vxSetReferenceName( pimpl, name.c_str() ); }


    // The vxHint function allows implementations to define various
    // hints taking different data types; However, they must first
    // define the corresponding tagmap struct to map the hint to
    // the data type.
    template <enum vx_hint_e attribute>
    vx_status hint(typename tagmap<attribute>::vx_type & data )
    {
        return vxHint( pimpl, attribute, static_cast<void*>( data ),
            sizeof( data ) );
    }
```

```
// Other VxReference methods simply match directly to the OpenVX
// API:
vx_status directive( enum vx_directive_e directive ) { return
    vxDirective( pimpl, directive ); }

vx_status getStatus( void ) const { return vxGetStatus( pimpl ); }
};
```

11.10.2 VxReference with paranoia

We spoke earlier about the lack of clarity in the specification about containers. If you suspect that your implementation may be deficient in this area, that is, destroying a container destroys the contained object even if references to them exist, then you may like to consider a modification to the VxReference object that holds a reference to the parent object. This means that the constructor(s) will have an extra parameter, but since they are not called directly but rather by a factory function that is a member of the parent object, there will be no obvious change to the wrapped API. There will, of course, be an extra data member, doubling the memory footprint of the VxReference object. The constructor must call vxRetainReference() on the parent, and the destructor must call vxReleaseReference on the parent.

11.10.3 queryReference and the tagmap template

In the definition of the queryReference() member function in the previous listing, you will probably have noticed the use of a template called "tagmap"; this is the template discussed in the previous section about the Query and SetAttribute functions. Here we give the definitions of a few of the tagmap templates (a full listing may be found online at https://gitlab.com/StephenRamm/openvx-sc-plus/tagged_type.hpp):

```
// a tagMap associates a tag with a type, used for attributes and types
    generally
template <vx_enum t> struct tagmap {};
template <> struct tagmap<VX_TYPE_CHAR> { typedef vx_char vx_type;};
template <> struct tagmap<VX_TYPE_INT8> { typedef vx_int8 vx_type;};
template <> struct tagmap<VX_TYPE_UINT8> { typedef vx_uint8 vx_type;};
template <> struct tagmap<VX_TYPE_INT16> { typedef vx_int16 vx_type;};
template <> struct tagmap<VX_TYPE_UINT16> { typedef vx_uint16 vx_type;};
template <> struct tagmap<VX_TYPE_INT32> { typedef vx_int32 vx_type;};
```

```
template <> struct tagmap<VX_TYPE_UINT32> { typedef vx_uint32 vx_type;};
template <> struct tagmap<VX_TYPE_INT64> { typedef vx_int64 vx_type;};
template <> struct tagmap<VX_TYPE_UINT64> { typedef vx_uint64 vx_type;};
template <> struct tagmap<VX_TYPE_FLOAT32> { typedef vx_float32
    vx_type;};
template <> struct tagmap<VX_TYPE_FLOAT64> { typedef vx_float64
    vx_type;};
template <> struct tagmap<VX_TYPE_ENUM> { typedef vx_enum vx_type;};
template <> struct tagmap<VX_TYPE_SIZE> { typedef vx_size vx_type;};
template <> struct tagmap<VX_TYPE_DF_IMAGE> { typedef vx_df_image
    vx_type;};
template <> struct tagmap<VX_TYPE_BOOL> { typedef vx_bool vx_type;};


template <> struct tagmap<VX_REFERENCE_TYPE> { typedef vx_enum vx_type;};
template <> struct tagmap<VX_REFERENCE_NAME> { typedef const vx_char*
    vx_type;};
template <> struct tagmap<VX_REFERENCE_COUNT> { typedef vx_uint32
    vx_type;};
template <> struct tagmap<VX_GRAPH_STATE>    { typedef vx_enum vx_type;};
template <> struct tagmap<VX_GRAPH_NUMNODES> { typedef vx_uint32
    vx_type;};
template <> struct tagmap<VX_GRAPH_NUMPARAMETERS> { typedef vx_uint32
    vx_type;};
template <> struct tagmap<VX_GRAPH_PERFORMANCE> { typedef vx_perf_t
    vx_type;};
template <> struct tagmap<VX_IMAGE_WIDTH>    { typedef vx_uint32
    vx_type;};
```

Defined in the same file as the tagmap are some other templates used in this shim. For example, the following template is useful when a type needs to change according to the "usage" constant supplied to some OpenVX functions:

```
// Add const to a type T if tag is VX_READ_ONLY
template <typename T, vx_enum tag> struct const_if_RO
{
    typedef T vx_type;
    typedef T * vx_ptr;
    typedef T & vx_ref;
};

template <typename T> struct const_if_RO<T, VX_READ_ONLY>
```

```
{
     typedef const T vx_type;
     typedef const T * vx_ptr;
     typedef const T & vx_ref;
};
```

11.10.4 Arrays of references

Arrays of generic references to OpenVX objects are required when creating an import object. We define a class VxRefArray, which puts all the potentially unsafe stuff in one place. Using a std::vector to hold the references, we can have type-safe functions to put our VxReference-derived types and their usages into the array and get them out again, making sure that we keep track of reference counts while we do it. Unfortunately, the type checking is at run-time (provided by the constructors for each class), but at least we do have checking. The friend class VxContext is allowed to gain access to the underlying arrays of vx_reference and vx_enum by using the type-cast operators, but no other access is given.

```
class VxRefArray
{
     // Used to handle arrays of references for VxImport factory defined
     // in VxContext
     private:
     std::vector<vx_reference> ref_array;
     std::vector<vx_enum> use_array;
     operator vx_reference*() { return ref_array.data(); }
     operator const vx_enum*() { return use_array.data(); }

     // We don't allow copies of this.
     // If for some reason an assignment operator is
     // required, then remember to call vxRetainReference
     // for each non-nullptr entry.
     VxRefArray& operator=( VxRefArray& ) {}
     friend class VxContext;

     public:
     VxRefArray( vx_size numrefs )
     {
          ref_array.resize( numrefs );
          use_array.resize( numrefs );
```

```
}


~VxRefArray()
{
      for ( vx_reference ref : ref_array )
      {
            if ( nullptr != ref )
            {
                  vxReleaseReference( &ref );
            }
      }
}


vx_status put( vx_size index, const VxReference& obj, vx_enum use
      = VX_IX_USE_EXPORT_VALUES )
{
      vx_status status = VX_SUCCESS;
      if ( index < ref_array.size() )
      {
            if ( nullptr != ref_array[index] )
            {
                  vxReleaseReference( &ref_array[index] );
            }
            ref_array[index] = obj;
            use_array[index] = use;
            if ( nullptr != ref_array[index] )
            {
                  vxRetainReference( ref_array[index] );
            }
      }
      else
      {
            status = VX_FAILURE;
      }
      return status;
}


template <class TYPE>
TYPE getRef( vx_size index )
{
      // Only allowed to get VxReference & derived types from a
      // VxRefArray
```

```
        static_assert( std::is_base_of<VxReference, TYPE>::value,
            "VxRefArray::get<TYPE> : TYPE must be derived "
        "from VxReference" );
        if ( index < ref_array.size() && ( nullptr !=
            ref_array[index] ) )
        {
            vxRetainReference( ref_array[index] );
            return TYPE( ref_array[index] );
        }
        else
        {
            return TYPE( ( vx_reference ) nullptr );
        }
    }

    vx_enum getUse( vx_size index ) const
    {
        return ( index < use_array.size() ) ? use_array[index] :
            VX_IX_USE_APPLICATION_CREATE;
    }

    vx_size getSize() const { return ref_array.size(); }
};
```

11.10.5 vx_context – the VxContext object

The VxContext object in practice is defined after all the other objects, since it includes factories to make them; they are all made "inside the context."

Note that we provide some specialized nontemplate functions for three of the context attributes, getImplementation(), getExtensions(), and getUniqueKernelTable(). In the first instance, the function would have otherwise returned an array (not allowed!), and in the other two cases, extra information needs to be retrieved beforehand to know how big the items are.

In the deployment set, no context attributes may be changed, so there is no setContextAttribute() function:

```
class VxContext : public VxReference
{
    private:
    VxContext( vx_context ref )
```

```
    : VxReference( reinterpret_cast<vx_reference>( ref ),
      VX_TYPE_CONTEXT )
    {
    }


    operator const vx_context() const { return
        reinterpret_cast<vx_context>( pimpl ); }


    friend class VxReference;
    public:
    ~VxContext() {}
    // Standard constructor uses OpenVX API to create a context
    VxContext( void )
    : VxReference( reinterpret_cast<vx_reference>( vxCreateContext()
        ), VX_TYPE_CONTEXT )
    {
    }


    // deployment set Context queries
    template <vx_enum A>
    typename tagmap<A>::vx_type queryContext(typename
        tagmap<A>::vx_type init={0}) const
    {
        static_assert( (A & VX_TYPE_MASK) == (VX_TYPE_CONTEXT << 8),
            "You must use an Context type attribute!");
        auto data(init);
        if ( nullptr != pimpl )
        {
            vxQueryContext( *this, A, &data, sizeof( data ) );
        }
        return data;
    }


    std::string getImplementation() const
    {
        vx_char name[VX_MAX_IMPLEMENTATION_NAME];
        vxQueryContext( *this, VX_CONTEXT_IMPLEMENTATION, name,
            sizeof( name ) );
        return name;
    }


    std::string getExtensions() const
```

```
{
    vx_size xsize = 0;
    vxQueryContext( *this, VX_CONTEXT_EXTENSIONS_SIZE, &xsize,
        sizeof( xsize ) );
    vx_char name[xsize];
    vxQueryContext( *this, VX_CONTEXT_EXTENSIONS, name, xsize );
    return name;
}


std::vector<vx_kernel_info_t> getUniqueKernelTable() const
{
    vx_uint32 count = queryContext<VX_CONTEXT_UNIQUE_KERNELS>();
    std::vector<vx_kernel_info_t> table( count );
    vxQueryContext( *this, VX_CONTEXT_UNIQUE_KERNEL_TABLE,
        table.data(), count * sizeof( vx_kernel_info_t ) );
    return table;
}


vx_status exportObjectsToMemory( VxRefArray& refs, const
    vx_uint8*& ptr, vx_size& length )
{
    return vxExportObjectsToMemory( *this, refs.getSize(), refs,
        refs, &ptr, &length );
}


// Factories for objects of all the other classes are defined here

VxImport importObjectsFromMemory( VxRefArray& refs, const
    vx_uint8* ptr, vx_size length )
{
    return VxImport( vxImportObjectsFromMemory( *this,
        refs.getSize(), refs, refs, ptr, length ) );
}


VxImage createImage( vx_uint32 width, vx_uint32 height,
vx_df_image color ) // Standard image creation
{
    return VxImage( vxCreateImage( *this, width, height, color )
        );
}
```

```
VxImage createUniformImage( vx_uint32 width, vx_uint32 height,
    const vx_df_image_e color, const vx_pixel_value_t pixel )
{
    return VxImage( vxCreateUniformImage( *this, width, height,
        color, &pixel ) );
}


VxImage createImageFromHandle( const VxImageHandle& handle )
{
    return VxImage( vxCreateImageFromHandle( *this,
        handle.color(), handle, handle, handle.mem_type() ) );
}


VxObjectArray createObjectArray( VxReference& exemplar, vx_size
    count )
{
    return VxObjectArray( vxCreateObjectArray( *this, exemplar,
        count ) );
}


VxDelay createDelay( VxReference& exemplar, vx_size count )
{
    return VxDelay( vxCreateDelay( *this, exemplar, count ) );
}

// Create a scalar with compile-time Type
template <vx_enum tag>
VxScalar<tag> createScalar(typename tagmap<tag>::vx_type val)
{
    return vxCreateScalar(*this, tag, &val);
}


// Create a Scalar when type not known at compile-time
VxScalar<0> createScalar(vx_enum tag, const void * val)
{
    return vxCreateScalar(*this, tag, val);
}


template <vx_enum T>
VxLUT<T> createLUT(vx_size count)
{
    return vxCreateLUT(*this, T, count);
```

```
    }

    VxLUT<0> createLUT(vx_enum T, vx_size count)
    {
        return vxCreateLUT(*this, T, count);
    }

    // Create an Array with compile-time type
    template <vx_enum tag>
    VxArray<tag> createArray(vx_size capacity)
    {
        return vxCreateArray(*this, tag, capacity);
    }

    // Create an Array when type not known at compile-time
    VxArray<0> createArray(vx_enum A, vx_size capacity)
    {
        return vxCreateArray(*this, A, capacity);
    }

    // Create a Remap
    VxRemap createRemap(vx_uint32 src_width, vx_uint32 src_height,
        vx_uint32 dst_width, vx_uint32 dst_height)
    {
        return vxCreateRemap(*this, src_width, src_height,
            dst_width, dst_height);
    }

    // Create a Pyramid
    VxPyramid createPyramid(vx_size levels, vx_float32 scale,
        vx_uint32 width, vx_uint32 height, vx_df_image format)
    {
        return vxCreatePyramid(*this, levels, scale, width, height,
            format);
    }

    // Create a convolution
    VxConvolution createConvolution(vx_size columns, vx_size rows)
    {
        return vxCreateConvolution(*this, columns, rows);
    }
};
```

```
VxContext VxReference::getContext() { return VxContext( vxGetContext(
    pimpl ) ); }
```

11.10.6 vx_import

The `VxImport` class definition is quite short. The constructor is declared as private because a `VxImport` will actually be made by a factory defined in the context object; for this reason, `VxContext` needs to be a friend of this class. The only public function is a template wrapping the `vxGetImportReferenceByName` function call and returning the correct type. It is up to the programmer to select the correct type for the function when calling it; note that the constructor for the underlying `VxReference` will also check the type at runtime, and the OpenVX object will not be accessible at all if the wrong template type was given:

```
class VxImport : public VxReference
{
private:
    VxImport(vx_import ref) :
        VxReference(reinterpret_cast<vx_reference>(ref),
        VX_TYPE_IMPORT){}
    operator const vx_import() const
    {
        return reinterpret_cast<vx_import>(pimpl);
    }
    friend class VxContext;
public:
    ~VxImport(){}
    // factories
    template<class TYPE>
    TYPE getReferenceByName(const vx_char * name)
    {
        return TYPE(vxGetImportReferenceByName(*this, name));
    }
};
```

11.10.7 vx_graph

The class `VxGraph` wraps the OpenVX graph object. Note that this class definition is for the deployment feature set only, and hence the number of things that may be done with a graph is limited. The templated `queryGraph` function is defined, allowing graph attributes to be queried, but no graph attributes may be directly set. Note that the attribute must be supplied as a constant, and the value is checked at compile-time by the static_assert in the template function.

Apart from this, graphs may be processed, scheduled, and waited for. They cannot be created, but they may be retrieved from an import object. They can also appear in arrays of references, and for these reasons, the classes VxImport and VxRefArray must be friends:

```
class VxGraph : public VxReference
{
    private:
    operator const vx_graph() const { return reinterpret_cast<const
        vx_graph>( pimpl ); }

    VxGraph( vx_reference ref )
    : VxReference( ref, VX_TYPE_GRAPH )
    {
    }
    friend class VxImport;
    // Arrays of reference need access to the pimpl
    friend class VxRefArray;

    public:
    ~VxGraph() {}
    template <vx_enum tag>
    typename tagmap<tag>::vx_type queryGraph(typename
        tagmap<tag>::vx_type init={0}) const
    {
    static_assert( (tag & VX_TYPE_MASK) == (VX_TYPE_GRAPH << 8), "You
        must use a Graph type attribute!");
        auto data(init);
        if ( nullptr != pimpl )
        {
            vxQueryGraph( *this, tag, &data, sizeof( data ) );
        }
        return data;
    }

    vx_status setGraphParameterByIndex( vx_uint32 index, VxReference&
        value )
    {
```

```
        return vxSetGraphParameterByIndex( *this, index, value );
    }

    vx_status processGraph( void ) const
    {
        return vxProcessGraph( *this );
    }

    vx_status scheduleGraph( void ) const
    {
        return vxScheduleGraph( *this );
    }

    vx_status waitGraph( void ) const
    {
        return vxWaitGraph( *this );
    }
};
```

11.10.8 vx_image

As might be expected, we wrap a `vx_image` object in `VxImage` class and define query and set functions. We can also add `static_assert`s to restrict at compile time to only those attributes where queries and sets are allowed deployment features; this is left as an exercise for the reader. We have already mentioned how `vxCreateImageFromHandle()` and `vxSwapImageHandle()` could be used within functions to handle application-specific image data; in this example wrapping `vxSwapImageHandle()`, we encapsulate the pointers in a class `VxImageHandle`, which can be derived from `std::vector`, and require that input and output pointer arrays are of the same length and that the images described have the same color and memory types. There can also be more detailed checking of the addressing methods if the `vx_imagepatch_addressing_t` structure is also stored in the `VxImageHandle`:

```
template <vx_enum usage> class VxImageMap;
class VxImage : public VxReference
{
protected:
    friend class VxImageMap<VX_READ_AND_WRITE>;
    friend class VxImageMap<VX_READ_ONLY>;
    friend class VxImageMap<VX_WRITE_ONLY>;
```

```
    operator const vx_image() const
    {
        return reinterpret_cast<vx_image>( pimpl );
    }
public:
    VxImage( vx_image ref )
        : VxReference( reinterpret_cast<vx_reference>( ref ),
        VX_TYPE_IMAGE )
    {
    }


    VxImage( vx_reference ref )
        : VxReference( ref, VX_TYPE_IMAGE )
    {
    }
    ~VxImage() {}


    template <vx_enum A>
    typename tagmap<A>::vx_type queryImage(typename tagmap<A>::vx_type
        init={0}) const
    {
        static_assert( (A & VX_TYPE_MASK) == (VX_TYPE_IMAGE << 8),
            "You must use an Image type attribute!");
        auto data(init);
        if ( nullptr != pimpl )
        {
            vxQueryImage( *this, A, &data, sizeof( data ) );
        }
        return data;
    }


    template <vx_enum A>
    vx_status setImageAttribute(typename tagmap<A>::vx_type data)
    {
        static_assert( (A & VX_TYPE_MASK) == (VX_TYPE_IMAGE << 8),
            "You must use an Image type attribute!");
        return vxSetImageAttribute(*this, A, &data, sizeof(data));
    }


    // Copying and mapping
    template<vx_enum usage>
    vx_status copyImagePatch( const vx_rectangle_t &rect,
```

```
                        vx_uint32 plane_index,
                        const vx_imagepatch_addressing_t &addr,
                        void * ptr,
                        vx_enum mem_type=VX_MEMORY_TYPE_HOST)
{
      static_assert( (VX_READ_ONLY == usage) ||
      (VX_WRITE_ONLY == usage),
      "usage must be VX_READ_ONLY or VX_WRITE_ONLY");
      return vxCopyImagePatch(*this, &rect,   plane_index, &addr,
          ptr, usage, mem_type);
}


template <vx_enum usage>
auto mapImagePatch( const vx_rectangle_t& rect,
                    vx_uint32 plane_index,
                    vx_enum mem_type=VX_MEMORY_TYPE_HOST,
                    vx_uint32 flags=0 )
{
      return VxImageMap<usage>(*this, rect, plane_index, mem_type,
          flags);
}


// Child factories
VxImage createImageFromROI( const vx_rectangle_t* rect )
{
   return VxImage( vxCreateImageFromROI( *this, rect ) );
}


VxImage createImageFromChannel( enum vx_channel_e channel )
{
      return VxImage( vxCreateImageFromChannel( *this, channel ) );
}


vx_status swapImageHandle( const VxImageHandle& new_ptrs,
                    VxImageHandle& prev_ptrs )
{
      return ( new_ptrs.size() == prev_ptrs.size() &&
          new_ptrs.color() == prev_ptrs.color() &&
          new_ptrs.mem_type() == prev_ptrs.mem_type() )
          ? vxSwapImageHandle( *this, new_ptrs, prev_ptrs,
              new_ptrs.mem_type() )
          : VX_ERROR_INVALID_PARAMETERS;
```

```
    }

    vx_status setImageValidRectangle( const vx_rectangle_t& rect )
    {
        return vxSetImageValidRectangle( *this, &rect );
    }

    vx_status getImageValidRectangle( vx_rectangle_t& rect )
    {
        return vxGetValidRegionImage( *this, &rect );
    }
};
```

11.10.9 Mapping images

Note how we have wrapped the functions `vxMapImagePatch` but not
`vxUnmapImagePatch`. This is because once again we think that these functions are inherently unsafe because of the use of void pointers; also, you
may forget to unmap an image patch after use or get the associated addressing object and size of the patch confused with other ones. We define a
`VxImageMap` class to keep all these things tidy. It contains not just the addressing object filled in at the time the patch was created, but also the map id,
the data pointer, a copy of the memory type, usage, dimensions passed at
the time of creation, and a reference to the image. All these things then have
the same lifetime as the patch, which is unmapped when it is destroyed.
Furthermore, note that image patches may be read/write, write-only or
read-only, allowing the implementation to make optimizations. So we derived read/write, write-only, and read-only image patches to enforce the
rules chosen at creation time for the life of the object.

After saying all that, we have left `copyImagePatch` quite unchanged. Using
the techniques employed elsewhere in this chapter, can you create a safer
version?

```
VxImageMap( VxImage image_in,
        const vx_rectangle_t& rect_in,
        vx_uint32 plane_index,
        vx_enum mem_type_in=VX_MEMORY_TYPE_HOST,
        vx_uint32 flags=0 ):
        image(image_in),
        rect(rect_in),
        mem_type(mem_type_in),
```

```
    status(vxMapImagePatch( image, &rect, plane_index, &map_id, &addr,
        &ptr, usage, mem_type, flags ))
    {}

public:
    ~VxImageMap()
    {
        if ( VX_SUCCESS == status && image != nullptr )
        {
            status = vxUnmapImagePatch( image, map_id );
        }
    }

    typename const_if_RO<vx_pixel_value_t, usage>::vx_ptr
        formatImagePatchAddress1d( vx_uint32 index )
    {
        return ( VX_SUCCESS == status ) ?
            vxFormatImagePatchAddress1d( ptr, index, &addr ) :
            nullptr;
    }

    typename const_if_RO<vx_pixel_value_t, usage>::vx_ptr
        formatImagePatchAddress2d( vx_uint32 x, vx_uint32 y )
    {
        return ( VX_SUCCESS == status ) ?
            vxFormatImagePatchAddress2d( ptr, x, y, &addr ) :
            nullptr;
    }

    typename const_if_RO<void, usage>::vx_ptr getVoidPtr()
    {
        return ptr;
    }

    vx_status copyPatch( VxImage image_in, const vx_rectangle_t&
        rect_in, vx_uint32 image_plane_index, vx_enum usage_in )
    {
        auto my_size_x = rect.end_x - rect.start_y;
        auto my_size_y = rect.end_y - rect.start_y;
        auto copy_size_x = rect_in.end_x - rect_in.start_x;
        auto copy_size_y = rect_in.end_y - rect_in.start_y;
```

```
            return ( ( my_size_x < copy_size_x ) || ( my_size_y <
                copy_size_y ) )
                    ? VX_ERROR_INVALID_PARAMETERS
                    : vxCopyImagePatch( image_in, &rect,
                        image_plane_index, &addr, ptr, usage_in, mem_type
                        );
        }


        const vx_imagepatch_addressing_t* getAddressing() const { return
            &addr; }
};
```

11.10.10 Mapping other objects

We will not give examples here, but for the other objects that can be mapped and unmapped (LUT, Array, Distribution and Remap), there can be a similar abstraction. In fact, in the case of these other objects the classes may be templated.

11.10.11 The delay and object array classes

Wrapping vx_delay and vx_object_array is very similar, the only real difference being that when retrieving a reference from a delay, we must increment the reference count of the retrieved object because of the anomaly in the OpenVX specification that treats delays differently from other containers:

```
class VxDelay : public VxReference
{
private:
    VxDelay( vx_delay ref )
            : VxReference( reinterpret_cast<vx_reference>( ref ),
                VX_TYPE_DELAY )
        {
        }
    operator const vx_delay() const { return
        reinterpret_cast<vx_delay>( pimpl ); }
    friend class VxImport;
    friend class VxContext;
    friend class VxRefArray;

public:
    ~VxDelay() {}
```

```
template <vx_enum tag>
typename tagmap<tag>::vx_type queryDelay(typename
    tagmap<tag>::vx_type init={0}) const
{
    auto data(init);
    if ( nullptr != pimpl )
    {
        vxQueryDelay( *this, tag, &data, sizeof( data ) );
    }
    return data;
}


template <class TYPE>
TYPE getReferenceFromDelay( vx_uint32 index )
{
    vx_reference ref = vxGetReferenceFromDelay( *this, index );
    if ( nullptr != ref )
    {
        vxRetainReference( ref );
    }
    return TYPE( ref );
}

vx_status age() { return vxAgeDelay( *this ); }
};

class VxObjectArray : public VxReference
{
private:
    VxObjectArray( vx_object_array ref )
        : VxReference( reinterpret_cast<vx_reference>( ref ),
            VX_TYPE_OBJECT_ARRAY )
    {
    }

    VxObjectArray( vx_reference ref )
        : VxReference( ref, VX_TYPE_OBJECT_ARRAY )
    {
    }
    operator const vx_object_array() const { return
        reinterpret_cast<vx_object_array>( pimpl ); }
```

```
friend class VxImport;
friend class VxContext;
friend class VxRefArray;

public:
    ~VxObjectArray() {}
    // general-purpose query function.
    // (Could be made to raise an exception if vxQueryObjectArray
    // returns an error)
    template <vx_enum tag>
    typename tagmap<tag>::vx_type queryObjectArray(typename
        tagmap<tag>::vx_type init={0}) const
    {
        auto data(init);
        if ( nullptr != pimpl )
        {
            vxQueryObjectArray( *this, tag, &data, sizeof( data )
                );
        }
        return data;
    }


    template <class TYPE>
    TYPE getObjectArrayItem( vx_uint32 index )
    {
        return TYPE( vxGetObjectArrayItem( *this, index ) );
    }


    template <class T>
    T operator [](vx_size index) { return
        getObjectArrayItem<T>(index); }
};
```

11.11 Learning and modification of software in safety-critical systems

Annex G of ISO/PAS21448 discusses the implications of offline training for autonomous vehicles and is worth reading in this context.

To round this chapter off, it is worth discussing how deployed systems can learn from their environments when the division of OpenVX into development and deployment feature subsets would seem to make deployed systems invariant and not able to adapt. First, a little background.

In most safety-related specifications, it is generally considered a bad idea to change programs on the fly; update of stored data that affects program operation (usually called "calibration") requires some strict control, and methods of ensuring data integrity are well developed. The same rigorous controls and methods are required generally to ensure adherence to legislation or voluntary standards pertaining to the environment and public health or for commercial reasons. For example, automotive engine calibrations are believed to be so well tested and their modification so well controlled that legislation in most countries is able to accept exactly the same engine, and the same control software but with different calibrations as being distinct as far as road tax or import duty is concerned. The same Diesel engine used in a range of vehicles with rated power outputs from 140 hp to 190 hp is possible by change of calibration. These calibrations may be updated post-sales to improve the performance characteristics where legislation allows, for example, where the change would not be detrimental to the ratings of noxious emissions, where the change would not put the vehicle into a different tax bracket, and/or where it would not invalidate the manufacturer claims. Needless to say, there is a burden of proof required, and sufficient testing of a new calibration in a range of typical production units must be carried out, being required either by law or tested in the courts.

Manufacturers also allow dynamic switching of calibrations, for example, "eco" or "sport" modes, and they must declare the maxima and minima of items such as CO_2 emission and power output across all calibrations. In Diesel engines, there is a trade-off between fuel economy and emissions of particulates and gases such as oxides of nitrogen that effect health, which translates into a trade-off between social conscience and profit. Unfortunately, in several countries the pursuit of profit has won, and there have been many instances of the illegal recalibration of goods vehicles, and a major incident involving a well-known automotive group resulting in hefty fines, many recalls, and much loss of reputation. In the first case, companies and individuals were able to circumvent security measures to apply a different calibration, which was more suited to their pocket, and in the second, it is alleged that vehicles were fitted by the manufacturer with an algorithm that detected test cycles and switched to a calibration more suited to achieving legislated emissions levels, whereas in normal operation a calibration able to demonstrate good fuel economy at the expense of worse emissions was employed.

As a result of the experience gained from changing engine calibrations, the industry has reacted with a far greater degree of internal policing, recognizing that short-term gains do not always translate to long-term profit, and this is reflected in the new Adaptive AUTOSAR standard, which carefully addresses items such as security of data and methods for updating vehicles in the field.

Many manufacturers are now looking at how vehicle calibrations may be updated conveniently while heeding all the considerations arising from this recent experience, and the result is that security is becoming sufficiently advanced and that future standards will clearly specify how calibrations may be uploaded over the air. This will result in lower costs as, for example, a "recall" need not involve customers physically taking their car to a garage, and indeed customers may in future be able to "opt-in" to a program of automatic updates. As leasing and just-in-time transport provision takes over as the major source of income for manufacturers (e.g., should the 2019 investment by BMW and Mercedes in their joint venture to challenge UBER bear fruit), the customer will have less of a say in the actual specification and specific range of features required in one vehicle and more of a say in the general comfort and safety of all vehicles provided. This model makes it all the more important to share data immediately; anything learned by one vehicle should be instantly available to all others. Rival providers will want to protect their data, and legislators will want to ensure that where public health and safety are concerned, they share it.

Take, for example, a mythical pothole avoidance system. This is conceived with the following advantages:

- A smoother ride for the occupants, meaning they will prefer this vehicle
- Less wear and tear on the suspension, resulting in lower costs
- Potential safety benefits because the risk of failure of safety-related items such as tires and steering is reduced

The system results in the following design:

- A pothole recognition system based upon images of the road ahead from multiple cameras
- Knowledge of the positions, speeds and estimated trajectories of other road users from existing systems
- Positions of other obstacles detected by existing systems
- Knowledge of own speed and trajectory
- Knowledge of road conditions with respect to braking distance, incline, and so on from existing systems
- Trajectory planning system based upon input from the previous items

- Control of engine, steering, and brakes resulting in a smooth change of trajectory

The implementations of the pothole recognition system and of the trajectory planning system may both use OpenVX graphs, the first with emphasis on image processing and object recognition and the second using a neural network to plan an optimum trajectory around the pothole that minimizes the risk of any wheel falling into the hole while maintaining a safe distance from other obstacles. The trajectory is updated in real time as the relative positions of obstacles and trajectories of other road users change.

An important consequence of using OpenVX graphs for these two large and complex items is that it is possible to treat the entire graphs like a calibration and change it effectively by uploading new data. The software on the vehicle utilizes the "deployment feature set" and imports the graph that has been created using the "development feature set" off-road back at base. Of course, like any calibration, there must be strict test and security protocols in place.

Thus generally improved pothole detection and avoidance algorithms may be achieved simply by calibration updates. However, if new data sources are required, then most likely the program will also have to change unless the implementation contains vendor-specific nodes that allow interfacing to existing data sources. A similar situation arises in the case of persistent data.

As an exercise for the reader, consider the following changes that you, as the pothole recognition system manufacturer, would like to introduce into your product. How feasible would it be to upgrade in the field: are changes to "calibration data" required alone, or are changes to the program also required?

- improved pothole recognition algorithm
- improved trajectory planning system
- consideration of weather conditions on pothole: for example, if it is raining, then the pothole may be deeper than it looks
- remembering the previous positions of potholes
- recalling previous experiences of failing to avoid a particular pothole: was it worse or better than expected? This "nonavoidance experience" is quantified in terms of vertical acceleration and disturbance to the steering system.
- consideration of possible effects of weather on a pothole since last encountering it (rain/frost may have worsened it, or heavy snowfall may have filled it)

- recognition of mended potholes and removal of them from the pothole memory
- sharing of data via a database (not in real time) with other vehicles
- offline sharing of data to the agency responsible for road maintenance
- offline removal of pothole data from the database by the agency responsible for road maintenance
- sharing of pothole data with other vehicles in real time
- sharing of trajectories with other vehicles in real time
- recording of pothole images from different distances
- recording of pothole nonavoidance experiences along with the images
- offline refinement of the pothole recognition algorithm using image data and nonavoidance experiences
- acquisition of pothole data from other sources (e.g., available from road maintenance agency or from specially commissioned survey) to link with visual data and improve the recognition algorithm
- adding ultrasonic depth measurement of a pothole beneath the vehicle in real time
- revenue from the sale of anonymized acquired data to the agency responsible for road maintenance

What data privacy considerations are relevant in these items: where must data be pseudonymized, and where must it be anonymized? All data need to be kept and transmitted securely to ensure safety, but where is encryption for secrecy also required?

As another exercise, consider the following enhancements provided by a mythical OpenVX implementation and already built into your product. In what ways could they assist your field upgrade process?

- A vendor kernel that can load a data object from a data source identified by a string; if the source is not ready, then the kernel may block for a specified delay (give zero for no blocking), and a Boolean output parameter indicates timeout expiry. The data object is of a type determined by the string, and there are other input parameters to further qualify the source of the data.
- A vendor kernel that can send a data object to a data sink identified by a string and further parameters. Again, a timeout value is an input parameter, and timeout expiry is an output parameter.
- The data sources and sinks may be in persistent memory (surviving reset) or from items such as sensors, indicators, or even remote databases in the cloud.
- The data objects involved are allowed to be virtual.

- All data are transmitted or stored with an error detection and correction algorithm and may optionally be encrypted.

We hope that this section has helped you appreciate the power of OpenVX graphs, particularly with respect to export and import, the development and deployment feature sets, and custom vendor kernels provided by your OpenVX supplier.

CHAPTER 12

Efficient data input/output

Contents

12.1 Introduction to efficient data I/O in OpenVX

Most of the efficiency considerations for vision processing come down to data movement. The execution time and power consumption required to execute a mathematical operation such as add or even multiply are dwarfed by the time and power it takes to fetch the operands from external DRAM. The data sets we need to manipulate in vision processing are too large to fit in the on-chip SRAM of a typical embedded device, so we must carefully manage and minimize transfers from external DRAM to internal SRAM. This principle applies, in particular, to the initial input of data to OpenVX. In a real-time high-resolution system the initial input may be a video stream of HD or larger images. If each of these large input images must be copied from the camera input area of memory to the OpenVX system memory, then the battle is lost before it has begun. Fortunately, the OpenVX API includes functions for zero-copy import of image data from input sources to the OpenVX processing engine. In this chapter, we describe the details of these functions and provide examples of how to use them.

In this chapter, we also describe the related topic of mapping and unmapping images and other data objects. One of the features of OpenVX objects that enables implementations to minimize data copies is that they are "opaque" in that the underlying memory location and organization where the data are stored are unknown to the programmer, and the data objects can only be manipulated via the API for that object, and not

Copyright © 2020 Elsevier Inc.
All rights reserved.

by poking directly at the memory where the object is stored. This enables implementations to do optimizations such as keeping a data object in special-purpose memory (e.g., on accelerator hardware) or reuse memory for different purposes without changing the end results of the graph computation. However, there are cases where an OpenVX application program needs direct access to portions of data objects, perhaps to perform special calculations on them that are not provided by the OpenVX API. We also describe the map and unmap functions used for this purpose.

12.2 Efficient data I/O from and to external sources

We start with a discussion of the functions for efficient data I/O from external sources. In vision processing, most of the high-volume data is on the input side, such as high-resolution video capture. The output of vision processing is typically a much lower data volume, for example, classification labels or motor commands. However, if the output required for an application is, for example, a high-resolution annotated video, then these functions can be used on the output side as well. Here we will provide examples referencing the camera input side, but the same principles and functions can be applied to output data.

There are two OpenVX functions that enable efficient input of data from capture devices such as cameras and secondarily to output devices such as displays: `vxCreateImageFromHandle` and `vxSwapImageHandle`. The `vxCreateImageFromHandle` function creates an OpenVX `vx_image` data structure that references the pixel data from the camera but does not copy it. This enables downstream OpenVX processing to fetch pixel data directly from where the camera placed it, without an intermediate "import" copy step to move the entire image from the camera memory area to an OpenVX memory area. (Note that, technically, there is a device separate from the camera, often called the "frame-grabber," which digitizes the camera data and puts it in the computer memory. Although it is more accurate to refer to the frame-grabber separately from the camera, in this chapter, we will just refer to the frame-grabber/camera image-capture system as the "camera.") The `vxCreateImageFromHandle` function effectively "wraps" the pixel data from the camera in a `vx_image` data structure that OpenVX can understand and use.

A typical camera places images in an area of memory with configurable location and data organization. It may use a collection of memory areas, or "buffers" and cycle through them, putting images in each buffer in turn until all the buffers have been filled, and then start over with the first buffer.

The simplest form of this is "double buffering," in which two buffers are used, say buffer A and buffer B. The camera fills buffer A with an input image and then proceeds to fill buffer B. While buffer B is being filled, buffer A can be processed by a vision system such as OpenVX. This enables the "current" image to be processed while the "next" image is being captured in parallel. More complex processing can be enabled with more buffers (i.e., triple-buffering, quadruple, etc.). We focus here on double-buffering, but it is a simple matter to extend to more buffers.

When using double-buffering as an input to an OpenVX graph, the first thing to do is to use the vxCreateImageFromHandle function with each of the buffers in order to create an OpenVX vx_image data structure that references the memory area where the camera is putting the data. Here is the header for this function:

```
vx_image vxCreateImageFromHandle(
    vx_context                              context,
    vx_df_image                             color,
    const vx_imagepatch_addressing_t addrs[],
    void* const                             ptrs[],
    vx_enum                                 memory_type);
```

Like many OpenVX functions, vxCreateImageFromHandle takes a context as its first parameter. This is the vx_context in which the resulting image object will be created. The second parameter is a vx_df_image code that indicates the format of each pixel in the image. In most cases, you can configure your camera to deliver 8-bit grayscale images, in which case you will use VX_DF_IMAGE_U8. If your camera only delivers color images, then you will need to use one of the color formats and extract or convert to grayscale U8 data via vxCreateImageFromChannel or a vxColorConvertNode.

The third parameter is a vx_imagepatch_addressing_t data structure that describes the organization of the pixel data in the input buffer. The fourth parameter is an array of memory pointers to the actual pixel data from the camera, one pointer per plane. For a single-plane U8 image, there is just one pointer to the upper-left pixel. The final parameter indicates the memory type of the pixel location: typically VX_MEMORY_TYPE_HOST.

The image patch addressing data structure you will need to provide bears more explanation. The fields of this structure are as follows:

```
typedef struct _vx_imagepatch_addressing_t {
    vx_uint32 dim_x;
    vx_uint32 dim_y;
```

```
    vx_int32  stride_x;
    vx_int32  stride_y;
    vx_uint32 scale_x;
    vx_uint32 scale_y;
    vx_uint32 step_x;
    vx_uint32 step_y;
    vx_uint16 stride_x_bits;
} vx_imagepatch_addressing_t;
```

The first two fields of this structure are the width (dim_x) and height (dim_y) of the captured images in pixels. The next two fields are the distances in bytes between adjacent pixels in the horizontal and vertical directions, respectively. For U8 images, stride_x is typically 1, and stride_y is typically equal to the width of the image (i.e., dim_x). This can vary if your camera puts extra space between pixels on a line (which is very unlikely) or if your camera puts extra space at the end of each line, which can happen, for example, if your image is an odd width and your camera rounds this up to the nearest power of two. The scale and step parameters are used for multiplanar images with different-sized planes; for our single-plane U8 example, they are set to 1. The stride_x_bits field is only used for binary (VX_DF_IMAGE_U1) images and can be ignored here.

The return value from vxCreateImageFromHandle is an OpenVX vx_image object as you might expect. The combination of the addressing structure and memory pointers comprise the "handle" that the vx_image is created from. The resulting vx_image can be used in a graph just like any other vx_image. The underlying pixel data are not moved or copied during the creation of this vx_image object. When a graph using this image is executed, it fetches the pixel data directly from the memory buffer where the camera placed it.

Let us look at an example of how to create an array of OpenVX vx_image objects from raw pixel data pointers to camera input buffers. In this case, we will use two buffers (for double buffering), and each buffer is a single U8 grayscale image. We can declare the camera input buffers and the array of two vx_image objects that will wrap the pixel data for use by OpenVX like so:

```
const int NUM_PLANES = 1;
const int NUM_BUFFERS = 2;
void* cam_ptr[NUM_BUFFERS][NUM_PLANES];
vx_image cam_image[NUM_BUFFERS];
```

The `cam_ptr` void pointers declared need to be filled with the locations of the camera buffers. Check the documentation for your image-capture system to determine these locations. Now we can construct the addressing structure that indicates to OpenVX how the camera data are organized. In this example, we only need one addressing structure for both camera buffers since they have the same format. There is only one `U8` plane in this example: plane `0`. The code goes on to fill in the fields of the addressing structure appropriately for a `U8` image that is `h_in` pixels high by `w_in` pixels wide, with no space between the pixels or image rows. The addressing structure also has fields for image scaling; use `VX_SCALE_UNITY` for unscaled images:

```
vx_imagepatch_addressing_t cam_addr[NUM_PLANES];
cam_addr[0].dim_x = w_in; cam_addr[0].dim_y = h_in;
cam_addr[0].stride_x = 1; cam_addr[0].stride_y = w_in;
cam_addr[0].scale_x = VX_SCALE_UNITY;
cam_addr[0].scale_y = VX_SCALE_UNITY;
cam_addr[0].step_x = 1; cam_addr[0].step_y = 1;
```

Finally, we create the `vx_image` objects that wrap the two input buffers of the camera:

```
for (i = 0; i < NUM_BUFFERS; i++) {
  cam_image[i] = vxCreateImageFromHandle(context, VX_DF_IMAGE_U8,
      cam_addr, cam_ptr[i], VX_MEMORY_TYPE_HOST);
}
```

These images can now be used as inputs to an OpenVX graph just like any other `vx_image` object. We will show how to do this in a simple example that takes an HD input image, scales it down by a factor of 4 in each direction, and then runs a Canny edge detector over it. The graph for this is depicted in Fig. 12.1. There are just two nodes in the graph, one to scale the image and another to run the Canny edge detector. The input comes from the camera, and the output goes to a display.

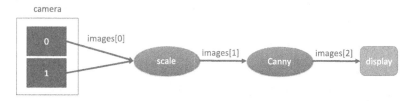

Figure 12.1 A simple graph that captures camera data, processes and displays it.

There are three `vx_image` objects in the graph as well. The first one (`images[0]`) is the input image from the camera. The second one (`images[1]`) is the intermediate scaled image, and the third one (`images[2]`) is the output Canny edge image to be displayed. Let's look at how these images are created. We start by defining a few constant values for the image sizes and threshold values for the Canny algorithm. Then we create the graph object itself:

```
const vx_uint32 w_in = 1080, h_in = 1920;
const int scale = 4;
const int w = w_in/scale; // scaled image width
const int h = h_in/scale; // scaled image height
vx_pixel_value_t hi_thresh, lo_thresh;
hi_thresh.U8 = (vx_uint8)120;
lo_thresh.U8 = (vx_uint8)15;
vx_context context = vxCreateContext();
vx_graph graph = vxCreateGraph(context);
```

Now we will create the images. We use the `vxCreateImageFromHandle` function to create `images[0]`, using the pointer to the camera's first buffer (`cam_ptr[0]`) and the camera addressing structure we created previously. The intermediate `images[1]` is created as a virtual image, and the output `images[2]` is a regular `vx_image`. Here is the code:

```
// Create images needed for the graph
vx_image images[] = {
  // 0. input:
  vxCreateImageFromHandle(context, VX_DF_IMAGE_U8, cam_addr,
      cam_ptr[0], VX_MEMORY_TYPE_HOST),
  // 1. scaled input (intermediate):
  vxCreateVirtualImage(graph, w, h, VX_DF_IMAGE_U8),
  // 2. Canny edge image (output):
  vxCreateImage(context, w, h, VX_DF_IMAGE_U8),
};
```

Now we can create the graph nodes. One of the nodes is the Canny edge detector, which requires a threshold object, so we will create that too. Finally, we will verify the graph.

```
// Create the threshold object needed for Canny
vx_threshold thresh =
  vxCreateThresholdForImage(context, VX_THRESHOLD_TYPE_RANGE,
      VX_DF_IMAGE_U8, VX_DF_IMAGE_U8);
```

```
// Set the threshold values
vxCopyThresholdRange(thresh, &lo_thresh, &hi_thresh, VX_WRITE_ONLY,
    VX_MEMORY_TYPE_HOST);

// Create the graph nodes
vx_node nodes[] = {
  vxScaleImageNode(graph, images[0], images[1], VX_INTERPOLATION_AREA),
  vxCannyEdgeDetectorNode(graph, images[1], thresh, 3, VX_NORM_L1,
      images[2]),
};
// Verify the graph
if (vxVerifyGraph(graph) != VX_SUCCESS) goto exit;
```

Now that we have constructed the graph depicted in Fig. 12.1, can feed it images from the camera. To do this, we will use the `vxSwapImageHandle` function that enables us to alternate between the two camera capture buffers. This function takes a `vx_image` object and a set of pointers to new pixel data, and replaces the image object's underlying data pointers with the given pointers. It returns the pointers to the previous image data. A final parameter just indicates the number of planes the image has:

```
vxSwapImageHandle(image, new_ptrs, prev_ptrs, NUM_PLANES);
```

Using this function, we can have the graph input image alternate between the two camera capture buffers. We will use two sets of pointers to the image pixels, `new_ptrs` and `prev_ptrs`, as declared as below, and set the `new_ptrs` to point to the second camera capture buffer:

```
void *new_ptrs[NUM_PLANES], *prev_ptrs[NUM_PLANES];
for (i = 0; i < NUM_PLANES; i++) new_ptrs[i] = cam_ptr[1][i];
```

Now we have the graph input image connected to the first camera capture buffer (`cam_ptr[0]`) and the `new_ptrs` connected to the second camera capture buffer (`cam_ptr[1]`), and we are ready to start our video processing loop. Here is the code for the processing loop:

```
int nextbuf = 1;

// Read the first input image into camera buffer 0
vx_bool newframe = myCaptureImage(0);
```

```
// Start the processing loop
while (newframe == vx_true_e) {

    // Launch the graph (could be in parallel with the capture below)
    if (vxScheduleGraph(graph) != VX_SUCCESS) goto exit;

    // Capture the next input image into the 'other' camera buffer
    //  while the graph runs
    newframe = myCaptureImage(nextbuf);

    // Wait for graph to complete
    if (vxWaitGraph(graph) != VX_SUCCESS) goto exit;

    // Display the output results
    myDisplayImage(images[2]);

    // Prepare for the next frame
    vxSwapImageHandle(images[0], new_ptrs, prev_ptrs, NUM_PLANES);

    // Save the returned ptrs for next iteration
    for (i = 0; i < NUM_PLANES; i++) new_ptrs[i] = prev_ptrs[i];
    nextbuf = (nextbuf == 0) ? 1 : 0; // toggle nextbuf
}
```

This code uses a hypothetical function called myCaptureImage to capture a live image into the indicated camera buffer (0 or 1) and myDisplayImage to display a given vx_image on a screen. The myCaptureImage function returns a Boolean value to indicate whether an image was successfully captured, and the processing loop exits when it returns false.

The first time the graph is run via vxScheduleGraph, it is run on the data captured into cam_ptr[0], because when we created images[0], we used vxCreateImageFromHandle to connect it to cam_ptr[0]. The first image capture inside the loop captures a live image into the other camera buffer (cam_ptr[1]). This capture can occur in parallel with the processing of the data in cam_ptr[0]. We wait for the processing to complete via vxWaitGraph and display the results.

Before looping back to the next image capture, we use vxSwapImageHandle to change the graph input image (images[0]) to point to the "other" camera buffer. Finally, we copy the prev_ptrs returned by vxSwapImageHandle to the new_ptrs to prepare for the next frame, and toggle the nextbuf indicator from 0 to 1 or vice versa. This code alternates processing between the two camera capture buffers without copying any of the pixel data; only the pointers to it are copied.

12.3 Gaining access to data objects via map and unmap

Having OpenVX object be opaque enables the implementation to perform optimizations that minimize memory movement and usage, but sometimes the application program needs to look at the data and perhaps manipulate it before allowing OpenVX to process it further. The map and unmap functions enable this capability. Mapping an OpenVX object places its underlying data in a fixed CPU-accessible location with a defined organization that can be read and written by the application program.

In some sense, this defeats the purpose of having opaque data objects, so this facility should be used with care. Depending on the implementation and the underlying hardware, using map and unmap can result in expensive data copies. For example, if the data object is a vx_image and the underlying hardware contains a GPU with a video memory separate from the CPU memory, then OpenVX may store the image in the GPU memory for efficient access by the GPU. Mapping the image may require copying its data from GPU memory to CPU memory, which can be expensive in terms of time and power consumption. On a different platform where the GPU or other accelerator shares a common memory with the CPU, map and unmap may just require some message and pointer passing without copying the underlying data. These potential differences in hardware platforms on which OpenVX runs can result in very different performance profiles for the same OpenVX program if map and unmap are heavily used, which defeats the goal of OpenVX being performance-portable. For these reasons, map and unmap should be used sparingly.

But almost every real OpenVX program needs some CPU access to object data, and when used appropriately, this is not an issue. OpenVX provided map and unmap functions for all the data objects that are (potentially large) collections of data, such as the vx_array and the vx_image, which is essentially a collection of pixels and some metadata. The full list of objects supporting map/unmap is as follows:

```
vx_array      vx_distribution    vx_image
vx_lut        vx_remap           vx_tensor
```

One way to think of the map/unmap feature is that it transfers ownership of the data from the OpenVX implementation to the application program and back again. The application data has no access or "owner-ship" of the data until it calls a map function. After mapping, the application "owns" the data and can do what it wants with it. When the application is done, it should unmap the data to transfer ownership back to OpenVX. Keep in mind that if you do not follow these ownership rules, then your program probably will not behave as expected. For example, if you forget to unmap an object when you are done with it and proceed to use that object in an OpenVX graph, then the object possibly will not have your updates, and different implementations will behave differently.

Another important thing to note is that you cannot map virtual objects. Virtual objects enable the implementation to perform optimizations that eliminate the existence of the object, so mapping the object would not make any sense. Declaring an object as virtual is a promise never to map the object to view its contents, so OpenVX can do what it wants with it, including optimizing it away. If you try to map a virtual object, then depending on the implementation, you might get an error, or it might work fine, or you might get strange behavior. It is unfair to the OpenVX implementation to declare an object as virtual and then try to map it. The flip side of this is that if you have objects that you never map, then you should declare them as virtual, so that OpenVX can do the best possible job of optimizing.

12.3.1 Mapping image patches

We start with an in-depth discussion of map/unmap using the vx_image functions as an example, and then briefly describe map/unmap for the other objects, which behave similarly. The map function for vx_image objects is vxMapImagePatch, which as you can tell by the name is designed to provide access to a small portion or rectangular "patch" of the image. Of course, you can get the entire image by requesting a patch that covers the entire thing, but if your application allows, then it is more efficient to map small subsets of the image. The function header and parameters of the vxMapImagePatch function are as follows:

```
vx_status vxMapImagePatch(
    vx_image                    image,
    const vx_rectangle_t*       rect,
    vx_uint32                   plane_index,
    vx_map_id*                  map_id,
    vx_imagepatch_addressing_t* addr,
    void**                      ptr,
```

```
vx_enum              usage,
vx_enum              mem_type,
vx_uint32            flags);
```

The first three parameters specify the image patch you want to access. The `image` parameter is simply the image object you want to access. The `rect` parameter defines the coordinates of the image patch you want and must be within the bounds of the image. If you want the entire image, then your rectangle should use (0, 0) for the upper left and (width-1, height-1) for the lower right. The `plane_index` parameter indicates which plane of the image you want to access; use 0 for a single-plane image.

The next three parameters are output parameters that describe the patch you receive from OpenVX as a result of this call. The first of these is a `map_id`, which is simply an identifying number for the patch you are retrieving. You will need this ID later when you unmap the patch to give it back to OpenVX. The next output parameter is an image patch addressing structure, which is the same structure we used when creating images from handles earlier in this chapter. However, in this case, it is an *output* parameter. So instead of the application telling OpenVX how the data are organized, OpenVX tells the application how the image patch data are organized. You will use this information when accessing the individual pixels. The last output parameter (sixth overall) is a pointer (`ptr`) to the actual patch data retrieved by the map call, typically the memory location of the upper left corner of the patch.

The last three parameters are input flags that specify a few details. The `usage` parameter tells OpenVX how the application intends to use the patch data. The options are VX_READ_ONLY, VX_READ_AND_WRITE, and VX_WRITE_ONLY. The most permissive of these options is VX_READ_AND_WRITE, which allows the application to read all the patch data and write over it, and when the patch is unmapped, the image object reflects any changes made to the image patch by the application. To accomplish this, the OpenVX implementation may have to copy the patch data back and forth. If your application needs to read or only write the image patch, then you should use one of the other parameters, which avoids one of the copies. If you use VX_READ_ONLY, then OpenVX does not have to copy the patch data back to the image object when you unmap. If you use VX_WRITE_ONLY, then OpenVX does not have to fill the initial image patch with data from the image object, since you are not going to read it, you only write. Be sure to write the *entire* image patch if you use this option; otherwise, you will put uninitialized data into the image object when you unmap. Do not lie to OpenVX about how you are going to access the patch. If you write to a patch you said you are only going to read or vice versa, your program has a bug and it's undetermined as to what actually happens. On one implementation, it may work as you might expect, whereas on another one, it will crash, so don't do it.

The mem_type parameter tells OpenVX what type of memory you want the image patch mapped to. The only legal value here in the standard is VX_MEMORY_TYPE_HOST, so the host CPU can access the data. Implementations from specific vendors may allow additional options; for example, a GPU vendor may offer an option to map the patch to GPU memory. The last parameter is flags and is mostly just for vendor extensions. You can usually just use 0 (no flags). The only other possible value defined by the spec is VX_NOGAP_X, which indicates that you do not want any space between pixels on the same line in the patch. In other words, this forces the stride_x field of the returned addressing structure to be 1.

OpenVX provides a couple of functions to help you address individual pixels in the image you just mapped, vxFormatImagePatchAddress1d and vxFormatImagePatchAddress2d. The first allows you to address the i_{th} pixel, treating the pixels as a long one-dimensional array. After mapping your patch, call it like this to write MY_NEW_VALUE into every pixel:

```
for (i = 0; i < addr.dim_x*addr.dim_y; i++) {
    vx_uint8 *ptr2 = vxFormatImagePatchAddress1d(ptr, i, &addr);
    *ptr2 = MY_NEW_VALUE;
}
```

The ptr and addr parameters are returned from vxMapImagePatch. In this case, we should have used VX_WRITE_ONLY when we mapped, since we just write the pixel data and do not read it.

The other method is to address the pixels in (x, y) fashion as a normal two-dimensional array using vxFormatImagePatchAddress2d like this:

```
for (y = 0; y < addr.dim_y; y+=addr.step_y) {
    for (x = 0; x < addr.dim_x; x+=addr.step_x) {
        vx_uint8 *ptr2 = vxFormatImagePatchAddress2d(ptr, x, y, &addr);
        *ptr2 = MY_NEW_VALUE;
    }
}
```

When we are done, we need to be sure to unmap to return ownership of the pixels back to OpenVX. This is a simple unmap call, using the same image we mapped in the first place and the ID returned by the map function:

```
vxUnmapImagePatch(image, map_id);
```

If all you want to do is copy an image patch from an image object to host memory, or from host memory to an image object, then OpenVX provides a short-cut for this called vxCopyImagePatch. The effect is to do a map-copy-unmap sequence, and the function looks like this:

```
vx_status vxCopyImagePatch(
    vx_image                            image,
    const vx_rectangle_t*               rect,
    vx_uint32                           plane_index,
    const vx_imagepatch_addressing_t*   user_addr,
    void*                               user_ptr,
    vx_enum                             usage,
    vx_enum                             user_mem_type);
```

The parameters are pretty much the same as those for vxMapImagePatch except that the addressing structure user_addr and data pointer user_ptr are *input* parameters describing the user memory area to copy the data to or from, and this user memory area must be preallocated and of the right size, or you will get a memory error. The usage parameter indicates whether the copy is to or from the image object. If the usage is VX_READ_ONLY, then the copy is from the image object to user memory, and if the usage is VX_WRITE_ONLY, then the copy is from the user memory to the image object.

12.3.2 More on pixel addressing

Now it is a good time to examine the pixel addressing structure in more detail. We used this structure as an argument to the image creation and mapping functions above. Recall that it has components for dim, stride, scale, and step in both the x and y directions:

```
typedef struct _vx_imagepatch_addressing_t {
    vx_uint32 dim_x;        vx_uint32 dim_y;
    vx_int32 stride_x;      vx_int32 stride_y;
    vx_uint32 scale_x;      vx_uint32 scale_y;
    vx_uint32 step_x;       vx_uint16 step_y;
    vx_uint16 stride_x_bits;
} vx_imagepatch_addressing_t;
```

So what is the purpose of each component and what is the difference between them? Looking at a diagram and the sample implementation of the vxFormatImagePatchAddress2d function can help clarify this. Consider the small 6-by-8 pixel image in the diagram of Fig. 12.2 below. It is a color image in YUV 4:2:0 format, which in OpenVX is indicated by the data format VX_DF_IMAGE_IYUV (see Section 6.1). In this color format the color channels (U and V) are half the resolution of the brightness channel (Y).

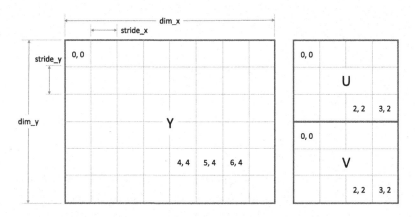

Figure 12.2 A small YUV 4:2:0 color image.

The dim component is straightforward, dim_x is 8 and dim_y is 6. Since the VX_DF_IMAGE_IYUV has 8-bit pixels, stride_x is 1. Note that whereas dim is in *pixels*, stride is in *bytes*. So stride_x is 1 because each pixel is one byte in size. If we had 16-bit pixels, we had have to move 2 bytes to get to the next pixel, and stride_x would be 2. In the y direction, stride_y is the number of bytes we have to move to get from a given pixel to the one immediately below it. If the rows of the image are contiguous in memory, then stride_y is dim_x times the pixel size, and so for 8-bit images, stride_y = dim_x. However, the rows of the image might *not* be contiguous in memory; there might be some extra space at the end of each line, so use stride_y instead of dim_x to move down a row.

The scale comes in when we consider the color channels. Each channel has its own scale relative to the "primary" channel, which in this case is channel 0, or the Y channel. This scale is a ratio that would naturally be indicated via a floating point number, but OpenVX avoids the use of floating point numbers for efficiency, which is where VX_SCALE_UNITY comes in. The numbers in the scale component of the addressing structure are implicitly divided by VX_SCALE_UNITY, which in the OpenVX sample implementation is set to 1024.

In the case of the Y channel the scale is the size of the Y channel relative to itself, so by definition the scale of the Y channel is 1.0. To express this in OpenVX, the scale of the Y channel should be set to VX_SCALE_UNITY, which when divided by VX_SCALE_UNITY (i.e., itself) yields 1.0. For the color channels, the scale is 0.5. To express this in OpenVX, the scale of the color channels is set to VX_SCALE_UNITY/2. In the sample implementation, this would be 512, and when this is divided by VX_SCALE_UNITY, we get 0.5. In general, set the scale factor to VX_SCALE_UNITY/$(1/f)$, where f is the scale factor you indeed want. Normally, the implementation does this for you, so you do not have to worry about it.

This all comes together in the expression used by vxFormatImagePatch-Address2d to find the location of a given pixel (x, y) in an image. The offset from the base pointer is computed as follows:

```
(addr->stride_y * ((addr->scale_y * y)/VX_SCALE_UNITY)) +
(addr->stride_x * ((addr->scale_x * x)/VX_SCALE_UNITY))
```

The x and y values are scaled using integer arithmetic, multiplying by the scale components of the addressing structure addr and dividing by VX_SCALE_UNITY. The resulting y value is multiplied by stride_y to get to the right row. The resulting x value is likewise multiplied by stride_x to get to the right byte in the row. The x and y values are added together to get the total byte offset.

We still have not used the step component of the addressing structure. It is a kind of way to undo the scale component, and you could argue that it can be computed from the scale, but OpenVX gives it to you, so you don't have to. The step component is in pixels, and the spec says it's "the number of logical pixel units to skip to arrive at the next physically unique pixel." In typical unscaled images the physical pixel is one pixel over or down, so the step is 1. In scaled images, it may be larger. In the YUV image above for example, the step for the Y component is 1, but for the U and V components, it is 2. To see why, consider pixels (4, 4) and (5, 4) in the Y channel. After applying the scale to (4, 4), the corresponding pixel in the U and V images is at (2, 2). Due to the truncation inherent in integer arithmetic, applying the scale to (5, 4) in the Y channel *also* maps to (2, 2) in the U and V channels, which is *not* the next physical pixel in U and V; it is the same pixel again. If you want to address your pixels using the `vxFormatImagePatchAddress2d` function, which applies the scale, then you need to step *two* pixels if you want to get to the next actual color value. If you want to walk through the values of the color channel using `vxFormatImagePatchAddress2d`, then you do not step by 1, but rather by `addr.step_x` and `addr.step_y` like this:

```
for (y = 0; y < addr.dim_y; y+=addr.step_y) {
    for (x = 0; x < addr.dim_x; x+=addr.step_x) {
        vx_uint8 *ptr = vxFormatImagePatchAddress2d(base, x, y, &addr);
        *ptr = value->U8;
    }
}
```

That's the story on accessing image data; now let's look at map/unmap for the other objects.

12.3.3 Mapping arrays

To map a portion of a `vx_array` object to host memory to read or write it, use `vxMapArrayRange`:

```
vx_status vxMapArrayRange(
    vx_array    array,
    vx_size     start,
    vx_size     end,
    vx_map_id*  map_id,
    vx_size*    stride,
    void**      ptr,
    vx_enum     usage,
    vx_enum     mem_type,
    vx_uint32   flags);
```

The parameters are similar to those for mapping an image patch. The first three parameters (`array`, `start`, and `end`) specify the array and the portion of it you want to map. Arrays are simpler than images, so instead of using a rectangle and plane index, all you need specify is a start and end of the array range you want to map. The next three parameters (`map_id`, `stride`, and `ptr`) describe the data area returned by the map operation: an ID, a stride, and a pointer to the data. The stride takes the place of the addressing structure in mapping image patches, since for arrays all you need to know is how far it is in bytes from one array element to the next. The last three parameters (`usage`, `mem_type`, and `flags`) function identically to the way they do in image mapping. When you are done with the array, just unmap it using `vxUnmapArrayRange(array, map_id)`. There is also a `vxCopyArrayRange`, which works the same as copying image patches:

```
vx_status vxCopyArrayRange(
    vx_array     array,
    vx_size      range_start,
    vx_size      range_end,
    vx_size      user_stride,
    void*        user_ptr,
    vx_enum      usage,
    vx_enum      user_mem_type);
```

12.3.4 Mapping distributions

Mapping distributions is even simpler, because you do not have the option to map a portion of it; you always map the whole thing. You do not need an addressing structure or even a stride because it is always an array of `vx_uint32` values. The parameters to `vxMapDistribution` behave identically to the other map functions:

```
vx_status vxMapDistribution(
    vx_distribution    distribution,
    vx_map_id*         map_id,
    void**             ptr,
    vx_enum            usage,
    vx_enum            mem_type,
    vx_bitfield        flags);
```

The `vx_bitfield` is just an integer like the other flags, and you should always use 0 here. Unmap with `vxUnmapDistribution(distribution, map_id)`. Here is the distribution copy function, which requires no further explanation:

```
vx_status vxCopyDistribution(
    vx_distribution    distribution,
    void*              user_ptr,
    vx_enum            usage,
    vx_enum            user_mem_type);
```

12.3.5 Mapping LUTs

The look-up table (vx_lut) map/unmap and copy functions are similarly trivial to the vx_distribution versions. One difference is the size of the elements, which depends on the VX_LUT_TYPE of a LUT. Otherwise, everything is the same as for distributions. Use vxUnmapLUT(lut, map_id) to unmap:

```
vx_status vxMapLUT(
    vx_lut      lut,
    vx_map_id*  map_id,
    void**      ptr,
    vx_enum     usage,
    vx_enum     mem_type,
    vx_bitfield flags);


vx_status vxCopyLUT(
    vx_lut      lut,
    void*       user_ptr,
    vx_enum     usage,
    vx_enum     user_mem_type);
```

12.3.6 Mapping remap objects

The remap object is an object that describes how to transform an image into a warped version of it. The warp is defined by a two-dimensional array of coordinates that specify where in the input image to find the pixel value that "maps" to the given output pixel, that is:

```
output(x,y) = input(mapx(x,y), mapy(x,y))
```

The word "map" here is overloaded to mean both the mapping of input pixels to output pixels by the vx_remap object and also the mapping of object data to user space as in the other "map" functions described in this chapter. This overloading results in the unfortunate names vxMapRemapPatch and vxUnmapRemapPatch for the functions that map and unmap portions of a vx_remap object data to user space where it can be manipulated by the application. The vxMapRemapPatch function header is as follows:

```
vx_status vxMapRemapPatch(
    vx_remap                remap,
    const vx_rectangle_t*   rect,
    vx_map_id*              map_id,
    vx_size*                stride_y,
```

```
void**              ptr,
vx_enum             coordinate_type,
vx_enum             usage,
vx_enum             mem_type);
```

This function bears similarities to the vxMapImagePatch function in that it returns a 2D portion or "patch" of data from the given object. The mapping of remap objects is a bit simpler that for image objects though, because we do not have to deal with multiple planes, for example. Moreover, the only value allowed by the OpenVX standard for the coordinate_type parameter is VX_TYPE_COORDINATES2DF, so the remap patch returned is always just an array of pairs of 32-bit floating-point numbers. The rows of this array are not necessarily contiguous, so we need a "stride" parameter to tell us how far it is from one row of the array to the next.

The first parameter to vxMapRemapPatch is the vx_remap object we are interested in, and the second parameter specifies the rectangular subset of the remap object we want. As with images, this rectangle can cover the entire object if we want the whole thing.

The next three parameters are the map function output values that describe the remap patch returned by the vxMapRemapPatch function. The map_id is as with previous functions and is needed when we unmap later. The stride_y parameter indicates the distance in bytes between a given remap coordinate and the one immediately below it in the patch. The ptr parameter is the pointer to the upper left corner of the remap patch's actual coordinate data.

The coordinate_type parameter specifies the coordinate structure of the remap patch; the only allowed value here is VX_TYPE_COORDINATES2DF. The usage and mem_type parameters are the same as in the other map functions described previously. Use vxUnmapRemapPatch(remap, map_id) to unmap.

As with the other mappable objects, a copy function is also provided, which behaves as the others, with the direction of the copy indicated by the usage parameter:

```
vx_status vxCopyRemapPatch(
    vx_remap                remap,
    const vx_rectangle_t*   rect,
    vx_size*                user_stride_y,
    void*                   user_ptr,
    vx_enum                 user_coordinate_type,
    vx_enum                 usage,
    vx_enum                 user_mem_type);
```

As with the other copy functions, the `user_ptr`, `user_stride`, and `user_mem_type` parameters are *input* parameters describing the user's memory area in the application space that is being copied to or from.

12.3.7 Mapping tensors

Finally, we have the mapping and unmapping functions for `vx_tensor` objects. These functions have similarities to the corresponding functions for images and remap objects, in that the data retrieved are a portion, or "patch" of the object data. Whereas the image and remap patches are two-dimensional, the tensor patches are *n*-dimensional. The number of dimensions can be as high as `VX_CONTEXT_MAX_TENSOR_DIMS`, which depends on the OpenVX implementation but must be at least 4. So the "patch" of a tensor is not just a 2D rectangle, but rather an *n*-dimensional rectangular prism. This rectangular prism is defined by *arrays* of start- and end-points, and the size of these arrays is specified by the `number_of_dims` parameter, which must be equal to the number of dimensions of the tensor itself. The rest of the parameters to `vxMapTensorPatch` should be familiar by now:

```
vx_status vxMapTensorPatch(
    vx_tensor        tensor,
    vx_size          number_of_dims,
    const vx_size*   view_start,
    const vx_size*   view_end,
    vx_map_id*       map_id,
    vx_size*         stride,
    void**           ptr,
    vx_enum          usage,
    vx_enum          mem_type);
```

The first two parameters are the tensor itself and the number of dimensions it has. The next two parameters define the corners of the rectangular prism we want to retrieve. The OpenVX spec refers to portions of tensors as "views," so these parameters are called `view_start` and `view_end`, and each is an array of indices with `number_of_dims` elements. For tensors, OpenVX provides a shortcut if you want to retrieve the entire tensor. The value `NULL` can be passed in for these arrays, in which case the `view_start` parameter defaults to an array of all zeros of appropriate size, and the `view_end` parameter defaults to the full dimensions of the tensor.

The next three parameters (`map_id`, `stride`, and `ptr`) are the output values of the `vxMapTensorPatch` function that describe the patch mapped into user space. The `map_id` is just for unmapping as usual, and the `ptr` points to the upper-left-front-whatever corner of the patch. The `stride` in this case is another *n*-dimensional array, and indicates how far it is in bytes from one element of the patch to the next one in the direction of the corresponding dimension. Unmap the patch with `vxUnmapTensorPatch(tensor, map_id)` when you are done with it.

The now-familiar copy-patch function is also provided, with the usual parameters, only in this case the `view_start`, `view_end`, and `user_stride` input parameters are arrays, each with `number_of_dims` elements, and they describe the data area in application space to be copied to or from, depending on the `usage` parameter:

```
vx_status vxCopyTensorPatch(
    vx_tensor          tensor,
    vx_size            number_of_dims,
    const vx_size*     view_start,
    const vx_size*     view_end,
    const vx_size*     user_stride,
    void*              user_ptr,
    vx_enum            usage,
    vx_enum            user_memory_type);
```

12.4 Conclusion

In this chapter, we have shown how to efficiently access OpenVX data, either from external devices or from the host CPU for manipulation by the application. The two OpenVX functions `vxCreateImageFromHandle` and `vxSwapImageHandle` efficiently capture and process data from a double-buffering camera capture device without requiring a data copy. By using the asynchronous `vxScheduleGraph` function you can process the current frame while the next frame is being captured, lowering overall latency. You can easily modify and extend the sample code provided to suit your capture device and processing and display needs, for example, to have more capture buffers or use a different capture or display interface.

The map and unmap functions enable access to the data inside various OpenVX objects that are collections of data. They may or may not require a data copy, depending on the access mode and implementation. Judicious use of these functions is required by nearly every production OpenVX program, but overuse can cause extra copies and poor performance, as well as performance that varies widely across implementations. Be sure to minimize the amount of data you access and use the most efficient access mode for your needs.

The copy functions require a data copy by definition, so you will want to minimize their use. If you know your mapping/unmapping will require a copy anyway, then these copy functions provide an easy-to-use shortcut. However, if you find you are spending a lot of time in data copies, then consider replacing them with map/unmap pairs, which can eliminate copies on some implementations. Be sure not to access and entire image/array/tensor/etc. when you only need a piece of it. Touching only the portion of the data you need can make a big difference in performance and power consumption from memory access.

CHAPTER 13

Interoperability between OpenVX and other frameworks

Contents

Software developers often prefer to use standard programming SDKs to accelerate their applications. So far you have read about how to accelerate vision and AI workloads using the standard OpenVX functions and OpenVX graphs. In real-world situations, you have to accelerate parts of the application that go beyond the standard OpenVX functions. These include application specific preprocessing and postprocessing on the OpenVX graph inputs/outputs, and new algorithms that may not map well to the standard OpenVX functions.

In such cases, you can implement these algorithms using OpenVX user kernels and insert them into OpenVX graphs seamlessly to take advantage of OpenVX graph optimizations. Unfortunately, the OpenVX standard currently only supports user kernels that can be scheduled on the host. Use of the `vxCopyXxx` or `vxMapXxx`/`vxUnmapXxx` APIs to exchange data buffers between OpenVX and any of the programming SDKs result in data copies back-and-forth between the target device and the host whenever a user kernel is scheduled. At times, it may not even be practical to wrap these

Copyright © 2020 Elsevier Inc.
All rights reserved.

functions inside OpenVX user kernels because of how the corresponding external components gets plugged into your application. This introduces additional data copies into the processing pipeline that cannot be optimized away by the OpenVX graph optimizer.

Most of the time, these copies between the target device and host are redundant because both the OpenVX graph and the other processing end up running on the same device or run on multiple devices with a direct DMA path between them. These host-side copies can end up significantly slowing down the overall system performance.

To overcome these inefficiencies, OpenVX supports a mechanism to exchange memory handles via the `vxCopyXxx`, `vxMapXxx/vxUnMapXxx`, `vxCreateXxxFromHandle`, and `vxSwapXxxHandle` APIs, where a handle represents pointer in the host address space, or device address space, or an opaque data object defined by the programmable SDKs. It is hard to standardize the device address space because of complexity and variety of memory hierarchy in heterogenous systems. This resulted in the OpenVX standard defining only the `VX_MEMORY_TYPE_HOST` handle type, which is meant for pointers in the host address space. Luckily, these APIs can be extended to support memory handles across various heterogenous systems that include GPUs, DSPs, FPGAs, and so on.

The use of the `vxCreateXxxFromHandle` and `vxSwapXxxHandle` for acquiring data from a camera has already been covered in Chapter 12. Here we review the data exchange model between OpenVX and OpenCV and then explain the basics of OpenCL and a mechanism for interoperation between OpenVX and OpenCL applications.

13.1 OpenCV

OpenCV http://opencv.org is one of the most widely adopted computer vision libraries, and OpenVX was designed to be used with OpenCV. Since OpenCV is not necessarily going to be available on a platform that supports OpenVX, the OpenVX API cannot depend on OpenCV. The most of OpenVX data structures is opaque, and an implementation can store data outside of the host memory, so making internal OpenVX data structures compatible with OpenCV is also out of question. So the only connection between the two libraries is through the OpenVX external data structures that are guaranteed to be stored in the host memory. The possible use cases of OpenVX with OpenCV fall into two categories:

1. Opencv is used outside of an OpenVX graph, either to create input data or process output data. A typical example is creating an application for a desktop platform that processes a video stream from a webcam with OpenVX. OpenCV can be used to fetch a video stream from a camera and feed it to an OpenVX graph. Also, OpenCV can be used to implement a part of vision pipeline outside the OpenVX graph. (However, we encourage developers to consider using user nodes for such scenarios.)

2. Opencv is used inside an OpenVX graph to implement user nodes. In practice, given the limited functionality of OpenVX, a developer has to resort to user nodes for any pipelines that are even moderately complex. Putting all functionality in one graph instead of running several graphs mixed with OpenCV code in between allows an OpenVX implementation to better plan data management, which on some platforms can give a significant performance benefit.

Both categories require efficient data transfer between the two libraries. This is why OpenVX `Map/Unmap` functions support data formats compatible with OpenCV. Let us look at the code of the open-source library VXA [31] to see how we can move data between the two frameworks. To simplify the examples in this chapter for readability, we sacrifice data exchange efficiency by creating full copies of images. See Section 13.2.1 and Chapter 12 for examples of more efficient data exchange implemented with `vxCreateXxxFromHandle` and `vxSwapXxxHandle`.

First, let us see how an OpenVX image can be created from an OpenCV image.

13.1.1 Convert an OpenCV image to OpenVX

The creation of an OpenVX image given an OpenCV `cv::Mat` object is implemented in the VXA function `vxa_cv2vx`. It starts by checking the OpenCV image type:

```
vx_image vxa_cv2vx(const cv::Mat& cv_img, vx_context context)
{
  vx_df_image img_type;
  switch(cv_img.type())
  {
    case CV_8UC1:
      img_type = VX_DF_IMAGE_U8;
      break;
```

```
case CV_8UC3:
  img_type = VX_DF_IMAGE_RGB;
  break;

default:
  return(NULL);
}
```

This function converts only 8-bit greyscale and RGB color images, re-turning an error for the rest of the image types. Images with other types, such as CV_16SC1, can also be efficiently converted to OpenVX images, but the implementation of this particular VXA function is limited to 8-bit im-ages only. Now we create an OpenVX image with the same dimensions as the input image. An OpenCV image is represented as a matrix, so the width and height of an OpenCV image are the numbers of columns and rows, stored in cv::Mat::cols and cv::Mat::rows, respectively. Note that an OpenVX context is an input argument to this function as it is required for the image creation functions:

```
int width = cv_img.cols, height = cv_img.rows;
vx_image image = vxCreateImage(context, width, height, img_type);
```

Now we prepare data for vxMapImagePatch (see Section 12.3.1) and make the call. Note the VX_WRITE_ONLY parameter; we are going to writing to the OpenVX image, so any data that was there will be overwritten:

```
vx_rectangle_t roi;
roi.start_x = 0;
roi.start_y = 0;
roi.end_x = width;
roi.end_y = height;

vx_map_id map_id;
vx_imagepatch_addressing_t addr;
unsigned char* ptr;

vx_status status = vxMapImagePatch(image, &roi, 0, &map_id, &addr,
  (void**)&ptr, VX_WRITE_ONLY, VX_MEMORY_TYPE_HOST, VX_NOGAP_X);
if(status != VX_SUCCESS)
{
  VXA_PRINT("vxMapImagePatch returned error with code %d\n", status);
  return(NULL);
}
```

The pointer to the image data and other information such as image stride (the length of a scanline in bytes) is contained in the structure `addr` of type `vx_imagepatch_addressing_t` (see Section 12.3.2). Now it is important to point out the difference in image layout between OpenCV and OpenVX. OpenCV uses dense representation of a scanline. For example, consider the greyscale 8-bit OpenCV image. The first pixel in a scanline has the address `p` of type `char*`, then the `n`th pixel will have the address `p + n`. There are no gaps between pixels. However, there may be a gap between different scanlines, so that the stride (the difference between pointers to the first pixels in the neighboring scanlines) is not always equal to the image width. One reason for such a gap is alignment of a scanline to a 32-bit or 64-bit memory block, making the processing more efficient. OpenVX prior to version 1.3 uses an even more flexible structure, which does not guarantee dense packing of pixels in a scanline. There is a horizontal stride `addr.stride_x` that defines the size of a memory block related to one pixel, so that the address of `n`th pixel in a scanline will be `p + n*stride_x`. The horizontal stride is not guaranteed to be equal to 1 for an 8-bit greyscale image or 3 for an 8-bit color image. This makes copying data between OpenCV and OpenVX quite inefficient. However, all OpenVX implementations that the authors are aware of use dense pixel packing, so VXA also makes this assumption. However, it checks for the stride value and returns an error if the assumption does not hold. We can create a fallback implementation that copies data pixel by pixel instead of a scanline by scanline. This situation is rectified in OpenVX 1.3, which requires dense pixel packing within a scanline:

```
if(addr.stride_x != 1 && addr.stride_x != 3)
{
  VXA_PRINT("addressing structure not supported, stride_x = %d\n",
    addr.stride_x);
  return(0);
}
```

Now that we are sure OpenVX image mapped to host memory uses dense pixel packing, we can copy data scanline by scanline:

```
for(int y = 0; y < height; y++)
{
  unsigned char* ptr_y = ptr + y*addr.stride_y;
  memcpy(ptr_y, cv_img.ptr(y), addr.stride_y);
}
```

Note that we are using `addr.stride_y` for OpenVX, and we are getting the address for each OpenCV image scanline using the function `cv::Mat::ptr`. Finally, we need to call `vxUnmapImagePatch` to release host memory holding the OpenVX image:

```
vxUnmapImagePatch(image, map_id);
```

Now the `image` object contains the data from the OpenCV image.

Note that the `vxa_cv2vx` function copies all data from an OpenCV image to an OpenVX image. We can avoid it by creating an externally allocated OpenVX image with the function `vxCreateImageFromHandle`. The difference is that with this method the memory used by the OpenCV image is managed by OpenVX, reading and writing to this memory between the call to `vxCreateImageFromHandle`, and the call to `vxMapImagePatch` will be undefined. So it is important to make sure that an OpenCV image is not used after its memory is given to OpenVX. The use of `vxCreateImageFromHandle` is extensively covered in Chapter 12; it is pretty straightforward to write a function similar to `vxa_cv2vx` that uses `vxCreateImageFromHandle`.

13.1.2 Convert an OpenVX image to OpenCV

Once OpenVX produces output results, it is easy to go back to OpenCV using the same set of functions. We will show this using another function from VXA called `vxa_vx2cv`. It takes an OpenVX image as input and creates an OpenCV image. It starts by obtaining the input OpenVX image dimensions and type:

```
int vxa_vx2cv(vx_image image, cv::Mat& cv_img)
{
    int width, height;
    vxQueryImage(image, VX_IMAGE_WIDTH, &width, 4);
    vxQueryImage(image, VX_IMAGE_HEIGHT, &height, 4);

    vx_df_image img_type;
    vxQueryImage(image, VX_IMAGE_FORMAT, &img_type, 4);
    int cv_type;
    switch(img_type)
    {
      case VX_DF_IMAGE_U8:
        cv_type = CV_8UC1;
        break;
```

```
case VX_DF_IMAGE_RGB:
  cv_type = CV_8UC3;
  break;

default:
  VXA_PRINT("Format %d not supported\n", img_type);
  return(-1);
}
```

Like `vx_cv2vx`, this function also supports only 8-bit greyscale and color images. The next step is getting the image data by mapping it into host memory:

```
vx_rectangle_t roi;
roi.start_x = 0;
roi.start_y = 0;
roi.end_x = width;
roi.end_y = height;

vx_map_id map_id;

vx_imagepatch_addressing_t addr;
unsigned char* ptr;

vx_status status = vxMapImagePatch(image, &roi, 0, &map_id, &addr,
  (void**)&ptr, VX_READ_ONLY, VX_MEMORY_TYPE_HOST, VX_NOGAP_X);
if(status != VX_SUCCESS)
{
  VXA_PRINT("vxMapImagePatch returned error with code %d\n", status);
  return(-1);
}
```

As before, we check that OpenVX has provided us with a dense pixel packing structure:

```
if(addr.stride_x != 1 && addr.stride_x != 3)
{
  VXA_PRINT("addressing structure not supported, stride_x = %d\n",
    addr.stride_x);
  return(0);
}
```

Then we create an OpenCV image with the same dimensions and type and copy data line by line:

```
cv_img = cv::Mat(height, width, cv_type);
for(int y = 0; y < height; y++)
{
    unsigned char* ptr_y = ptr + y*addr.stride_y;
    memcpy(cv_img.ptr(y), ptr_y, addr.stride_y);
}
```

We finish by releasing the host memory mapping:

```
status = vxUnmapImagePatch(image, map_id);
if(status != VX_SUCCESS)
{
    VXA_PRINT("vxUnmapImagePatch failed...\n");
    return(0);
}
```

13.1.3 Converting other data types

Images are not the only data that can be converted between OpenVX and OpenCV. The VXA library can also handle importing of remap data structures prepared by OpenCV into OpenVX; let us look at how this is done. The function vxa_import_opencv_remap is implemented in the "opencv-import.cpp" file of the VXA library. First, it reads the OpenCV remap matrix from file:

```
int vxa_import_opencv_remap(const char* filename, const char* nodename,
    vx_context context, vx_remap* remap, int* _dst_width, int* _dst_height)
{
    FileStorage fs(filename, FileStorage::READ);

    Mat cv_remap;
    fs[nodename] >> cv_remap;
    int src_width, src_height, dst_width, dst_height;
    fs[(std::string(nodename) + std::string("_src_width")).c_str()] >>
        src_width;
    fs[(std::string(nodename) + std::string("_src_height")).c_str()] >>
        src_height;
    fs[(std::string(nodename) + std::string("_dst_width")).c_str()] >>
        dst_width;
```

```
fs[(std::string(nodename) + std::string("_dst_height")).c_str()] >>
    dst_height;

if(cv_remap.type() != CV_32FC2)
{
    return(0);
}
```

The `cv::FileStorage` class from OpenCV is used to read a matrix from a file (xml or yml) also created by this class. Since this file can contain several matrices, the `nodename` parameter is used to find a specific matrix that we need. Since this is a remap, we check that the `cv_remap` matrix is of type `CV_32FC2`, storing two 32-bit floating-point values per pixel (the source image horizontal and vertical coordinates).

Once we have the remap matrix in memory, it is time to create a remap transformation and use the `vxCopyRemapPatch` function to copy data from OpenCV to OpenVX. This function is capable of copying to a rectangular subset of a remap matrix, so we supply a region of interest in the form of a `vx_rectangle_t`. OpenVX requires a remap to store a pair of 32-bit floating-point values per each pixel, just like the OpenCV matrix, so we use the `VX_TYPE_COORDINATES2DF` argument for `vxCopyRemapPatch`:

```
vx_rectangle_t roi;
roi.start_x = 0;
roi.start_y = 0;
roi.end_x = cv_remap.cols;
roi.end_y = cv_remap.rows;

*remap = vxCreateRemap(context, src_width, src_height,
    dst_width, dst_height);

if(vxCopyRemapPatch(*remap, &roi, cv_remap.step, cv_remap.ptr(),
    VX_TYPE_COORDINATES2DF, VX_WRITE_ONLY, VX_MEMORY_TYPE_HOST) !=
        VX_SUCCESS)
{
    return(0);
}

return(1);
}
```

Once `vxCopyImagePatch` returns, we have a remap transformation in OpenVX. Note that this function, unlike the image conversion functions we considered before, does not use a C++ interface, because instead of taking a `cv::Mat` as an input argument, it uses a file name. This can come handy if your platform has a file system but has no C++ compiler.

13.2 OpenCL

The OpenCL™(Open Computing Language) is the open, royalty-free standard for cross-platform, parallel programming of diverse processors, like CPUs, GPUs, and other processors, found in personal computers, servers, mobile devices, and embedded platforms. It is specifically developed for efficient compute across platforms.

In this section, we review the basics of OpenCL and interoperation between OpenVX and OpenCL applications.

13.2.1 OpenCL in a nutshell

The OpenCL consists of a host-side API for scheduling computation across heterogeneous processors and a cross-platform language specially designed for a data parallel programming model. The OpenCL memory model abstracts device physical memory, which is a key for interoperability with other APIs.

13.2.1.1 OpenCL C programs

It is easy to write a kernel using the OpenCL C programming language, which is a subset of C and has a good collection of math functions. Let us consider a simple kernel that computes *hard sigmoid* activation function:

```
////
// OpenCL kernel to compute hard sigmoid activation
// alpha : float constant
// beta : float constant
// X    : input 16-bit fixed-point Q7.8 buffer
// Y    : output 16-bit fixed-point Q7.8 buffer
//
__kernel void hard_sigmoid(
        float alpha,
        float beta,
        __global const short * X,
        __global short * Y)
```

```
{
  // get the index of current data element
  size_t i = get_global_id(0);

  // read and convert input into float from Q7.8
  float x = X[i]/256.0;

  // compute hard sigmoid for the current data element
  float y = fmin(fmax(alpha * x + beta, 0), 1);

  // convert the output to Q7.8 and write
  Y[i] = (short)(y * 256.0);
}
```

This example uses the OpenCL __global address space. OpenCL buffers are used to allocate the device memory in the __global address space. The OpenCL buffers can be mapped to the host address space when the application needs to access data in the device memory.

An OpenCL kernel is a function that gets executed as multiple threads, which are called work-items and assigned a global id. Usually, these work-items are grouped into work-groups and executed parallelly on multiple compute units in a target device.

13.2.1.2 The OpenCL context

The host-side OpenCL API controls the execution of these kernels on the compute devices. All the OpenCL compute resources, such as target devices, device memory, kernels, and so on, will be captured in an OpenCL context. Command queues will be used to schedule jobs on a device:

```
// OpenCL API header file
#include <CL/cl.h>


    ...
    // select an OpenCL device
    cl_platform_id platform_id;
    cl_device_id device_id;
    cl_int err;
    err = clGetPlatformIDs(1, &platform_id, NULL);
    if (err != CL_SUCCESS) {
      // error handling
    }
```

```
err = clGetDeviceIDs(platform_id, CL_DEVICE_TYPE_DEFAULT,
    1, &device_id, NULL);

// create the OpenCL context
cl_context opencl_ctx;
cl_context_properties ctxprop[] = { CL_CONTEXT_PLATFORM,
    (cl_context_properties)platform_id, 0, 0 };
opencl_ctx = clCreateContext(ctxprop, 1, &device_id, NULL, NULL,
    &err);

// create an OpenCL command-queue for scheduling jobs on the device
cl_command_queue opencl_cmdq;
opencl_cmdq = clCreateCommandQueue(opencl_ctx, device_id, 0, &err);
```

13.2.1.3 OpenCL just-in-time compiler

To execute a kernel on a device, you must first compile the source and get an OpenCL kernel object.

OpenCL allows applications to create program objects directly from source code in the OpenCL C programming language. The OpenCL just-in-time compiler takes a kernel program source as input and creates program executables. The program source is a string of characters that can be passed directly to clCreateProgramWithSource to create a cl_program object. Once a cl_program object is created, the clBuildProgram call will prepare program binaries specific to the devices in the OpenCL context.

An OpenCL program may consist of one or more kernels identified as functions declared with the __kernel qualifier in the program source. The cl_kernel object encapsulates a __kernel function and all its argument values to be used when executing the __kernel function. You need to use the clCreateKernel call to create a kernel object for a specific kernel function. Then use clSetKernelArg calls to set the values of function parameters.

The tensor objects in OpenVX use VX_TYPE_INT16 data types with signed Q7.8 fixed-point representation. You need to write OpenCL kernels to take data in the native OpenVX format for efficiency. The following example has a slightly different version of OpenCL kernel compared to the earlier hard_sigmoid example. This performs the data conversion between Q7.8 and float when accessing the data directly in tensor buffers:

```
////
// keep the OpenCL C program source into a char array
// alpha : float constant
```

```
//  beta : float constant
//  X    : input 16-bit fixed-point Q7.8 buffer
//  Y    : output 16-bit fixed-point Q7.8 buffer
//
static const char hard_sigmoid_program_source[] =
  " // OpenCL kernel to compute hard sigmoid activation \n"
  " __kernel void hard_sigmoid(float alpha, float beta, \n"
  "      __global const short * X, __global short * Y) \n"
  " {                                              \n"
  "   // get the index of current data element \n"
  "   size_t i = get_global_id(0);                 \n"
  "                                                 \n"
  "   // read and convert input into float from Q7.8 \n"
  "   float x = X[i]/256.0;                         \n"
  "                                                 \n"
  "   // compute hard sigmoid for the current data element \n"
  "   float y = fmin(fmax(alpha * x + beta, 0), 1); \n"
  "                                                 \n"
  "   // convert the output to Q7.8 and write \n"
  "   Y[i] = (short)(y * 256.0);                    \n"
  " }                                              \n";

////
// compile OpenCL C program from source
//
const char * program_strings[] = {
   hard_sigmoid_program_source
};
size_t program_sizes[] = {
   sizeof(hard_sigmoid_program_source)
};

cl_program hard_sigmoid_program = clCreateProgramWithSource(
      opencl_ctx, 1, program_strings, program_sizes, &err);

err = clBuildProgram(hard_sigmoid_program, 1, &device_id,
      NULL, NULL, NULL);

////
// get kernel object for the "hard_sigmoid" kernel function in program
//
cl_kernel hard_sigmoid_kernel = clCreateKernel(hard_sigmoid_program,
```

```
"hard_sigmoid", &err);
```

13.2.1.4 OpenCL buffers

Now that the kernel object is ready, you need to allocate memory on the device for input and output buffers in the __global address space. The clCreateBuffer call returns an opaque memory object for device memory, similar to OpenVX data objects. Each argument of the kernel needs a separate call to clSetKernelArg:

```
////
// create memory buffers for hard_sigmoid input and output
//  16-bit fixed-point Q7.8 buffers
//
cl_mem x_mem = clCreateBuffer(opencl_ctx, CL_MEM_READ_WRITE,
            num_tensor_elem * sizeof(short), NULL, &err);
cl_mem y_mem = clCreateBuffer(opencl_ctx, CL_MEM_READ_WRITE,
            num_tensor_elem * sizeof(short), NULL, &err);

// set "hard_sigmoid" kernel arguments:
//   argument #0: "float alpha"
//   argument #1: "float beta"
//   argument #2: "__globla const short * X"
//   argument #3: "__globla short * Y"
float alpha = 0.2f;
float beta = 0.5f;
err = clSetKernelArg(hard_sigmoid_kernel, 0, sizeof(float), (void
    *)&alpha);
err = clSetKernelArg(hard_sigmoid_kernel, 1, sizeof(float), (void
    ʌ)&beta);
err = clSetKernelArg(hard_sigmoid_kernel, 2, sizeof(cl_mem), (void
    *)&x_mem);
err = clSetKernelArg(hard_sigmoid_kernel, 3, sizeof(cl_mem), (void
    *)&y_mem);
```

13.2.1.5 OpenCL kernel execution

Once the buffers on device are created and kernel argument are set, the kernel is ready for execution. The clEnqueueNDRangeKernel call will enqueue a command to execute the kernel on device. The information about how much data to process by this kernel is specified as the number of work-items.

Before executing the kernel, the input buffer must be initialized with input data. Note that the OpenCL buffers are opaque, just like OpenVX objects. So you need to call `clEnqueueMapBuffer` and `clEnqueueUnmapMemObject` to access to the device memory for initialization or reading:

```
////
// initialize input buffer:
// 1. map OpenCL buffer to host address space for writing
//    (no copy from device to host)
// 2. initialize input values
// 3. unmap host address space so that kernel can access OpenCL
//    buffer on device
//
short * x_buf = (short *)clEnqueueMapBuffer(opencl_cmdq, x_mem,
                    CL_TRUE, CL_MAP_WRITE, 0,
                    num_tensor_elem * sizeof(short),
                    0, NULL, NULL, &err);

... copy input values into x_buf[] ...

err = clEnqueueUnmapMemObject(opencl_cmdq, x_mem, x_buf, 0, NULL,
    NULL);

////
// run hard_sigmoid kernel parallelly across "num_tensor_elem"
//    work-items
// just queue up the job to execute after input buffer write is
//    completed
//
size_t global_item_size = num_tensor_elem;
err = clEnqueueNDRangeKernel(opencl_cmdq, hard_sigmoid_kernel,
    1, NULL, &global_item_size,
    NULL, 0, NULL, NULL) );


////
// read output from "hard_sigmoid" and compare with reference output
// the clEnqueueMapBuffer will return after the kernel execution
// as well as the read of output data from device to host address
// space is completed
//
short * y_buf = (short *)clEnqueueMapBuffer(opencl_cmdq, y_mem,
```

```
                    CL_TRUE, CL_MAP_READ, 0,
                    num_tensor_elem * sizeof(short),
                    0, NULL, NULL, &err);

            ... process output values from y_buf[] ...

            err = clEnqueueUnmapMemObject(opencl_cmdq, y_mem, y_buf, 0, NULL,
                NULL);
```

The following outline summarizes the basic steps essential to writing an OpenCL program to accelerate an algorithm:

- Write your algorithm in OpenCL C language as a kernel
- Initialize OpenCL environment: context and command-queue from an OpenCL platform and device
- Compile and create an OpenCL kernel object from the OpenCL C source code
- Create OpenCL buffers and set kernel arguments
- Write inputs to device memory, execute kernels, and read output from device memory

13.2.2 Interoperability with OpenCL

OpenCL is specifically developed for efficient compute across platforms, which can be used to extend OpenVX functionality for implementing application-specific algorithms. To enable a standard interoperation (or "interop" for short) between OpenVX and OpenCL, the Khronos has developed the OpenVX OpenCL Interop Extension (vx_khr_opencl_interop), which can be used by the OpenVX applications and user-kernels for efficient data exchange as in the following use cases:

- Access OpenVX data objects as OpenCL data objects
- Import OpenCL data objects into OpenVX context
- Synchronize resources shared between OpenVX and OpenCL using fully asynchronous APIs

13.2.2.1 OpenVX context with OpenCL interoperability

In order for the interop to work, both OpenVX and the application must use the same cl_context object, an OpenCL context that encapsulates all compute and memory resources accessible to the host. For the coordination between OpenVX and the OpenCL application/user-kernel, a common in-order cl_command_queue object is shared by the OpenVX context and the application/user-kernel.

To enable OpenCL interop, you must create the OpenVX context using the `vxCreateContextFromCL` API with the shared OpenCL context and command queue:

```
// OpenVX OpenCL interop header
#include <VX/vx_khr_opencl_interop.h>


...

// create the OpenVX context by specifying the OpenCL context and
// the global coordination command queue
vx_context context = vxCreateContextFromCL(opencl_ctx, opencl_cmdq);
...
```

13.2.2.2 OpenCL buffer access

The OpenVX standard supports more than one memory type (`vx_memory_type_e`) for data access. The default memory type is `VX_MEMORY_TYPE_HOST` for memory in the host address space. As you have seen in earlier chapters, the `vxMapXxx/vxCopyXxx` APIs used the `VX_MEMORY_TYPE_HOST` enum for OpenVX data object read/write operations.

The OpenCL interop extension comes with a new memory type `VX_MEMORY_TYPE_OPENCL_BUFFER` to access OpenVX data object memory as an OpenCL buffer (`cl_mem`).

The opaqueness of OpenVX objects allows an OpenVX implementation to manage device memory efficiently across heterogenous hardware. For example, an OpenVX object may be residing on a GPU as an OpenCL buffer when it is computed on a GPU.

- If the OpenVX object is accessed as `VX_MEMORY_TYPE_HOST`, then the data buffer is mapped to the host address space or copied into a host buffer and returned from `vxMapXxx`
- If the OpenVX object is accessed as `VX_MEMORY_TYPE_OPENCL_BUFFER`, then the OpenCL buffer on GPU is returned immediately without any copies

Similarly, when `vxUnmapXxx` is called for a buffer mapped with `VX_MEMORY_TYPE_HOST`, it may be copied back to GPU, if the next kernel is scheduled to run on the GPU. If the buffer is mapped with `VX_MEMORY_TYPE_OPENCL_BUFFER`, then it can be directly processed on GPU without any additional overhead.

Note that the following example uses 3-D tensors unlike the `hard_sigmoid` example in the previous example:

```
// get OpenCL buffer from a 3-D OpenVX tensor object for read access
```

```
//  inside the "hard_sigmoid" OpenCL kernel ("X" parameter)
cl_mem x_mem;
vx_map_id x_map_id;
vx_size x_stride[3];
vxMapTensorPatch(tensor_x, 3, NULL, NULL, &x_map_id, x_stride,
        (void **)&x_mem, VX_READ_ONLY, VX_MEMORY_TYPE_OPENCL_BUFFER);

// get OpenCL buffer from 3-D OpenVX tensor object for write access
//  inside the "hard_sigmoid" OpenCL kernel ("Y" parameter)
cl_mem y_mem;
vx_map_id y_map_id;
vx_size y_stride[3];
vxMapTensorPatch(tensor_y, 3, NULL, NULL, &y_map_id, y_stride,
        (void **)&y_mem, VX_WRITE_ONLY, VX_MEMORY_TYPE_OPENCL_BUFFER);

// set OpenCL kernel arguments
data->params.x_stride_1 = x_stride[1] / sizeof(short);
data->params.x_stride_2 = x_stride[2] / sizeof(short);
data->params.y_stride_1 = y_stride[1] / sizeof(short);
data->params.y_stride_2 = y_stride[2] / sizeof(short);
clSetKernelArg(data->opencl_kernel, 0,
        sizeof(hard_sigmoid_params), (void *)&data->params);
clSetKernelArg(data->opencl_kernel, 1, sizeof(cl_mem), (void
    *)&x_mem);
clSetKernelArg(data->opencl_kernel, 2, sizeof(cl_mem), (void
    *)&y_mem);

// queue the "hard_sigmoid" kernel for execution in the OpenVX
    internal
// command-queue for optimal performance the OpenVX will queue up
// other OpenCL kernel in the graph so that the device can execute
// several OpenCL kernels until there is a data dependency for
// processing/data-access outside the device (like host).
clEnqueueNDRangeKernel(data->opencl_cmdq, data->opencl_kernel,
        3, NULL, data->global_work_size, NULL, 0, NULL, NULL);

// give the ownership of the OpenCL buffers back to the OpenVX
vxUnmapTensorPatch(tensor_x, x_map_id);
vxUnmapTensorPatch(tensor_y, y_map_id);

// NOTE: the x_mem & y_mem can't be used by after the above calls
// since the application is not the owner of these objects
```

It is also important to note that the execution of "hard_sigmoid" kernel does not have to complete before making the vxUnmapTensorPatch calls, because it is scheduled using the command-queue that is shared with the OpenVX graph.

Any OpenVX API that has vx_memory_type_e as an input will interop with OpenCL when VX_MEMORY_TYPE_OPENCL_BUFFER is used, for example, using the functions below:

- vxCopyXxx to copy OpenVX data object to/from OpenCL buffer
- vxMapXxx/vxUnmapXxx to access an OpenVX data object as an OpenCL buffer
- vxCreateXxxFromHandle to create OpenVX data objects from externally created OpenCL buffers
- vxSwapXxxHandle to swap OpenCL buffers with previous handles in OpenVX data objects

The vxCreateXxxFromHandle and vxSwapXxxHandle provide a mechanism to use OpenCL buffers created by the application directly the OpenVX. This is required in scenarios where the application is managing all the OpenCL buffers used across OpenVX and other modules in the application:

```
// 3-D tensor dimensions
size_t dims[3] = { 512, 32, 1 };

// allocate OpenCL buffers in the application for sharing with OpenVX
size_t num_tensor_elem = dims[0] * dims[1] * dims[2];
cl_mem a_mem = clCreateBuffer(opencl_ctx, CL_MEM_READ_WRITE,
        num_tensor_elem * sizeof(short), NULL, &err);
cl_mem b_mem = clCreateBuffer(opencl_ctx, CL_MEM_READ_WRITE,
        num_tensor_elem * sizeof(short), NULL, &err);

// create tensors using application specific OpenCL buffers
size_t strides[3] = { sizeof(vx_int16), sizeof(vx_int16)*dims[0], ...
    };
vx_tensor tensor_a = vxCreateTensorFromHandle(context, 3, dims,
        VX_TYPE_INT16, 8, strides, &a_mem,
            VX_MEMORY_TYPE_OPENCL_BUFFER);
vx_tensor tensor_b = vxCreateTensorFromHandle(context, 3, dims,
        VX_TYPE_INT16, 8, strides, &b_mem,
            VX_MEMORY_TYPE_OPENCL_BUFFER);

// build OpenVX graph
...
```

```
// schedule preprocessing using another compute module
extPreprocessor(opencl_cmdq, ..., a_mem);

// schedule OpenVX graph that consumes a_mem and computes b_mem
vxProcessGraph(graph);

// schedule post-processing using another compute module
extPostprocessor(opencl_cmdq, b_mem, ...);
```

13.2.2.3 User kernels with OpenCL acceleration

OpenVX provides a mechanism to create user kernels for custom function-ality and insert them in the middle of an OpenVX graph, so that a complete graph can be scheduled at once. The OpenVX specification supports user kernels that can be scheduled on the host only. However, the OpenCL interop extension provides a mechanism to create user kernels that can execute OpenCL kernels in the middle of an OpenVX graph without re-quiring the data to be copied to the host and back. To specify that a user kernel needs OpenCL interop, the user kernel must be registered by setting the kernel VX_KERNEL_USE_OPENCL attribute to vx_true_e as in the following example:

```
// register user kernel for "hard_sigmoid"
vx_kernel kernel = vxAddUserKernel(context,
        "app.userkernels.hard_sigmoid", USER_KERNEL_HARD_SIGMOID,
        hard_sigmoid_opencl_function, 4,
        hard_sigmoid_validator,
        hard_sigmoid_init,
        hard_sigmoid_uninit);

// set user kernel arguments
vxAddParameterToKernel(kernel, 0, VX_INPUT,
        VX_TYPE_SCALAR, VX_PARAMETER_STATE_REQUIRED);
vxAddParameterToKernel(kernel, 1, VX_INPUT,
        VX_TYPE_SCALAR, VX_PARAMETER_STATE_REQUIRED);
vxAddParameterToKernel(kernel, 2, VX_INPUT,
        VX_TYPE_TENSOR, VX_PARAMETER_STATE_REQUIRED);
vxAddParameterToKernel(kernel, 3, VX_OUTPUT,
        VX_TYPE_TENSOR, VX_PARAMETER_STATE_REQUIRED);

// specify that the user kernel is using OpenCL interop
```

```
vx_bool use_opencl_interop = vx_true_e;
vxSetKernelAttribute(kernel, VX_KERNEL_USE_OPENCL,
    &use_opencl_interop, sizeof(vx_bool));

// finalize the user kernel after setting VX_KERNEL_USE_OPENCL
    attribute
vxFinalizeKernel(kernel);
```

Once a user kernel is registered with the OpenCL interop feature, OpenVX will optimize its internal scheduler so that the user kernel can access OpenCL buffers and schedule OpenCL kernels without any overhead:

```
vx_status hard_sigmoid_opencl_function(vx_node node,
        const vx_reference * arg, vx_uint32 num_args)
{
    // get user kernel arguments
    vx_scalar scalar_alpha = (vx_scalar)arg[0];
    vx_scalar scalar_beta = (vx_scalar)arg[1];
    vx_tensor tensor_x = (vx_tensor)arg[2];
    vx_tensor tensor_y = (vx_tensor)arg[3];

    // get node local data from VX_NODE_LOCAL_DATA_PTR
    hard_sigmoid_local_data * data;
    vxQueryNode(node, VX_NODE_LOCAL_DATA_PTR, &data, sizeof(data));

    // get OpenCL buffer from OpenVX tensor object as the input
    // of "hard_sigmoid" OpenCL kernel ("X" parameter)
    cl_mem x_mem;
    vx_map_id x_map_id;
    vx_size x_stride[3];
    vxMapTensorPatch(tensor_x, 3, NULL, NULL,
        &x_map_id, x_stride, (void **)&x_mem,
        VX_READ_ONLY, VX_MEMORY_TYPE_OPENCL_BUFFER);

    // get OpenCL buffer from OpenVX tensor object as the output
    // of "hard_sigmoid" OpenCL kernel ("Y" parameter)
    cl_mem y_mem;
    vx_map_id y_map_id;
    vx_size y_stride[3];
    vxMapTensorPatch(tensor_y, 3, NULL, NULL,
        &y_map_id, y_stride, (void **)&y_mem,
```

```
        VX_WRITE_ONLY, VX_MEMORY_TYPE_OPENCL_BUFFER);

    // set OpenCL kernel arguments
    data->params.x_stride_1 = x_stride[1] / sizeof(short);
    data->params.x_stride_2 = x_stride[2] / sizeof(short);
    data->params.y_stride_1 = y_stride[1] / sizeof(short);
    data->params.y_stride_2 = y_stride[2] / sizeof(short);
    clSetKernelArg(data->opencl_kernel, 0,
          sizeof(hard_sigmoid_params), (void *)&data->params);
    clSetKernelArg(data->opencl_kernel, 1,
          sizeof(cl_mem), (void *)&x_mem);
    clSetKernelArg(data->opencl_kernel, 2,
          sizeof(cl_mem), (void *)&y_mem);

    // enqueue the "hard_sigmoid" kernel for execution using
    // the OpenVX internal command queue:
    //  for optimal performance the OpenVX will enqueue other
    //  OpenCL kernel in the graph using the same command queue,
    //  so that the device can execute several OpenCL kernels
    //  until there is a data dependency for processing/data-access
    //  outside the device (like host)
    cl_command_queue opencl_cmdq;
    vxQueryNode(node, VX_NODE_CL_COMMAND_QUEUE,
          &opencl_cmdq, sizeof(cl_command_queue));
    clEnqueueNDRangeKernel(opencl_cmdq, data->opencl_kernel,
          3, NULL, data->global_work_size, NULL, 0, NULL, NULL);

    // give the ownership of the OpenCL buffers back to the OpenVX
    vxUnmapTensorPatch(tensor_x, x_map_id);
    vxUnmapTensorPatch(tensor_y, y_map_id);

    return VX_SUCCESS;
}
```

13.2.3 Summary

With the set of six essential features listed below, the OpenCL interop extension supports efficient implementation of applications and user algorithms within OpenVX.

- share a common `cl_context` object between OpenVX and the OpenCL application

- share a set of common in-order `cl_command_queue` objects for coordination between OpenVX and the OpenCL application/user-kernel
- mechanism for an OpenCL application to export `cl_mem` buffers to OpenVX
- mechanism for an OpenCL application to reclaim exported `cl_mem` buffers back from OpenVX
- mechanism for an OpenCL application/user-kernel to temporarily map OpenVX data objects into `cl_mem` buffers
- mechanism to copy between `cl_mem` buffers and OpenVX data objects.
  See https://www.khronos.org/registry/OpenVX for the complete specification of the Khronos OpenVX OpenCL Interop Extension (`vx_khr_opencl_interop`).

CHAPTER 14

Existing implementations and platforms for OpenVX

Contents

One of the primary goals of the OpenVX API was to enable programmers to write code that is efficiently portable to a broad range of hardware architectures. Specific architectures considered in the design of OpenVX were CPUs, GPUs, DSPs, FPGAs, and special-purpose hardware. Now that the API has been published for some time, we can look to the available implementations to gauge the portability of the API.

A list of all of the existing conformant OpenVX implementations is available on the Khronos web page at https://www.khronos.org/conformance/adopters/conformant-products/openvx. This is an ever-growing list, and at the time of this writing, there were over three dozen conformant implementations. These include implementations running on a conventional CPU (Intel), a GPU (AMD, Imagination, NVIDIA, Verisilicon), a DSP (Cadence, Synopsys, Texas Instruments), and platforms that include special-purpose hardware blocks (Elvees, Socionext). Although there is no specific FPGA-based implementation, many of the platforms supporting OpenVX were prototyped on FPGA hardware. Based on the existing implementations alone, we can see that the OpenVX API has been successful in the goal of supporting a broad range of architectures. Let's look at the advantages that OpenVX brings to implementations on each platform. This chapter discusses each class of architecture generally. Consult the documentation for your specific implementation of OpenVX to determine its features and optimizations.

OpenVX Programming Guide
https://doi.org/10.1016/B978-0-12-816425-9.00020-6
Copyright © 2020 Elsevier Inc.
All rights reserved.
311

14.1 CPU implementations

Aside from commercial implementations, the open-source OpenVX sample implementation is designed to be built and run on a CPU. Although the core computations are not optimized in the sample implementation, it is a complete functional implementation of the OpenVX standard, which anyone can easily obtain and run on their standard-issue PC. It also forms a starting point for the development of optimized code for CPUs and other platforms. Most of the lines of code in the sample implementation are for the framework features for building graph data structures, verifying their validity, maintaining reference counts to objects, and so on. Since it does not operate on image pixel data, it generally need not be highly optimized, so it can be used as-is even in optimized commercial implementations on any platform with a C compiler. The implementor of an optimized version can focus on replacing only the compute-intensive pixel-processing code that consumes most of the compute cycles in most computer vision applications.

Optimized commercial CPU implementations additionally benefit from the OpenVX graph infrastructure to enable cache-optimized data access patterns. Modern compute platforms of all types, including common CPU architectures, employ a memory hierarchy with a combination of small, fast, and relatively expensive memory and large, relatively slow, and cheap memory. In CPUs, this usually takes the form of a data cache, in which once a memory location or area in the large memory is used, it is copied, or cached, in the small fast memory, so that the next time the data at that location is referenced, the cached copy can be used instead. This is often very effective because in most (non-vision) applications, once a piece of data is used, it is very likely that it will be used again soon, so most of the time the CPU is working with cached data, and the large slow memory is only accessed during the relatively rare cache "misses" when the data has not been previously brought into the cache.

However, with the large volumes of image and video data processed in computer vision applications, a naïvely constructed program can access the data in a pattern that does not use the cache effectively. Using a standard (nongraph-based) API, the user is encouraged to string together a series of simple computations, each of which operates over an entire image. Since the entire image may not fit in the small cache (especially on embedded platforms with limited memory), the cache is filled before the first simple operation over the entire image completes. This necessitates ejecting older data from the cache, including the results of the first operation. By the time the next operation starts, the results of the previous operation are no longer in the cache, so they need to be fetched again. These data fetches to the large slow memory can impose a very high performance penalty. This bad cache behavior can be alleviated by processing the image as "tiles," breaking it into pieces small enough that several of the resulting tiles can fit in the cache. If the tiles are sized appropriately, then entire chains of operations can be performed in which the data are all in the cache. When the first simple operation is performed on a tile, the input data must be fetched into the cache, but the results of the computation on one tile can remain in cache for the next operation if the tiles are small enough. The user of a non-graph-based API can do this tiling by hand, executing the API functions over tiles instead of full images, but it can be quite tedious to code this and can impose an overhead that negates the benefits of tiling if not done properly. Many operations (such as convolution) have "neighborhoods" or "halos" that must be accounted for at the edges of the tiles. In practice, users take the source code of the API and edit the series of kernels into a single function. This can be efficient, but after further optimization, the resulting code is generally not portable to alternative platforms.

Via the graph-based OpenVX API, users can write their code in a natural "full-image" style, stringing together a series of simple operations on entire images. Since the code is executed in the context of a graph, the vxVerifyGraph function can transform the computation from being full-image based as expressed to tile based for execution. This can be done automatically with a high degree of optimization to the specific hardware, for example, accounting for the sizes and relative access speeds of the cache memories, which can be organized in a hierarchy several layers deep in a modern CPU. Since the full chain of computation is known to the OpenVX implementation at the time vxVerifyGraph is called, the tiling pattern can be further optimized to account for the specific operations being performed. So we do not need to be running on exotic special-purpose hardware to enjoy the benefits of the OpenVX graph API.

Modern CPUs also often have a rich set of vector-based multimedia instructions, which can be used to process large volumes of data. These instructions can process chunks of data in a single cycle, where the same operation is performed on a number of data elements. A compiler can sometimes "vectorize" the computation to take advantage of such instructions, but full optimization typically requires hand coding that accounts for tedious details such as memory alignment. Such code can be incorporated into the OpenVX implementation such that the user of the implementation can reap the benefits of hand vectorization without coding it themselves. This optimization could also be done with non-graph-based APIs. The OpenVX API brings the additional advantage of a conformance test suite to ensure portability of applications written on top of it. Existing CPU implementations of the OpenVX API make extensive use of multimedia instruction sets.

Modern CPUs often come in clusters of 2, 4, 8, or more. Multithreading techniques are used to spread the computation across the available CPUs. The tile-based compute pattern used to optimize for cache performance also well lends itself to multithreading. Each tile or group of tiles can be assigned a thread that may run on a different CPU. Again, this can be done by the OpenVX implementation itself, so the application programmer can reap the benefits of multithreading without having to deal with the intricacies of things like synchronization primitives.

14.2 DSP implementations

DSP platforms may have data caches like CPUs, but they usually also have direct-memory access (DMA) engines that can be explicitly programmed to move data between the tiers of the memory hierarchy. A modern DMA engine can be programmed to move complex patterns of data, such as two-dimensional image data with strides between scanlines. Triggers can be set up so that the completion of one DMA launches another. Triggers can also come from external events (such as an image capture) or from the DSP main processor. Since the DMA engine runs independently from the main processor, it can run in parallel with it so that data transfers occur while the main processor is doing something else. The DMA engine itself may have multiple channels, so it can perform multiple transfers in parallel.

The DSP DMA engine enables the programmer to use image tiling techniques to set up a processing pipeline in which a stream of tiles is fed to the main processor in the fastest available memory. The input image is conceptually divided into tiles, and the DMA engine moves a tile at a time from the large slow memory, where the entire input image is stored, to the small fast memory that can contain only a few tiles. The main processor works only on data in the fast memory, usually with single-cycle access. While the main processor is computing on the current tile, the DMA engine is bringing in the next input tile. When the output based on the current tile is complete, the DMA engine moves the result back out to the main memory. Once the pipeline gets going, the main processor simply computes using data in the fast memory, reading its inputs from there and writing its outputs there as well. In parallel, the DMA engine is reading in the next tile and writing out the previous tile to the large slow memory.

The DMA-based architecture can be more efficient than a cache-based architecture, since instead of waiting for a cache miss to bring in the data, the DMA engine can proactively pull in the data that will be needed ahead of time. (A similar effect can be achieved on cache-based architectures via prefetching.) Since the data access pattern is known ahead of time (typically sequencing though tiles), the DMA engine can be programmed to anticipate it. Multiple DSPs, possibly with multiple DMA engines, can be used to accelerate the processing similar to what was previously described for CPUs. This can be done via data parallelism (e.g., one DSP does the left half of the image, and another does the right half) or functional parallelism (e.g., with one DSP doing the first half of the computation and the other one doing the second half) with DMA (or just shared memory) managing the data movement between the DSPs.

The DMA pipelining described above in a sense decouples the speed of computation from the speed of the large slow memory. All of the computation happens in the fast single-cycle memory, but the decoupling is not complete. The latency to the large memory can be significant, on the order of 200 cycles. If the computation is very fast, then even with the pipelining, the main DSP processor will spend most of its time waiting for data to come in via DMA. In this case the algorithm is said to be "data-bound" or "memory-bound" because the time it takes is completely determined by how long it takes to move the data in and out of the main memory. The computation itself happens in parallel with this data movement, so it does not contribute to the overall run time.

If the computation time is sufficiently large, then the situation is reversed, and the algorithm is said to be "compute-bound." If the computation on each tile takes a few hundred cycles or more, then the DMA engine can keep up and have new data ready by the time the main processor completes the current tile. In this case the data movement is said to be "hidden" behind the compute, since it happens in parallel with the computation. With the exception of a pipeline delay to bring in the first tile and write out the last one, the data movement time does not contribute to the overall run time, and the main processor computes continuously.

The processor and algorithm are often designed so that the computation is "balanced" with neither the DMA engine nor main compute processor time dominating. This maximizes the utilization of both the processor cycles and memory bandwidth. Depending on the specifics of the hardware and the application, this can be the most power efficient implementation. In addition to the time latency associated with moving data from the large memory, there is typically a large power penalty to such data accesses. Ideally, the input data is read from the large memory only once, all intermediate computations are done in fast memory, and only the final result is written back out to the large memory. The DSP architecture is designed to operate in this way and can provide a unique combination of high performance and low power, which has found success on many embedded platforms.

The OpenVX graph structure can help achieve such results on a DSP. In a DSP implementation the entire OpenVX graph can be set up to run on tiles in the fast memory. The input data is read only once, and then several processing kernels (perhaps the entire graph) can be run on the tile while still in the fast memory, and only the output of the entire graph is written to the large memory. This is not always achievable, since some kernels do not lend themselves well to tiling, or the fast memory is too small to hold all the intermediate values necessary, but even having one intermediate result stay in the fast memory and avoiding the trip to the large memory can be a significant improvement in power and performance.

Programming the DMA engine on a DSP can be a challenge. They have proprietary interfaces and run in parallel with the main processor, so there can be race conditions that are difficult to debug. Fortunately, an OpenVX implementation can manage all this DMA for you. The graph structure can be analyzed by a compiler and mapped to an appropriate sequence of DMAs and computations on tiles, transparent to the OpenVX programmer. The user of the OpenVX API can enjoy the high-performance and low-power benefits of a DMA-based DSP architecture without directly programming the DMA engine. The OpenVX conformance tests ensure that the application code is portable to DSPs with different DMA engines, with different proprietary interfaces, or to an entirely different architecture.

14.3 GPU implementations

GPUs use a different approach to tackle the memory-hierarchy issues discussed previously. GPUs have specific hardware to support large-scale multithreading. When used for image processing, the image is conceptually divided into tiles similar to the architectures described above, and then each tile can be assigned a thread to execute the processing of that tile. Conceptually, all the threads start at once, and then are immediately blocked while their input data is loaded into cache from the large memory. As soon as a thread's input data are available, it can start executing. Some threads get their data first and can start, while the data for other threads are loaded in parallel with the execution of the first group of threads. Although this description is a bit of a simplification, it illustrates how the GPU can hide the memory latency via multithreading. Of course, the GPU hardware can contain hundreds or thousands of physical processors to execute the threads, so OpenVX programs running on GPUs can achieve high performance via parallelism.

In practice, GPUs are paired with CPUs in a heterogenous system. Most commonly, the CPU and GPU have separate main memories, both of which are relatively slow compared to the fast cache memory that both processors need to use for good performance. This means that there is often a large memory transfer between the CPU memory and GPU memory before, after, and perhaps during the computation. This data transfer can easily dominate the run time, and minimizing it is a key component of using GPUs for computer vision processing. The OpenVX graph structure, the opaque nature of the OpenVX data objects, and the availability of virtual objects enable GPU-based implementations to keep most of the data objects in GPU memory only, transferring a minimum amount of data to the CPU memory.

Even when only considering the GPU side of this system, GPUs themselves often have a variety of memory types with advantages and disadvantages of each. Which type of memory to use is under programmer control via CUDA or OpenCL directives. A GPU implementation of OpenVX can analyze the graph during the vxVerifyGraph function to automatically determine what memory type to use for intermediate data objects to maximize performance.

OpenCL incorporates an online kernel compiler that can be use to generate kernels at run time. Using this facility, an OpenVX implementation written in OpenCL can analyze the graph during vxVerifyGraph and generate optimized OpenCL kernel code specific to that graph, fusing kernels for efficiency, perhaps even generating one large highly optimized OpenCL kernel that executes the entire OpenVX graph. At least one existing GPU implementation leverages this feature of OpenCL.

By writing application code using the OpenVX API and running on a GPU implementation of OpenVX, the OpenVX programmer can gain the GPU performance benefits of large-scale multithreading, a complex memory hierarchy with special-purpose memories, and kernel optimization in OpenCL or CUDA without having to write special-purpose OpenCL or CUDA code. The OpenVX application will be portable across GPUs running OpenCL or CUDA, as well as non-GPU architectures.

14.4 Special-purpose hardware implementations

Special-purpose hardware can implement highly optimized versions of specific functions. There is a trade-off between dedicating a silicon block for one specific function versus the performance and power benefits of the block. If a function is frequently used and consumes a large number of cycles on a standard processor, the it is a candidate for custom hardware acceleration. Less frequently used functions or those that can be run quickly on standard hardware are generally best left on the standard processor to make most efficient use of silicon area. For this reason, OpenVX implementations incorporating special-purpose hardware blocks also have conventional processors that execute some or even most of the OpenVX functions. Special-purpose blocks are dedicated to only a few functions that achieve the most benefits. For example, convolution is a common computer vision function that can consume a lot of cycles on a standard processor architecture, so it is a popular function for dedicated hardware. Image processing operations such as resizing and color conversion may also run on a dedicated image signal processor or ISP. From the application programmer's point of view, there is no change to their OpenVX code, but if their graph incorporates a function with a dedicated hardware block, then it will just run faster and consume less power than it would on a fully general processor.

14.5 FPGA implementations

Whereas there is no conformant implementation of OpenVX specifically targeted to an FPGA platform, implementations on other types of platforms can be instantiated on an FPGA. This has been done for demonstration purposes for at least one of the DSP implementations. The FPGA is used to implement a DSP, which runs OpenVX. Of course, an FPGA can be used to implement OpenVX functions more directly with custom FPGA blocks. A commercial FPGA implementation would likely be similar to the special-purpose hardware implementations in that there would probably be a traditional processor executing a large portion of the API, with special-purpose FPGA blocks for a few functions that benefit from custom hardware. Given the flexibility of both the FPGA platform and the OpenVX API, there are many possibilities.

14.6 Hybrid System-on-Chips (SoCs)

Modern SoCs as the heart of today's mobile phones and autonomous vehicles typically contain an assortment of processors, including multiple CPUs, a GPU, a DSP, an ISP, and a few special-purpose hardware blocks. An OpenVX implementation designed for an SoC may leverage all these processors. Depending on the relative performance and power consumption of each of these processors, specific functions or portions of graphs may be sent to different processors, with shared memory or DMA for communication between the blocks. A single graph can run on several processors and thereby achieve higher performance via parallelism. As OpenVX is deployed on more complex SoCs, we can expect to see implementations that leverage a variety of compute resources. The OpenVX application programmers need not even know which processor(s) their application is running on—they will just see high performance at low power.

CHAPTER 15

Changes in OpenVX 1.3

Contents

The Khronos OpenVX working group released version 1.3 of the OpenVX specification in August of 2019. The main change in 1.3 versus previous releases of the spec is the introduction of Feature Sets. Feature sets enable implementations to support well-defined subsets of the spec without necessarily supporting every function the spec describes. OpenVX 1.3 also introduces support for binary images, adds information for implementing safety-critical applications, removes support for bidirectional parameters, and makes several other minor changes. In this chapter, we provide an overview of these changes.

15.1 Feature sets

Prior to OpenVX version 1.3, support for all APIs and features described in the main specification document was mandatory for all implementors of OpenVX. To market an implementation as compliant with the OpenVX specification and use the associated Khronos trademarks, it must be submitted to a conformance process that checks that every function described in the spec is supported. Over the years, more and more functions were added to the specification as the field evolved, and not all of these functions are useful for every application. If an implementor wanted to focus on customers within a specific application area of OpenVX, they still had to implement all the functions, even if they were not useful to them. Part of this is by design, since having a standard set of functions that application developers can rely on to be supported is essential to making sure that applications are portable. As the list of functions in the standard grew, the burden of implementing all the functions in the spec on diverse and

OpenVX Programming Guide
https://doi.org/10.1016/B978-0-12-816425-9.00021-8
Copyright © 2020 Elsevier Inc.
All rights reserved.

specialized hardware became too large, and the OpenVX working group introduced Feature Sets to address this problem.

Feature sets strike a balance between requiring everyone to implement everything and having a free-for-all where every implementor decides independently what to support, which would have the result that application developers cannot assume any function works. Feature sets are well-defined coherent subsets of the spec tailored for a particular application space. Application developers can rely on support for all the functions in each of a few feature sets, so they only need to check that the feature set they need is supported by the implementation they use, and then they can use all the functions in that feature set.

The feature sets of OpenVX are defined in a separate document from the main spec. The initial feature set document can be found at [19]:

https://www.khronos.org/registry/OpenVX/specs/1.3/vx_khr_feature_ sets/1.0/html/vx_khr_feature_sets_1_0.html

The feature set document describes a few different categories of feature sets, but the two most important types are *conformance* feature sets and *optional* feature sets. Conformance feature sets are important for implementors, because at least one conformance feature set must be supported in its entirety in order for the implementation to be advertised as OpenVX conformant, or even as "OpenVX" at all. Optional feature sets are as you would expect: the implementation may support them or not, *in addition to* at least one conformance feature set. Optional feature sets are similar to OpenVX extensions in this way, and in fact the only technical difference between an extension and an optional feature set is that feature sets are defined in the feature set document, referencing subsets of the main spec, whereas extensions are defined in entirely different documents. If an implementation supports an optional feature set or extension, then it must support it in its entirely–it cannot pick and choose individual functions within that feature set or extension. The feature set spec also makes the minor distinctions of *organizational* and *informational* feature sets and defines one of each, which we will describe below.

The first feature set described in the spec is the **Base** feature set, and it contains the basic framework elements needed to construct OpenVX graphs and execute them. It is neither a conformance feature set nor optional–it is organizational. It is not a conformance feature set because implementations cannot get OpenVX conformance certification by implementing only this feature set. The logic here is that actually you cannot do anything with the base feature set without also defining some actual functions to use in the framework. It is not optional either: all OpenVX implementations must support all the functions in the base feature set. The base feature set is mainly used to refer to this core set of functions in conformance feature set descriptions without having to repeat them all, and hence it is called "organizational."

The feature set spec then defines three conformance feature sets: (1) **Vision**, (2) **Neural Network**, and (3) **NNEF**. The **Vision** feature set contains a set of basic classical vision functions and roughly corresponds to the set of functions that was available in version 1.1 of the OpenVX specification. The **Neural Network** feature set contains a set of common neural network "layer" functions and corresponds to the neural network extension defined for version 1.2 of the OpenVX spec. The **NNEF** feature set refers to the Khronos Neural Network Exchange Format specification and enables applications to import and execute neural networks defined using the domain-specific language described in the NNEF specification. It is basically an alternative implementation of neural networks, which is more flexible and feature rich than the layer functions defined in the **Neural Network** feature set. Refer to https://www.khronos.org/nnef for details on NNEF. An OpenVX implementation must support one or more of these conformance feature sets, as demonstrated by passing the conformance tests for the given feature sets, to be marketed as an implementation of OpenVX. An implementation may also support more than one conformance feature set, so in that sense, once at least one conformance feature set is supported, the others become "optional" for that implementor.

The feature set document also defines two specific optional feature sets: (1) the **Binary Image** feature set and (2) the **Enhanced Vision** feature set. Both of these depend on the Vision conformance feature set, that is, they can only be implemented if the Vision feature set is also implemented, because they depend on Vision features. The Enhanced Vision feature set roughly corresponds to the set of functions introduced in version 1.2 of the OpenVX spec. A table can be found in the feature set specification. The Binary Image feature set bears further discussion.

15.1.1 Binary images

The Binary Image feature set introduces images in which each pixel is represented by a single bit, with the data format VX_DF_IMAGE_U1. Prior to the introduction of this data format, binary images had to be represented with a full 8-bit byte, with zero being represented as 0x00 (all bits zero) and one represented as 0xFF (all bits set to one), that is, 255 in decimal. If an implementation supports the Binary Image feature set, then such images can efficiently represented with only one bit per pixel, saving data space and enabling a potentially considerable execution speed-up for key binary operations. The obvious cases is for logical operations (And, Or, Not, Xor), all of which are supported in the binary image feature set. Another common use of binary images is for nonlinear filters, which of course includes the general vxNonLinearFilter function and also the functions for specific 3 × 3 morphology operations of Dilate, Erode, and Median. If your OpenVX implementation supports the Binary Image feature set, then you can use the binary versions of these functions simply by setting the input and output image parameters to images that you created with the VX_DF_IMAGE_U1 data format.

The Binary Image feature set also provides support for conversion between U1 images and the integer types U8 and S16 using the existing vxConvertDepth function. Simply set one parameter of vxConvertDepth to a U1 image and the other to the U8 or S16 image you want to convert to or from. When converting from U8 or S16 to U1, pixels set to zero (0x00 or 0x0000) in the input will of course be set to "0" bits in the U1 output, and all nonzero pixels in the input will be set to "1" bits in the U1 output. When converting from U1 to the larger types, "0" bits will be set to all zeros in the output (0x00 or 0x0000), and "1" bits will be set to all ones in the output (i.e., 0xFF or 0xFFFF, which have decimal values 255 and -1 in U8 and S16, respectively).

You can also scale and warp U1 images using vxScaleImage and vxWarpAffine. Both the input and output images must be U1. Format mixing is not allowed; if you want to change the format, then you must do it explicitly using the vxConvertDepth function.

The output of some OpenVX functions are naturally binary, but until now, these had to be represented with 8 bits per pixel. However, if the binary image feature set is supported, then you can make the output of vxCannyEdgeDetector and vxThreshold be truly represented as binary, simply by setting the output parameter to an image with the VX_DF_IMAGE_U1 format.

Three more functions will accept binary images as input: vxHoughLinesP, vxMeanStdDev, and vxNonMaxSuppression. You can search for lines in a binary image with vxHoughLinesP. The vxMeanStdDev function with a binary image as input will give you the fraction of "1" pixels in the image for the mean, and a standard deviation ranging between 0 (all 0s or all 1s) and about 0.5

(about half 0s and half 1s). The vxNonMaxSuppression function has a "mask" input, which can now be represented with a truly binary image. The functions in the Binary Image feature set that support U1 parameters are summarized as follows:

- **Logical:** And, Not, Or, Xor
- **Nonlinear:** Dilate3x3, Erode3x3, Median3x3, NonLinearFilter
- **Reshape:** ConvertDepth, ScaleImage, WarpAffine
- **Binary output:** CannyEdgeDetector, Threshold
- **Binary input:** HoughLinesP, MeanStdDev, NonMaxSuppression (mask only)

15.2 Safety-critical application support

A significant enhancement to the OpenVX 1.3 specification is the incorporation of features supporting safety-critical applications, such as self-driving cars. Safety-critical applications were first addressed by OpenVX as an entirely separate OpenVX-SC specification document based on the OpenVX 1.1 main spec. It was developed in parallel with OpenVX 1.2, and so it does not incorporate OpenVX 1.2 features. In OpenVX 1.3 the safety critical features are merged back into the main specification, so there is no longer a need for a separate safety-critical spec. As described in Chapter 11, one of the main things needed for safety-critical support is the identification of a "deployment" subset of the entire spec that will actually run on the target system, for example, on a car's computer. OpenVX 1.3 identifies this subset in the feature set specification as the **Safety-Critical Deployment** feature set. As can be seen in Fig. 15.1, which is taken from the OpenVX feature set spec, the Safety-Critical Deployment feature set contains data objects such as images and tensors, high-level context, graph, and reference structures, and an "import" object that enables loading and executing graphs. It does *not* contain internal graph details like kernels, nodes, or parameters. The idea is that all these details used to construct and verify graphs are only used offline, and at run-time the graphs are just loaded as-is and executed. Again, see Chapter 11 for details.

The other main enhancement of the OpenVX 1.3 specification is the incorporation of requirements tags into the main 1.3 spec document. Requirements tags are identifiers of the form **[REQ-XXXX]**, where "XXXX" is a unique numerical identifier for that requirement. These were first introduced in the separate OpenVX-SC document, and in OpenVX

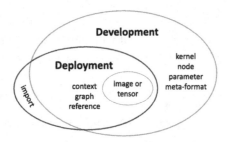

Figure 15.1 Illustration of the OpenVX deployment feature set.

1.3 they are included in the main spec. These tags uniquely identify each requirement that must be implemented and verified. Having unique tags like this enables OpenVX implementors and application developers to apply the strict tracking techniques required by safety-critical development methodologies such as ISO-26262. In these methodologies, each requirement must be specified, implemented, and verified, with clear documentation of each step. The tags enable each requirement to be tracked throughout this process.

There are a few other minor changes that were made to the specification document in support of safety-critical applications. The only one we will mention here is the change of the use of the word "undefined" to be "implementation-defined" instead. There are several places in the specification where a rule for how to correctly write programs using the standard is described. In previous versions of the spec, it said that if such a rule is violated, the behavior of the program that breaks the rule is "undefined." For safety-critical applications, it is not acceptable to have any behavior be undefined, so this phrasing was changed to "implementation-defined." In safety-critical implementations of OpenVX the implementor has to define what happens when the rule is broken, even though it is not defined by the OpenVX spec itself.

Examples of implementation-defined behavior can be seen in the map and unmap functions for various objects. When you map an object, you get a chunk of memory with a base pointer and a size. If you try to access memory outside of this chunk, either before the base pointer or beyond the end of the memory region, the result is implementation-defined. If you try to write to read-only memory or read write-only memory, then the result is implementation-defined. Safety-critical implementations of OpenVX need to specify what happens when you do these things, for example, when you try to read beyond the end of the memory area, an error is generated, and the result read is all zeros. A non-safety-critical implementation is allowed to do whatever is easiest, which may include reading a random result or even crashing. Safety-critical implementations must prohibit this sort of thing.

15.3 Removal of bidirectional parameters

Another change to the specification in OpenVX 1.3 is the removal of bidirectional parameters. Running a graph with bidirectional parameters both reads and writes the bidirectional parameter data, which technically makes a cycle in the graph. This can be a problem for some optimization techniques and requires a lot of rules about when the data was read versus written to make sure the behavior is well-defined. These rules are no longer needed now that the bidirectional parameters are removed.

The only kernels in the standard that used bidirectional parameters in OpenVX 1.2 and earlier were the accumulate nodes: Accumulate, Accumulate Squared, and Accumulate Weighted. The functionality of the Accumulate node can be easily reconstructed without bidirectional parameters using an Add node. By also using a Multiply node, the Accumulate Squared node functionality can also be achieved. The Accumulated Weighted functionality is a little harder to construct with OpenVX 1.2 nodes, so OpenVX 1.3 adds a "Weighted Average" node to make this easier:

```
vx_node vxWeightedAverageNode(
    vx_graph    graph,
    vx_image    img1,
    vx_scalar   alpha,
    vx_image    img2,
    vx_image    output);
```

It accepts two input images and an "alpha" parameter between 0 and 1, which indicates how much to weight each image. Each pixel in the output image is set to the sum of the first input image weighted by alpha and the second input image weighted by $1 - $ alpha:

```
output(x,y) = alpha * img1(x,y) + (1 - alpha) * img2(x,y)
```

This simple computation is also called *alpha blending*, since it produces a "blend" of the two input images controlled by the alpha parameter. It works analogously to the alpha parameter in the removed Accumulate Weighted node, so this functionality can easily be reproduced using the new Weighted Average node.

This removal of bidirectional parameters removes the implicit cycle they cause but adds some burden on implementations of OpenVX to optimize efficient implementations. The accumulate nodes explicitly operated on the accumulation parameter "in place," so that a separate image object was not needed for the output image. To prevent cycles in their graphs, the user must create a separate output image when constructing the accumulate functionality. To efficiently execute this, the implementation must detect that the computation can be done in-place and optimize appropriately.

15.4 User structures

The OpenVX standard has always had a vx_array object, which can be used to hold collections of data structures. When creating a vx_array object, the programmer must provide an item_type parameter, which identifies the data type of the items in the array. In the previous versions of OpenVX, these data types were limited to a subset of the enumerated vx_type_e values defined by the OpenVX standard. Vendors, that is, implementors of OpenVX, can add a few types with values between VX_TYPE_VENDOR_STRUCT_START and VX_TYPE_VENDOR_STRUCT_END, but the application programmer cannot. OpenVX 1.3 introduces the concept of a "user struct" that can be created by the application programmer. Once this structure is "registered" with the OpenVX implementation, the user can create vx_arrays of them. All the user has to do is to register their structure using the vxRegisterUserStruct function, providing the size of their structure in bytes. The register function returns an enumeration value, which can be used to create arrays of this user struct.

Optionally, the user can associate their structure with a name by registering it instead with the vxRegisterUserStructWithName function and providing a name string in addition to the size. If they do this, then they can map between the name and the enum using the functions vxGetUserStructNameByEnum and vxGetUserStructEnumByName.

15.5 Miscellaneous changes

There are a number of small changes in OpenVX 1.3 including minor clarifications and corrections of typos that are not worth going into here, but there are two new functions worth mentioning, vxCreateTensorFromHandle and vxQueryMetaFormatAttribute. They are really just oversights in the previous versions, holes that are filled in by OpenVX 1.3.

The first, vxCreateTensorFromHandle, is an analog of vxCreateImageFromHandle described in Chapter 12. It enables the creation of a tensor object from existing data and has a number of parameters that describe the tensor to be created:

```
vx_tensor vxCreateTensorFromHandle(
    vx_context      context,
    vx_size         number_of_dims,
    const vx_size*  dims,
    vx_enum         data_type,
    vx_int8         fixed_point_position,
    const vx_size*  stride,
    void*           ptr,
    vx_enum         memory_type);
```

There is also vxSwapTensorHandle analogous to vxSwapImageHandle, with the obvious parameters, and the map and unmap tensor functions previously described in Chapter 12.

The other new function is vxQueryMetaFormatAttribute. OpenVX kernel parameter objects have various metaformat data associated with them, which are specific to the object type. For example, vx_image objects have a height and width, and vx_array objects have a capacity and an item type. The previous versions of OpenVX allowed users to set the metaformat values in a kernel output validator, but not query what the existing metaformat values of a kernel parameter are. OpenVX 1.3 enables queries via the new vxQueryMetaFormatAttribute function. It takes a metaformat object and an attribute identifier as input and returns a pointer to the value and size of the returned value:

```
vx_status vxQueryMetaFormatAttribute(
    vx_meta_format  meta,
    vx_enum         attribute,
    void*           ptr,
    vx_size         size);
```

Those are the high points of the new OpenVX 1.3 specification. See the spec itself for additional details.

The list of OpenVX data objects and their attributes

Here is the list of OpenVX data objects, arranged in alphabetical order, along with their attributes.

- vx_array The object representing an array of primitive data types like floating point values vx_float32 or an array of structures, like keypoints vx_keypoint_t and 2D coordinates vx_coordinates2d_t. The attributes of vx_array are:
  - VX_ARRAY_ITEMTYPE the type of elements in the array, vx_enum data type (see vx_type_e), read-only. For primitive OpenVX data types and structures, use enums with a prefix VX_TYPE, such as VX_TYPE_FLOAT32 and VX_TYPE_KEYPOINT
  - VX_ARRAY_NUMITEMS the number of elements in the array, vx_size data type, read-only
  - VX_ARRAY_CAPACITY the maximum number of elements the array can hold, vx_size data type, read-only
  - VX_ARRAY_ITEMSIZE the size of each array element in bytes, vx_size data type, read-only
- vx_convolution a user-defined rectangular convolution kernel for a linear image filter. It has the following attributes:
  - VX_CONVOLUTION_ROWS the number of rows of the convolution matrix, vx_size data type, read-only
  - VX_CONVOLUTION_COLUMNS the number of columns of the convolution matrix, vx_size data type, read-only
  - VX_CONVOLUTION_SCALE the scale of the convolution matrix. The function vxConvolveNode, which applies a convolution to an image and divides the result of a convolution in each pixel by the value of this attribute. vx_uint32 data type, read-write (use vxSetConvolutionAttribute function to set its value). OpenVX 1.0 supports only scale values that are a power of 2 up to 2^{31}
  - VX_CONVOLUTION_SIZE the total size of the convolution matrix in bytes, vx_size data type, read-only
- vx_delay A manually controlled list of objects for processing a temporal sequence of data, with the following attributes:

- VX_DELAY_TYPE the type of objects stored in the delay object, vx_enum data type (use vx_type_e), read-only
- VX_DELAY_SLOTS the number of items in the delay object, vx_size parameter, read-only
- vx_distribution an object that contains a frequency distribution, such as a histogram. It has the following attributes:
  - VX_DISTRIBUTION_DIMENSIONS the number of dimensions in the distribution, vx_size data type, read-only
  - VX_DISTRIBUTION_OFFSET the start of the values to use in the distribution. The function vxHistogramNode subtracts the value of this attribute from pixel intensity before calculating the bin to increment; the pixels with intensities lower than this value are ignored. vx_int32 data type, read-only
  - VX_DISTRIBUTION_RANGE the total number of the consecutive values of the distribution interval. The function vxHistogramNode only takes into account the pixels with intensities lower than VX_DISTRIBUTION_OFFSET + VX_DISTRIBUTION_RANGE. vx_uint32 data type, read-only
  - VX_DISTRIBUTION_BINS the number of bins in the distribution, vx_size data type, read-only
  - VX_DISTRIBUTION_WINDOW the width of each bin in the distribution. It is equal to the value of the range (VX_DISTRIBUTION_RANGE) divided by the number of bins (VX_DISTRIBUTION_BINS). vx_uint32 data type, read-only
  - VX_DISTRIBUTION_SIZE the total size of the distribution in bytes, vx_size data type, read-only
- vx_image Image object with the following attributes:
  - VX_IMAGE_WIDTH image width, vx_uint32 data type, read-only
  - VX_IMAGE_HEIGHT image height, vx_uint32 data type, read-only
  - VX_IMAGE_FORMAT image format, vx_df_image data type, read-only
  - VX_IMAGE_PLANES the number of planes in an image, vx_size data type, read-only
  - VX_IMAGE_SPACE image color space, vx_enum data type (see vx_color_space_e), read-write (use vxSetImageAttribute to change its value)
  - VX_IMAGE_RANGE image channel range, vx_enum data type (see vx_channel_range_e), read-only
  - VX_IMAGE_MEMORY_TYPE image memory type (used only for images created by vxCreateImageFromHandle function), vx_enum data type (see vx_memory_type_e), read-only

- VX_IMAGE_IS_UNIFORM used to check whether an image is uniform, that is, all pixel values are the same, vx_bool data type, read-only
- VX_IMAGE_UNIFORM_VALUE the value of each pixel in a uniform image, vx_pixel_value_t data type, read-only
- vx_lut the Lookup Table object that is used for pixel-by-pixel intensity transformations. It has the following attributes:
  - VX_LUT_TYPE the value type of the LUT. Can be VX_TYPE_UINT8 or VX_TYPE_INT16, vx_enum data type (see vx_type_e), read-only
  - VX_TYPE_COUNT the number of elements in the LUT. Cannot be greater than 256 for VX_TYPE_UINT8 type and 65536 for VX_TYPE_INT16.
  - VX_LUT_SIZE the total size of a LUT in bytes, vx_size data type, read-only
  - VX_LUT_OFFSET the index of an input value equal to zero. It is equal to 0 for VX_TYPE_UINT8, and (vx_uint32)(VX_TYPE_COUNT/2) for VX_TYPE_INT16
- vx_matrix contains a matrix of scalar values and has the following attributes:
  - VX_MATRIX_TYPE the type of matrix elements. Can be VX_TYPE_UINT8, VX_TYPE_INT16 and VX_TYPE_FLOAT32. vx_enum data type (see vx_type_e), read-only
  - VX_MATRIX_ROWS the number of rows in the matrix, vx_size data type, read-only
  - VX_MATRIX_COLUMNS the number of columns in the matrix, vx_size data type, read-only
  - VX_MATRIX_SIZE the total size of the matrix in bytes, vx_size data type, read-only
  - VX_MATRIX_ORIGIN the origin of the matrix with the default value of [floor(VX_MATRIX_COLUMNS/2), floor(VX_MATRIX_ROWS/2)]. These coordinates are used by the function vxNonLinearFilterNode to adjust the mask defined by a matrix with the input image pixel to compute the transformation for. vx_coordinates2d_t data type, read-only
  - VX_MATRIX_PATTERN matrix pattern. If the matrix was created by vxCreateMatrixFromPattern and vxCreateMatrixFromPatternAndOrigin functions, the value of this attribute is set by the corresponding input argument of these functions; in this case, it can take on values VX_PATTERN_BOX, VX_PATTERN_CROSS and VX_PATTERN_DISK. If the matrix is created with vxCreateMatrix, then the value of this attribute is VX_PATTERN_OTHER. vx_enum data type (see vx_pattern_e), read-only
- vx_pyramid represents an image pyramid with the following attributes:

- VX_PYRAMID_LEVELS the number of pyramid levels, vx_size data type, read-only
- VX_PYRAMID_SCALE the scale factor for the subsequent pyramid levels sizes, the OpenVX implementation has to support VX_SCALE_PYRAMID_HALF and VX_SCALE_PYRAMID_ORB, although support for other positive values is not prohibited. vx_float32 data type, read-only
- VX_PYRAMID_WIDTH the width of the image on the highest level (level 0) of the pyramid. vx_uint32 data type, read-only
- VX_PYRAMID_HEIGHT the height of the image on the highest level (level 0) of the pyramid. vx_uint32 data type, read-only
- VX_PYRAMID_FORMAT the format of each image in the pyramid, vx_df_image data type (see vx_df_image_e), read-only
- **Remap** the object for describing arbitrary image geometric transformations with the following attributes:
  - VX_REMAP_SOURCE_WIDTH the source image width, vx_uint32 data type, read-only
  - VX_REMAP_SOURCE_HEIGHT the source image height, vx_uint32 data type, read-only
  - VX_REMAP_DESTINATION_WIDTH the destination image width, vx_uint32 data type, read-only
  - VX_REMAP_DESTINATION_HEIGHT the destination image height, vx_uint32 data type, read-only
- vx_scalar an object that contains a single primitive data type, with the attribute
  - VX_SCALAR_TYPE the data type contained in the scalar object, vx_enum parameter (see vx_type_e), read-only
- vx_threshold contains the parameters of the threshold image function, with the following attributes:
  - VX_THRESHOLD_TYPE the type of the threshold function, vx_enum data type (see vx_threshold_type_e: can be VX_THRESHOLD_TYPE_BINARY and VX_THRESHOLD_TYPE_RANGE), read-only
  - VX_THRESHOLD_INPUT_FORMAT the format of the input image for the threshold function, vx_enum data type (see vx_df_image_e), read-only
  - VX_THRESHOLD_OUTPUT_FORMAT the format of the output image for the threshold function, vx_enum data type (see vx_df_image_e), read-only

Note that the threshold values (one value for VX_THRESHOLD_TYPE_BINARY and two values for VX_THRESHOLD_TYPE_RANGE) and the output values (two values, for true and false threshold comparison condition value) are not attributes, but the object data.

- `vx_object_array` an array of any data object, except for `vx_delay` and `vx_object_array`, with the following attributes:
  - `VX_OBJECT_ARRAY_ITEMTYPE` the type of the items in the object array, `vx_enum` data type (see `vx_type_e`), read-only
  - `VX_OBJECT_ARRAY_NUMITEMS` the number of elements in the object array, `vx_size` data type, read-only
- `vx_tensor` a multidimensional data object, used in Histogram of Oriented Gradient functions and in the Neural Network extension. It has the following attributes:
  - `VX_TENSOR_NUMBER_OF_DIMS` the number of tensor dimensions, `vx_size` data type, read-only
  - `VX_TENSOR_DIMS` the dimension sizes, `vx_size*` data type, with the value pointing to an allocated memory block of size `sizeof(vx_size)*VX_TENSOR_NUMBER_OF_DIMS`
  - `VX_TENSOR_DATA_TYPE` the type of tensor elements, `vx_enum` data type (see `vx_type_e`), read-only
  - `VX_TENSOR_FIXED_POINT_POSITION` the position of a fixed point to represent floating point value with integer values, `vx_int8` data type, read-only

The list of computer vision graph API nodes

This appendix lists the computer vision kernels of OpenVX. The list is organized by category and contains only graph nodes, as there is almost 1-to-1 correspondence between graph nodes and immediate node functions. We also provide a reference to an example of usage for each function.

B.1 Image arithmetics and control flow

Name	Function	Usage example
vxAbsDiffNode	Absolute difference between two images	Chapter 7, "vx_bg.c" sample
vxAddNode	Per-pixel sum of two images	Chapter 8, "stitch.c" sample
vxSubtractNode	Per-pixel subtraction of two images	Chapter 8, "stitch-multiband.c" sample
vxAndNode	Per-pixel bitwise AND of two images	
vxXorNode	Per-pixel bitwise XOR of two images	
vxOrNode	Per-pixel bitwise OR of two images	Chapter 2, "example4.c" sample
vxNotNode	Per-pixel bitwise NOT of an image	Chapter 5, "graphFactory.c" sample
vxCopyNode	Copy a data object	Chapter 9, "example4a.c" sample
vxSelectNode	Selects one of two data objects depending on a condition	Chapter 4
vxScalarOperationNode	Scalar operations for control flow	

continued on next page

(*continued*)

Name	Function	Usage example
vxMagnitudeNode	Computes a per-pixel magnitude for two images, such as image gradients in x- and y-directions	Chapter 6, "houghLines.c" sample
vxPhaseNode	Computes a per-pixel phase for two images, such as image gradients in x- and y-directions	
vxMax	Computes a per-pixel maximum for two images	
vxMin	Computes a per-pixel minimum for two images	
vxMultiplyNode	Per-pixel multiplication for two images	Chapter 8, "stitch.c"
vxTableLookupNode	Per-pixel arbitrary mapping of intensity values	Chapter 8, "stitch-multiband.c" sample
vxWeightedAverageNode	Computes a weighted average for two images	

B.2 Image format conversions

Name	Function	Usage example
vxChannelCombineNode	Combine several single channel images into a multiple channel image	Chapter 6, "changeImage.c" and "houghLines.c"
vxChannelExtractNode	Extract a single channel image from a multiple channel image	Chapter 6, "changeImage.c" and "houghLines.c"
vxColorConvertNode	Convert color space of an image	Chapter 6, "changeImage.c" and "houghLines.c" sample
vxConvertDepthNode	Transform a single channel image to an image with a different element size (for example, 8-bit unsigned to 16-bit signed)	Chapter 8, "example4a.c" and "stitch.c" samples

B.3 Image filtering and statistics

Name	Function	Usage example
vxBilateralFilterNode	Bilateral filtering of an image	
vxBox3x3Node	Box filter with 3 × 3 kernel	
vxConvolveNode	Arbitrary linear convolution	Chapter 6, "filterImage.c" sample
vxDilate3x3Node	Image dilatation	Chapter 6, "houghLines.c" sample
vxErode3x3Node	Image erosion	Chapter 7, "vx_bg.c" sample
vxGaussian3x3Node	Gaussian 3 × 3 image filter	Chapter 6, "filterGaussImage.c" sample
vxLBPNode	Computes a local binary pattern image	
vxMeanStdDevNode	Computes mean and standard deviation	
vxMedian3x3Node	Median filter of an image	
vxMinMaxLocNode	Computes the maximum and minimum pixel intensities in an image along with the corresponding pixel locations	
vxNonLinearFilterNode	Computes a nonlinear filter, such as a median function over a window	
vxSobel3x3Node	Computes a 3 × 3 Sobel filter for an image	Chapter 6, "houghLines.c" sample
vxThresholdNode	Threshold operation	Chapter 6, "houghLines.c" sample

B.4 Geometric transformations

Name	Function	Usage example
vxGaussianPyramidNode	Create a Gaussian pyramid from an image	Chapter 8, "stitch-multiband.c" sample
vxLaplacianPyramidNode	Create a Laplacian pyramid from an image	Chapter 8, "stitch-multiband.c" sample

continued on next page

(*continued*)

Name	Function	Usage example
vxLaplacianReconstructNode	Reconstructs an image from a Laplacian pyramid	Chapter 8, "stitch-multiband.c" sample
vxRemapNode	Arbitrary geometric transformation of an image	Chapter 6, "undistort-remap.c" sample
vxHalfScaleGaussianNode	Scale an image 2 times each direction with a Gaussian blur	Chapter 8, "stitch-multiband.c" sample
vxScaleImageNode	Image resize	Chapter 6, "houghLines.c" sample
vxWarpAffineNode	Affine transformation on an image	Chapter 6
vxWarpPerspectiveNode	Perspective transformation on an image	Chapter 6, "birdsEyeView.c" sample

B.5 Feature extraction

Name	Function	Usage example
vxCannyEdgeDetectorNode	Canny edge detector	Chapter 6, "filterImageROIvxu.c" sample
vxFastCornerNode	Fast feature detector	Chapter 9, "example4a.c" sample
vxHOGCellsNode	Performs cell calculations for the average gradient magnitude and gradient orientation histograms	
vxHOGFeaturesNode	Produces HOG features in a sliding window over the whole image	
vxHarrisCornersNode	Harris corner detector	Chapter 4
vxHistogramNode	Computes image histogram	
vxEqualizeHistNode	Equalize image histogram	

continued on next page

(continued)

Name	Function	Usage example
vxHoughLinesPNode	Computes a probabilistic hough transformation	Chapter 6, "houghLines.c" sample
vxIntegralImageNode	Computes an integral image	
vxMatchTemplateNode	Template-based object detection	
vxNonMaxSuppressionNode	Computes a nonmaximum suppression, to be used with nodes like vxHarriscornersNode	
vxOpticalFlowPyrLKNode	Lukas–Kanade optical flow for a sequence of images	Chapter 9

B.6 Tensor functions

Name	Function	Usage example
vxTensorAddNode	Elementwise sum of two tensors	
vxTensorConvertDepthNode	Transform a tensor to a tensor with a different element size (for example, 8-bit unsigned to 16-bit signed)	
vxTensorMatrixMultiplyNode	Generalized matrix multiplication node	
vxTensorMultiplyNode	Elementwise multiplication of two tensors	
vxTensorSubtractNode	Elementwise subtraction of one tensor from another	
vxTensorTableLookupNode	Elementwise transformation of tensor element values with a lookup table	
vxTensorTransposeNode	Performs a transpose transformation on an input tensor	

References

[1] Openvx: an open, royalty-free standard for cross platform acceleration of computer vision applications, https://www.khronos.org/openvx/.

[2] The Khronos group, https://www.khronos.org.

[3] P. Viola, M. Jones, Robust real-time object detection, Int. J. Comput. Vis. (2001).

[4] E. Rosten, T. Drummond, Machine learning for high-speed corner detection, in: Proceedings of the 9th European Conference on Computer Vision - Volume Part I, ECCV'06, Springer-Verlag, Berlin, Heidelberg, 2006, pp. 430–443, ISBN 3-540-33832-2, 978-3-540-33832-1.

[5] M. Calonder, V. Lepetit, M. Ozuysal, T. Trzcinski, C. Strecha, P. Fua, Brief: computing a local binary descriptor very fast, IEEE Trans. Pattern Anal. Mach. Intell. 34 (7) (2012) 1281–1298, https://doi.org/10.1109/TPAMI.2011.222.

[6] E. Rublee, V. Rabaud, K. Konolige, G. Bradski, Orb: an efficient alternative to sift or surf, in: Proceedings of the 2011 International Conference on Computer Vision, ICCV'11, IEEE Computer Society, Washington, DC, USA, ISBN 978-1-4577-1101-5, 2011, pp. 2564–2571.

[7] G.R. Bradski, V. Pisarevsky, Intel's computer vision library: applications in calibration, stereo, segmentation, tracking, gesture, face and object recognition, in: 2000 Conference on Computer Vision and Pattern Recognition, CVPR 2000, 13–15 June 2000, Hilton Head, SC, USA, 2000, p. 2796.

[8] J. Fung, S. Mann, OpenVIDIA: parallel GPU computer vision, in: Proceedings of the 13th Annual ACM International Conference on Multimedia, MULTIMEDIA'05, ACM, New York, NY, USA, ISBN 1-59593-044-2, 2005, pp. 849–852.

[9] G. Dedeoğlu, B. Kisačanin, D. Moore, V. Sharma, A. Miller, An optimized vision library approach for embedded systems, in: CVPR 2011 WORKSHOPS, 2011, pp. 8–13.

[10] FastCV computer vision SDK, https://developer.qualcomm.com/software/fastcv-sdk.

[11] G.P. Stein, E. Rushinek, G. Hayun, A. Shashua, A computer vision system on a chip: a case study from the automotive domain, in: 2005 IEEE Computer Society Conference on Computer Vision and Pattern Recognition (CVPR'05) - Workshops, 2005, p. 130.

[12] The OpenCL™ Specification, https://www.khronos.org/opencl/.

[13] E. Trucco, A. Verri, Introductory Techniques for 3-D Computer Vision, Prentice Hall PTR, Upper Saddle River, NJ, USA, ISBN 0132611082, 1998.

[14] OpenVX conformance tests, https://www.khronos.org/openvx/adopters/.

[15] OpenVX open source conformance tests implementation, https://github.com/KhronosGroup/OpenVX-cts.

[16] T.J. Olson, J.R. Taylor, R.J. Lockwood, Programming a pipelined image processor, Comput. Vis. Image Underst. 64 (1996) 351–367.

[17] The OpenVX neural network extension, https://www.khronos.org/registry/OpenVX/extensions/vx_khr_nn/1.3/html/vx_khr_nn_1_3.html.

[18] The OpenVX kernel import extension, https://www.khronos.org/registry/OpenVX/extensions/vx_khr_import_kernel/1.3/html/vx_khr_import_kernel_1_3.html.

[19] The OpenVX feature set definitions, https://www.khronos.org/registry/OpenVX/specs/1.3/vx_khr_feature_sets/1.0/html/vx_khr_feature_sets_1_0.html.

[20] Neural network exchange format (NNEF), https://www.khronos.org/nnef.

[21] Open Source Computer Vision Library, http://opencv.org.

[22] J. Coombs, R. Prabhu, G. Peake, Overcoming the challenges of porting opencv to TI's embedded ARM + DSP platforms, Int. J. Electr. Eng. Educ. 49 (3) (2012) 260–274, https://doi.org/10.7227/IJEEE.49.3.6.

[23] Stephen Neuendorffer, Thomas Li, Devin Wang, Accelerating OpenCV Applications with Zynq-7000 All Programmable SoC using Vivado HLS Video Libraries, tech. rep., Xilinx, 2015, https://www.xilinx.com/support/documentation/application_notes/xapp1167.pdf.

[24] H. Sugano, R. Miyamoto, Highly optimized implementation of opencv for the cell broadband engine, Comput. Vis. Image Underst. 114 (11) (2010) 1273–1281, https://doi.org/10.1016/j.cviu.2010.03.022.

[25] D.A. Forsyth, J. Ponce, Computer Vision: A Modern Approach, Prentice Hall Professional Technical Reference, ISBN 0130851981, 2002.

[26] R. Hartley, A. Zisserman, Multiple View Geometry in Computer Vision, 2nd ed., Cambridge University Press, New York, NY, USA, ISBN 0521540518, 2003.

[27] R. Szeliski, Computer Vision: Algorithms and Applications, 1st ed., Springer-Verlag, Berlin, Heidelberg, 2010, ISBN 1848829345, 9781848829343.

[28] G. Bradski, A. Kaehler, Learning OpenCV: Computer Vision in C++ With the OpenCV Library, 2nd ed., O'Reilly Media, Inc., 2013, ISBN 1449314651, 9781449314651.

[29] OpenVX tutorials and examples under MIT license, https://github.com/rgiduthuri/openvx_tutorial.

[30] OpenVX sample implementation, https://github.com/KhronosGroup/OpenVX-sample-impl.

[31] VXA: convenience functions for OpenVX, https://github.com/relrotciv/vxa.

[32] S.V.C. Ramm, A C++ wrapper for the openVX API, https://gitlab.com/StephenRamm/openvx-sc-plus, 2018.

[33] E. Anderson, Z. Bai, J. Dongarra, A. Greenbaum, A. McKenney, J. Du Croz, et al., Lapack: a portable linear algebra library for high-performance computers, in: Proceedings of the 1990 ACM/IEEE Conference on Supercomputing, Supercomputing'90, IEEE Computer Society Press, Los Alamitos, CA, USA, ISBN 0-89791-412-0, 1990, pp. 2–11, http://dl.acm.org/citation.cfm?id=110382.110385.

[34] R. Fisher, S. Perkins, A. Walker, E. Wolfart, Canny edge detector, https://homepages.inf.ed.ac.uk/rbf/HIPR2/canny.htm, 2003.

[35] J. Matas, C. Galambos, J. Kittler, Robust detection of lines using the progressive probabilistic hough transform, Comput. Vis. Image Underst. 78 (1) (2000) 119–137, https://doi.org/10.1006/cviu.1999.0831.

[36] Camera calibration with openCV, https://docs.opencv.org/3.1.0/d4/d94/tutorial_camera_calibration.html.

[37] P.J. Burt, E.H. Adelson, A multiresolution spline with application to image mosaics, ACM Trans. Graph. 2 (4) (1983) 217–236, https://doi.org/10.1145/245.247.

[38] M. Brown, D. Lowe, Automatic panoramic image stitching using invariant features, Int. J. Comput. Vis. 74 (1) (2007), https://doi.org/10.1007/s11263-006-0002-3.

[39] B.D. Lucas, T. Kanade, An iterative image registration technique with an application to stereo vision, in: International Joint Conference on Artificial Intelligence, 1981, pp. 674–679, http://cecas.clemson.edu/~stb/klt/lucas_bruce_d_1981_1.pdf.

[40] C. Tomasi, T. Kanade, Detection and Tracking of Point Features, tech. rep., 1991, http://cecas.clemson.edu/~stb/klt/tomasi-kanade-techreport-1991.pdf.

[41] J.Y. Bouget, Pyramidal implementation of the Lucas Kanade feature tracker description of the algorithm, tech. rep., https://robots.stanford.edu/cs223b04/.

[42] ISO, The international organization for standardization, https://iso.org.

[43] C. Naden, Keeping safe on the roads: series of standards for vehicle electronics functional safety just updated, https://www.iso.org/news/ref2358.html, 2018.

[44] ISO, Road vehicles — functional safety — part 6: product development at the software level, https://www.iso.org/standard/68388.html, 2018.

[45] MIRA-Limited, Guidelines for the use of the C language in critical systems, MIRA Limited, 2013, ISBN 978-1-906400-10-1.

[46] MIRA-Limited, Guidelines for the use of the C++ language in critical systems, 2008, ISBN 978-1-906400-03-3, MIRA Limited.

[47] HORIBA-MIRA-Limited, Achieving compliance with MISRA Coding Guidelines, HORIBA MIRA Limited, ISBN 978-1-9060400-13-2 PDF, https://misra.org.uk/LinkClick.aspx?fileticket=w_Syhpkf7xA%3D&tabid=57, 2016.

[48] AUTOSAR, Guidelines for the use of the C++14 language in critical and safety-related systems, https://www.autosar.org/fileadmin/user_upload/standards/adaptive/17-03/AUTOSAR_RS_CPP14Guidelines.pdf, 2017.

[49] ISO, Road vehicles — safety of the intended functionality, https://www.iso.org/standard/70939.html.

[50] RTCA, Software considerations in airborne systems and equipment certification, https://my.rtca.org/NC__Product?id=a1B36000001IcmqEAC.

[51] https://en.wikipedia.org/wiki/DO-178C.

[52] https://en.wikipedia.org/wiki/Radio_Technical_Commission_for_Aeronautics.

[53] CENELEC, European standards (en), https://www.cenelec.eu/standardsdevelopment/ourproducts/europeanstandards.html, 2019.

[54] Railway applications - the specification and demonstration of reliability, availability, maintainability and safety (rams) - part 1: generic rams process, https://www.cenelec.eu/dyn/www/f?p=104:110:1382593971855801::::FSP_ORG_ID,FSP_PROJECT,FSP_LANG_ID:1257173,60236,25, 2017.

[55] CENELEC, Railway applications - the specification and demonstration of reliability, availability, maintainability and safety (rams) - part 2: systems approach to safety, https://www.cenelec.eu/dyn/www/f?p=104:110:1382593971855801::::FSP_ORG_ID,FSP_PROJECT,FSP_LANG_ID:1257173,60237,25, 2017.

[56] CENELEC, Railway applications - communication, signalling and processing systems - software for railway control and protection systems, https://www.cenelec.eu/dyn/www/f?p=104:110:1382593971855801::::FSP_PROJECT,FSP_LANG_ID:43626,25, 2011.

[57] CENELEC, Railway applications - communication, signalling and processing systems - safety related electronic systems for signalling, https://www.cenelec.eu/dyn/www/f?p=104:110:1382593971855801::::FSP_ORG_ID,FSP_PROJECT,FSP_LANG_ID:1258773,60242,25, 2018.

[58] RSSB, Guidance on high-integrity software based systems for railway applications, https://catalogues.rssb.co.uk/rgs/standards/GEGN8650%20Iss%201.pdf, 2017.

[59] JWG CB, Industry standard on software maintenance of shipboard equipment, version 1.0, http://www.cirm.org/publications/industry_standards/Industry%20Standard%20on%20Software%20Maintenance%20of%20Shipboard%20Equipment%20v1-0.pdf, 2017.

[60] IEC, International electrotechnical commission, https://iec.ch.

[61] IMO, Publications, http://www.imo.org/en/Publications/Pages/Home.aspx.

[62] International safety management code, https://en.wikipedia.org/wiki/International_ Safety_Management_Code.

[63] International maritime organization, https://www.imo.org.

[64] ISO, Systems and software engineering – systems and software quality requirements and evaluation (square) – system and software quality models, https:// web.archive.org/web/20160314115231/http://www.iso.org/iso/catalogue_detail. htm?csnumber=35733, 2011.

[65] IEC, Medical device software — software life cycle processes, https://www.iso.org/ standard/38421.html, 2006.

[66] IEC 60601, https://en.wikipedia.org/wiki/IEC_60601, 2019.

[67] IEC, Functional safety - safety instrumented systems for the process industry sector - part 1: framework, definitions, system, hardware and application programming requirements, https://webstore.iec.ch/publication/24241, 2016.

[68] IEC, Safety of machinery - functional safety of safety-related electrical, electronic and programmable electronic control systems, https://webstore.iec.ch/publication/6426.

[69] ISA, Instrumented systems to achieve functional safety in the process industries, https:// www.isa.org/isa84/.

[70] ANSI, Machine safety standards, https://www.b11standards.org/standards.

[71] ISO, Safety of machinery — general principles for design — risk assessment and risk reduction, 2010.

[72] IEC, Functional safety and IEC 61508, https://www.iec.ch/functionalsafety/?ref= extfooter, 2019.

Index

Printed in the United States
By Bookmasters